HACK
IVERSITY

KYLE WINEY

"Everything you want is out there waiting for you to ask. Everything you want also wants you. But you have to take action to get it."

– JACK CANFIELD, *CHICKEN SOUP FOR THE SOUL*

HACKING COLLEGE FRAMEWORK

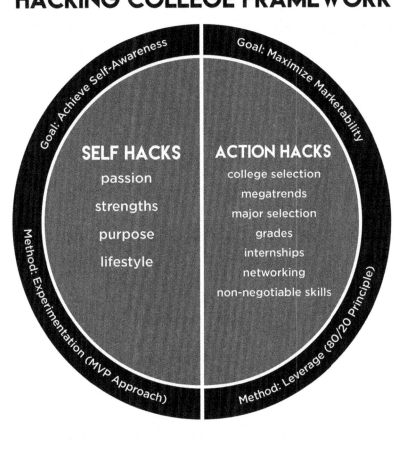

Table of Contents

FAQ: Skeptics Read This   1
My Story and Why You Need This Book   3
A Timeline of How I Got Here   7
The Basics of College   10
CORNERSTONE #1 Self-Awareness   18
Self HACK #1: Passion   29
Self HACK #2: Strengths   41
Self HACK #3: Purpose   51
Self HACK #4: Lifestyle   64
CORNERSTONE #2 Execution   72
Action HACK #1: College Selection   84
Action HACK #2: Megatrends   102
Action HACK #3: Major Selection   115
Action HACK #4: Grades   133
Action HACK #5: Internships   150
Action HACK #6: Networking   162
Action HACK #7: Non-Negotiable Skills   178
Bringing it to a Close   188
Notes   205

FOREWORD

By Richard Koch
Author, *The 80/20 Principle*

The world has changed. It used to be true that hard work and diligent study would guarantee, if not dramatic success, at least a pleasant middle-class lifestyle. No more. And no class of people is more affected by this change than the students of today and tomorrow. The realities students face today are quite different than they used to be even ten or twenty years ago. A new approach is required. Fortunately one is available, in the form of the book by Kyle Winey that you hold in your hands.

Deans and professors are still handing out the obsolete advice. "Go to college," they say, "study hard, get good grades, and everything will work out." It won't. Chances are you'll end up saddled with debt and a good, well-paying job will be hard to find. You would be much better off not going to college at all, or going but playing the game totally differently. Winey tells you how.

Today's students face soaring college costs, an ever-growing mountain of debt, and a world of climbing unemployment rates once they graduate. The post-college environment is barren, raw, windswept and cold. If you're not properly prepared for it—by the strategy you adopt while you are still a student—you are going to suffer.

Happily, *HACKiversity* provides practical, battle-tested solutions created by students for students. Winey does a masterful job of telling how he went wrong and corrected his mistakes, with detailed stories from dozens of highly successful recent college graduates, who had only one thing in common. They rejected the "study hard, get good grades" mantra and developed skills that could be used in the brave new world.

The great news—which fits perfectly with my own message that hard work is a delusion that nobody today should buy—is that you don't have to work harder. In fact, you should work less to achieve more. By following the steps in this book, you will discover how to work less in college and get ahead afterwards by focussing ruthlessly on the few things that matter most to you—and ignoring the many things that are hard to do but don't matter.

I often get asked to write Forewords, and I nearly always say No. But Kyle sent me his book and I thought, this is really excellent stuff. It's original, and the many interesting stories in the book ring true and are thought-provoking. The book itself is easy to read, yet incredibly helpful. Kyle has applied the 80/20 principle—how to get more with less effort—to college success, and

I take my hat off to him: I couldn't have done it nearly as well. I believe this book will introduce a whole new generation around the world to the magic insights of 80/20—enjoying at least eighty percent of results from less than twenty percent of hard work. Since I've devoted a good chunk of my life to writing and broadcasting this gospel, I see Kyle as a fellow-traveller and comrade-in-arms.

Despite its breezy style, this book is an important and inventive work. Its fresh perspective offers you students a way to lead your life in college and immediately afterwards that you won't get from your parents, professors, or counselors. I'd recommend any enlightened parent to read the book and give it to your sons and daughters. And to students I'd say this—success, even fantastic success, can be yours and can be enjoyable rather than a grind. But only if you rig the odds in your favor.

Why wouldn't you want to do that?

Richard Koch
Sunny Gibraltar, Summer 2017

FAQ: Skeptics Read This

Is HACKing college for you? If I were a betting man (I am), I would say yes. When talking about the concepts in this book, here are the most common objections, fears, and doubts people have about leaping in and joining the ranks of the college HACKers:

1. **Is HACKing college and "achieving more by doing less" encouraging students to be lazy?**
No. HACKing college is all about results, and in particular, achieving a higher *per hour* output. By focusing on the things that matter most, students can accomplish more with less time. This is difficult for most to accept because we live in a culture that rewards personal sacrifice instead of personal productivity. Completing fewer hours of meaningless work so students can focus on things that matter more is *not* laziness.

2. **I'm a high school/college student who is too busy studying, working, and hanging out with friends to read about college. Why should I add one more thing to my list?**
The point of this book is not to *add* anything to your workload. Instead, the point is to help you *eliminate* the many college activities that provide little value. The reality of college is that most things don't matter all that much. If you organize your college experience around the few things that matter most, which are outlined in this book, and ignore everything else, your life will be simpler and your results better.

3. **I have college advisors. Why do I need you?**
Many college advisors played the college game twenty to thirty years ago, a period when simply going to college, getting good grades, and graduating with a degree virtually guaranteed a great job. Today, it no longer does. Unfortunately, many college advisors haven't adapted to the new world, mainly because they're convinced the old way still works. To excel in college, however, students must discard the conventional model and adapt to new realities.

4. **College seems hard. Reading about it stresses me out.**
With the right game plan, excelling in college is simple. Honestly. It's the *absence* of planning that complicates college. This book aims to take out the uncertainty of college, thereby reducing anxiety, while maximizing chances for college success.

5. **New approaches are risky. I don't want to gamble with something as important as college.**
   New approaches are risky, but only if they are new. The college approach I outlined, however, has worked beautifully for thousands of students, including those highlighted within this book. What's perhaps the riskiest choice of all is continuing to do the "same old, same old" inside a world changing faster than ever.

6. **Why "HACKiversity" and not "hackiversity?"**
   Emphasis. HACKiversity is radical about productivity, so I created a name to say as much.

MY STORY AND WHY YOU NEED THIS BOOK

Today, virtually every college student receives the same advice. I was no different. "Attend college and study hard," they said. "Everything will work out."

In 2006, as an incoming Penn State freshman, I fully bought into this advice. I believed that employers wanted students with the highest grades, because great grades meant you were smart. And what employer doesn't want to hire the smartest students? As a result, I spent countless hours in the library cramming for exams and writing papers to earn the best grades possible. As you'll see, my hard work paid off. Or did it?

In 2007, halfway through my college career, the Great Recession struck. I witnessed an already limited job pool shrivel to almost nothing. Being the driven guy that I am (but mainly not knowing any better) I studied even harder. Although I was previously scoring 3.70 - 3.90 GPAs and making Dean's List every semester, I decided those grades were no longer good enough. In the wake of increasingly limited job prospects, I needed perfection. I was determined to get it. And I did. Junior year I started landing 4.0s every semester. Ultimately, I achieved precisely what I wanted: I graduated at the top of my class from the Penn State College of Business, one of the best business schools in the country.

In light of my accomplishments, I expected to land a great job with a great company and launch the beginning of a successful career. After all, I perfectly executed the game plan everyone promised worked so well. But there was just one problem: I graduated with no job offers. *Zero.* Think about that. I graduated at the top of my class from one of the best business schools with absolutely no employers knocking on my door. I don't think they even knew I existed.

How My Fraternity Brother Landed an Elite Job Without Going to Class

While I was studying hard, I watched one of my fraternity brothers do everything I was told not to do. He frequently slept in after watching movies all night, and skipped class to perfect his FIFA skills on Xbox. The rare times my fraternity brother studied occurred a day or two before an exam, when he would do the least amount possible just to get by. In short, my fraternity brother was one of the biggest slackers I knew in college.

The great irony was, during my junior year, my fraternity brother interned at one of the elite investment banks on Wall Street, where he eventually worked following graduation. Although Wall Street receives a lot of (much deserved) flack, that's where nearly every ambitious business student wants to work. I was no different. But landing on Wall Street is highly competitive and not many make it.

From the outside, you would think that I—not my fraternity brother—would be the one working on Wall Street. But, in spite of his lackadaisical college approach, my fraternity brother landed the prized job everyone wanted.

Following my graduation from Penn State, I enrolled in law school, mainly because I didn't want to be unemployed after college.

I distinctly remember a telephone call with my fraternity brother during my first year of law school:

"How is law school going?" he asked.

"It's pretty rough, man," I complained. "I'm studying 60 to 80 hours a week just trying to stay afloat. How's Wall Street going for you?"

In response, my fraternity brother roared with laughter. No, I didn't crack a joke. He was laughing *at* me. Throughout college, I had poked fun at my fraternity brother for not taking college seriously. But here he was, excelling in one of the most coveted jobs of my college class. And there I was, taking on $100,000+ in student loans with job prospects no better than a year earlier.

After the laughter stopped, my fraternity brother finally said, "Dude I'm helping to manage $300 million! I'm killing it here!" Yes, he was. But there I was, studying harder than ever, and getting burned out doing it.

How could such different college approaches lead to two radically different career paths? I was supposed to be on Wall Street, not my fraternity brother. What was going on?

The Birth of HACKing College

After my phone call with my fraternity brother, a long, overdue light bulb exploded in my brain. I finally realized what should have occurred to me much earlier. My story, along with millions of others like it, demonstrates that hard work, good grades, and a college diploma no longer guarantee a job. Period.

My fraternity brother understood that better than anyone. In fact, he was a pure genius at identifying what he needed to do at college (not much) and what he didn't need to do (most things) in order to achieve precisely what he wanted. The secret to unlocking college success is not simply about working hard and doing well. Turns out there's much more to it. "HACKing college" explores this topic—and most importantly—how students can succeed as a result.

Writing the HACKs

"The dominant culture of education has come to focus on not teaching and learning but testing," said Sir Ken Robinson, who was knighted for his contribution to education. Yes, college is one big test. But with testing comes standardization, and that's great news for you. Standardization means the college process can be learned, which means it can be taught, which means it can be mastered.

Regrettably, students enter college with no approach, and no one encourages them to develop one, either. Instead, everyone celebrates when the admission letter arrives in the mail and when students walk the stage at graduation, but little attention is paid during the four years in between. It's almost as if people say to students, "We'll see you in four years. Hope you have it figured out by then!" That's why many students underperform during college and early in their careers.

Each of the secrets to college success contained in this book—or "HACKs"—are designed to equip students with a devastatingly effective college approach. By drilling down on the things that matter most, students can unlock college success faster than ever before. Unlike every other college approach out there, HACKing college does not necessarily mean raising your calculus grade from a B to an A. That move no longer produces meaningful results. Instead, HACKing college focuses on only the biggest opportunities, those capable of changing your life—opportunities that I call "Big Wins."

Fortunately, there is a group of people who best know where the Big Wins are in college: recent college graduates. In general, recent college graduates have freshly walked the college path, affording them the unique ability to have experienced both college *and* the workplace inside the new economy. Conversely, all non-recent college graduates advising students do so on the basis of analyzing—*from the outside*—the lives and experiences of recent college graduates.

I, as a recent college graduate, have relied on my seven years of playing the college game—four on the undergrad level and three on the doctorate level—as well as my experiences in the working world to develop a new college approach. In addition, I've collected 40+ real-world testimonies from people who have previously—and recently—walked the college path, including a:

- Team USA Hockey gold medalist and former professional hockey player, retired from NHL circuit (age 22);
- Patent designer turned professional YouTuber with 75+ million views (age 27);
- Startup founder, crowdfunded $100,000+ to build a school in Africa, raised $150,000 in venture capital to launch startup company (age 26);
- Networking superstar who leveraged LinkedIn to score job with presidential campaign, works in White House (age 23);
- Harvard near-flunkee turned NFL office insider (age 23);
- Fulbright Scholar, drafted laws as part of state legislative committee (age 24);
- U.S. Army veteran and Bronze Star recipient, oversees multi-million dollar projects (age 32);
- Refugee resettlement expert at U.S. Embassy, Baghdad, Iraq (age 27);
- Aerospace engineer, works on projects that support the International Space Station (age 26);

- Women's tennis Coach of the Year award winner at collegiate level (age 27);
- Videographer and small business owner, filmed 2014 Super Bowl (age 24); and
- Superstar scientist, serial publisher of scholarly articles, and former presenter at prestigious Mayo Clinic (age 28).

I hand-selected these stories—and more—to show current and upcoming college students exactly how it's possible to construct a college career that allows them to succeed in the modern economy.

Unfortunately, I fell behind my college classmates, largely because I had no college plan, no approach to college success. I learned too late. Unlike me, however, you don't have to play "catch up." You don't have to keep pace with the crowd, either. You can be different.

Thanks to these stories, this how-to manual represents insights costing literally tens of millions of dollars and centuries worth of time to acquire. Ultimately, this book represents an account of every practical lesson I wish I had known when I started my first day of college. If I had possessed this resource on Day 1 of freshman year, I'm confident that it would have changed my life. I've written this book to change yours.

A TIMELINE OF HOW I GOT HERE

Before diving into this life-changing advice, let's look at how I got here. Although I now know enough about college to rival even the best of college advisers, how I accumulated my knowledge is a bit less glamorous:

Early Childhood and High School

- **1987:** Born and raised in central Pennsylvania to a working class family. My small hometown owns the world record for the longest banana split ever made at 4.55 miles.

- **Spring 2006:** After completing a childhood filled with activities that showcased my promise for "success," I capped off high school by: leading the varsity football team in tackles, serving as captain of the wrestling team, and starting on the varsity tennis team, all while scoring high enough grades to land in my high school's top 10 percent. Never a question *if* I would attend college, but rather *where*. On the fast-track to success.

College and Law School

- **Spring 2006:** Parents promised to pay for the cost of attending Penn State. I took my parents' free ride.

- **Fall 2006:** Days after starting college, I opened and funded my first online poker account. The winnings would end up paying for my books and other expenses for my four years in college. Getting a taste for the benefits of playing life outside the norm.

- **Fall 2006 – Spring 2007:** Two college semesters down and two Dean's List honors later (a recognition I would achieve every semester), success looks like I couldn't miss.

- **Summer 2007:** Setback strikes. Despite my high grades, I failed to score an internship the summer after my freshman year. I returned home and worked for my grandparents' family-owned business. I repeated this process every summer leading up to law school, believing that I didn't need prestigious internships to land a job after graduation. Turns out, I was dead wrong.

- **Spring 2010:** Graduated at the top of my Penn State class. Despite my academic honors, however, I received zero job offers. I didn't know what to do, so I applied to 30+ law schools, spending all my Christmas money on application fees. I eventually received a full-ride offer to the University of Baltimore School of Law, which I rejected. I instead enrolled in the higher-ranked George Mason School of Law, where I paid (or borrowed) the full price of tuition, expecting to earn $160,000 at graduation (what George Mason said) from the "better" school. In the end, I took on $140,000 in student loans.

- **Spring 2010:** Apply to legal internships. However, because I failed to gather practical work experience (internship at family business was a tough sell), and because of mediocre grades following my first semester, I couldn't find any takers. Dumbfounded by the rigidness of the whole system. Disdain for rule-following builds.
- **Summer 2012:** Interned at Morgan Stanley, a Wall Street bank, the job I wanted in college. How did I score this position? *Through my fraternity brother.* Confident that the "enroll-study-graduate" system is broken beyond repair.

Law Student Turned Entrepreneur

- **September 2012:** Thanks to a friend's recommendation, I read *The 4-Hour Work Week* by Tim Ferriss, one of the top-three most influential books of my life. In the book, Ferriss laid out how people could escape the 9-5 grind, travel anywhere, and make even more money by simply doing things differently. This contradicted everything I had been taught up to this point in my life, including everything inside law school. *And I loved it.*
- **Fall 2012:** A friend introduces me to the founder of MIT's *Entrepreneurship Review* (later became my mentor), who encouraged me to (1) start a business—any business—in order to get into the entrepreneurial game, and (2) focus on something where I already had an edge. Soon thereafter I founded my first business, Gate1Tailgating, LLC, a cornhole board manufacturer.
- **Winter 2012:** Gate1Tailgating, LLC flopped. I quickly realized that a better business model doesn't require me to manufacturer a new product each time I make a sale. Shortly later, founded InvestConnect.com, a business that sought to help part-time investors invest like big banks.

Law School Graduation

- **May 2013:** What should have been an uninhibited celebration instead marked a pause to my entrepreneurial dreams. Plus, the reality of just having spent $140,000—a decision scheduled to take 20 years to repay—had a way of tempering the excitement coming from the stage.

Entry into Fulltime Employment

- **October 2013:** After receiving news that I had passed the Bar (exam that authorizes lawyers to practice) on my first try, I resumed working as a law clerk for one of the most well-respected trial judges in Virginia, something I had begun my third year of law school. Looks like I had finally achieved the "success" everyone expected.
- **Fall 2014:** Despite my best efforts to believe otherwise, nothing I did convinced me I was a "success." I realized that my life was on a trajectory

to work 60-hours a week, every week, for the next 40 years of my life, just so I could (hopefully) retire at the age of 65. That was not a life I wanted. So I did something radical: took two months off from my clerkship and rode my bicycle 3,167 miles across America.

- **Spring 2015:** After settling back into my clerkship, I rekindled my love for investing and launched nuwaverly.com, a socially responsible investing company meant for one thing: to revolutionize economics by investing exclusively in "socially responsible" companies. I once heard that the best businesses shoot for the moon, and nuwaverly was my moonshot. Soon realize that nuwaverly was more than I could chew. In search of a new entrepreneurial project.

- **July 2015:** Left my clerkship to pursue a job that afforded me the ability to repay my student loans before turning gray and wrinkly.

- **Fall 2015:** Hired by a law firm. Despite the handsome salary, working there turned out to be the worst job of my life. From the outside, everyone was trying to get in. From the inside, everyone was trying to get out.

- **Summer 2016:** In less than a year from being hired, the law firm president informs me that the firm no longer has sufficient work to justify my salary. Welcome to unemployment.

Enough Is Enough

- **Fall 2016:** Fed up with the brokenness and unfulfillment of playing by the rules, I resolved to (1) fully embrace my entrepreneurial, rule-breaking spirit (something that dated back to my poker days), (2) create a product that I could sell again and again without having to reproduce another after each sale (something I learned from Gate1Tailgating, LLC), and (3) deep-dive into an industry that I knew boatloads about (something I learned from my MIT mentor).

- **Summer 2017:** Launched *HACKiversity* to share everything I had learned, wished I had known, and wanted other students to know before setting out to play the college game.

THE BASICS OF COLLEGE

College Basic #1: *What is the Purpose of College?*

Skip the content in school. We'll teach it to you at Goldman Sachs.
—LLOYD BLANKFEIN, CEO OF GOLDMAN SACHS

In 2010, when I began my first year of law school, I saw up close what it looks like to have a brilliant mind. Nearly all of my classmates had graduated at the top of their college classes.

After our first year of law school, several students decided to transfer to higher-ranked law schools. One of my friends transferred to the University of Pennsylvania, a prestigious, Ivy League law school. When I saw him the next year, I asked about the differences between the two law schools.

"Basically, man, everything in terms of student quality, professor quality, and learning is the same," my friend said. "If any difference exists, I would say that students at Mason actually work harder than the students at Penn, because Mason students know they can't rely solely on their degree's reputation to open doors, whereas mostly everyone at Penn has something already locked up before graduation, simply because they go to Penn."

I couldn't believe it. How could the essence of a law school experience—students, professors, and the teaching curriculum—be mostly the same, while leading to vastly different career prospects?

This conversation caused me to ask a question that I should have asked long before: *what is the purpose of college?* In other words, what is the point to pulling all-nighters, cramming for exams, and paying thousands of dollars for this experience?

Generally speaking, people perceive the purpose of college as falling under one of the two belief systems:

- Getting a job, or
- Learning.

Those who focus on learning say, "College helps young people discover themselves and provides the skills necessary to pursue those things."

But if college were truly about learning, why do students pay hundreds of thousands of dollars to learn the same lessons accessible in thousands of scholarly articles on Google, hundreds of millions of videos on YouTube, and hundreds of online courses—all available for *free*? For example, today, anyone can take a semester's worth of online courses—*for free*—in MIT's top-ranked Supply Chain Management master's program. MIT's online program has no admissions requirements and is completely open to anyone. Harvard, Yale, and Princeton offer similar free programs. In reality, everyone is willing to pay a fortune to graduate from Harvard, but not many are willing to learn from Harvard professors without getting a degree.

That's because college is *not* about learning. It's about getting a job. A college degree is simply the mechanism for doing so. The value of college is what the degree—and the school behind the degree—says about the student. A college degree tells employers, "You can trust that I'll provide value to your company. For proof, just look at my diploma."

While it's true that there are many smart people without college degrees, there are also many not-so-smart people who don't have college degrees. In general, employers don't have time to find and select smart, non-college graduates from a stack of resumes, even if they exist. It's just easier to look at a diploma as evidence of an applicant's abilities. That's why a college degree is essentially no more than a certificate employers want to see, a box that needs checked, because employers believe—whether correctly or not—the best employees are college graduates.

I'm not suggesting that learning does not occur in college. Of course it does. If you spend thousands of dollars and four years (five or six years, for some) doing anything, there's no doubt you will learn something. The fact that learning *occurs*, however, does not make it the purpose of college. Learning is purely the *byproduct* of college. Learning is not why students go to college in the first place.

Still not convinced? Let's just suppose college were about learning. If that's the case, college is failing miserably at teaching students much of anything. A groundbreaking study found that 45 percent of students make no gains in their writing, complex reasoning, or critical-thinking skills during their first two years of college. After four years, the news isn't much better: 36 percent failed to show any improvement. If college students are spending a fortune to learn, they sure are getting a lousy deal.

Why does this matter? Once students know the purpose of college, they can reverse engineer a path that makes sense for them and achieve their goals. Academy Award-winning actor Kevin Spacey says it like this:

> I very often watch a lot of young people sort of meander around without any idea about why they're doing what they are doing…To know what you want, to understand why you're doing it… then there is nothing you can't achieve.

By knowing, from the start, that the purpose of college is to score a job, students can invest 100 percent of themselves in activities that help them reach this goal and trim away everything else.

Obviously, getting a job isn't the *only* thing that matters from your college career. The job has to be the right job. It has to bring you fulfillment and make you happy. That's why HACKing college is broken down into two sections: (1) learning *what* to do at college, and (2) teaching students *how* to do it. Ultimately, the HACKing college playbook is organized as follows:

HACKING COLLEGE FRAMEWORK

Discovering *What* to Do: The Self-Awareness Cornerstone. This is everything to the left of the centerline. The Self-Awareness Cornerstone provides the principles for helping students figure out the things that drive, motivate, and bring them to life—ingredients that form the foundation for building a successful college experience and career.

Two main concepts shape the Self-Awareness Cornerstone. The first concept is the goal of achieving self-awareness. This goal shapes everything inside the Self-Awareness Cornerstone. The second concept is experimentation, the fastest and most effective way to achieve self-awareness.

Inside these two concepts are the "Self-HACKs," or the step-by-step action items designed to identify specific resources and exercises to help students pinpoint—with warp speed—the things that make them tick. The four Self-HACKs are:

1. Passion
2. Strengths
3. Purpose
4. Lifestyle

All of these ideas—including the four Self-HACKs and the two basic concepts—are known as the "Self-Awareness" Cornerstone.

Learning *How* to Do College: The Execution Cornerstone. This is everything to the right of the centerline. The Execution Cornerstone provides the principles for helping students achieve success—both during and after college—faster than ever before.

Similar to the Self-Awareness Cornerstone, two main concepts shape the Execution Cornerstone. The first concept is the goal of maximizing a student's marketability in the eyes of employers. This goal shapes everything inside the Execution Cornerstone. The second concept is leverage, the idea that only a small amount of things matter in achieving any goal.

Inside these two concepts are the "Action HACKs," the step-by-step action items designed to maximize a student's marketability by honing in on the few things that matter most in college. The seven Action HACKs are:

1. College Selection
2. Megatrends
3. Major Selection
4. Grades
5. Internships
6. Networking
7. Non-Negotiable Skills

All these ideas—including the seven Action HACKs and the two basic concepts—are known as the "Execution" Cornerstone.

In total, "HACKing College" contains two Cornerstones (providing the conceptual framework for the HACKs) and their accompanying HACKs (providing actionable, step-by-step advice).

Before diving in, however, it's important to understand what happens if students do *not* HACK college. Read on and buckle up!

College Basic #2: *Why Your Current College Approach Will Fail*

"The What:" The Same Bad Advice Every Student Is Given Today

Adults are always asking kids what they want to be when they grow up because they're looking for ideas.
—PAULA POUNDSTONE, COMEDIAN

I call it "conventional wisdom." It's based on this misguided belief that nearly every student needs to attend college, work really hard, and graduate with a stellar GPA from a top university. Then, upon graduation, the student takes his or her freshly-minted diploma to an employer, who is supposed to be so amazed that someone as gifted as this student is standing in their presence. Out of this amazement, the employer rushes to offer the student a job, and the student lives happily ever after. It's like a three-step process for 18-year olds.

Once employed, conventional wisdom instructs recent college graduates to stay working inside their career for the next 40 years of their life. Conventional wisdom believes that stability is king, which means few job changes, little exploration, and no variety in life until retirement.

It's only once the student hits retirement that conventional wisdom believes the student can actually live an enjoyable life. Suddenly, it's permissible to do fun things like travel, spend time with friends and family, or generally do whatever he or she wants. Until then, it's a race to accumulate as many material possessions necessary to bridge the period between retirement and death. Oh, and if the student dies before retirement, they never receive any of the benefits conventional wisdom has to offer. This is the life that everyone wants *you* to live.

Amazingly, conventional wisdom forces students into this rigid process in their teens. This twisted approach to college in particular, and life in general, has caused great damage to students seeking to use college to jumpstart their careers. Stories of crushing debt and widespread underemployment are no longer isolated incidents, but are increasingly becoming the norm. Nevertheless, conventional wisdom advocates continue to trumpet their message in every school, home, and office, despite clear signs it no longer works.

"The Why:" Why More of the Same Is a Bad Idea

Truth is like poetry. And most people hate poetry.
—The Big Short, 2015

Today, college graduates are flocking into lower-quality jobs that have not traditionally required a college degree, something known as "underemployment." Think of the college graduates now waiting tables, working at a coffee shop, or pouring drinks as a bartender in jobs that do not fit their education level.

In 2008, more than 35 percent of recent college graduates were under-employed. By 2015, that number jumped to 50 percent. Next time you're in class, look to your left and right. Chances are, one of those people will wear a green Starbucks apron after graduation. (And they're thinking the same thing about you).

Students' deteriorating employment prospects are made worse by the sky-rocketing cost of college tuition. "A major source of worry and concern for Millennials is debt," reported a leading survey. "Their number one financial concern, following day-to-day bills, is paying off student loans."

The economics of a college education have gotten so out of control that today over 40 million people carry $1.2 trillion in student loan debt. Nationwide, student loan debt grows by $2,700 every second. "What you thought you were going to get in quality of life by going to that college, you've just undermined with the amount of debt you're taking on," said Mark Cuban, billionaire and owner of the Dallas Mavericks basketball team.

Why are employment prospects for college graduates disappearing? There are many reasons, but none bigger than something known as "academic inflation," the process by which a college degree loses value as a result of too many people having one. Think of it like this: the more college degrees there are, the less valuable each degree becomes.

Consider the staggering amount of students who attended some sort of American higher education institution in 2015 alone: an eye-popping 27.8 million students. That's more people than the populations of New York, Los Angeles, Chicago, Houston, Philadelphia, Phoenix, San Antonio, San Diego, Dallas, and San Jose...*combined.*

But America's college numbers do not reflect the entire story. Consider the state of college around the world today: there are over 150.6 million college graduates or current students globally. That's more than Russia's *total* population. What's more, experts project that in the next thirty years, more people will hold a college degree than *since the beginning of human history.* Feeling lost in the crowd yet? You should.

This flood of college graduates has fundamentally reshaped the value of college. Sir Ken Robinson explains:

> Between 1950 and 1980, a college degree was pretty much a guarantee of a good job. If you had a degree, employers formed a line to interview you. They don't now. The essential problem is not the quality of the degrees, but the quantity…A college degree used to be so valuable because relatively few people had one. In a world bristling with graduates, a college degree is no longer the distinction it once was.

College degrees have now become the new high school diploma, and jobs that used to require a bachelor's degree now require a master's degree. The reality is that college students today are no more special than the millions of other similarly qualified graduates out there.

But there are more problems. Today, globalization is offshoring more jobs, including white-collar jobs, than ever before. Thomas Friedman in his famous piece about globalization, *The World Is Flat*, interviewed a CEO of a tech company located in Bangalore, India (think America's Silicon Valley), who explained how, through the Internet, anyone willing to work at a cheaper rate can perform *any* work previously completed by an American college graduate. As a result, jobs that have traditionally required a college degree—such as doctors, lawyers, and engineers—are now disappearing thanks to global competition.

A friend and former college classmate said it best when, six years after college graduation, she reflected on her decision to blindly follow conventional wisdom:

> As a 17 year old, a big name school was all that I saw, not what my future would really be like. Four years later, as a senior about to graduate college, I cried in my advisor's office after realizing I wouldn't be able to pay rent and my student loan at the same time.

Millions of recent college graduates are like my friend: over-indebted, underemployed, and defeated by the empty promises of conventional wisdom. Fortunately, it doesn't have to be this way. But in order to bring about a different outcome, students must first understand that what it takes for college graduates to get a "good job"—and increasingly, a job, period—has changed.

"The Who:" Traditional College Advisors Don't Get It

One of the perils of being seventeen is that lots of people think
they have good advice for you. But what they really have is good
advice for them when they were seventeen.
—SETH GODIN, AUTHOR

Family, friends, school teachers, and administrators. These are the people who have traditionally given college advice. They are also the ones responsible for ingraining conventional wisdom deep into students' minds.

"I learned everything about college from my parents," said Ben Bailey (Susquehanna '10, Environmental Science). "They said that I needed to bust my butt, that I needed to study way harder than I did in high school. I went into college thinking, 'This is another thing I've got to do to get ahead,' instead of relishing it."

Despite their good intentions, traditional sources of conventional wisdom don't understand that studying hard and graduating with a shiny diploma no longer guarantees anything. Fortunately for them, the stock market *doubled* over a four-year period in the 1980's and more than *tripled* over a four-year period in the 1990's. Working inside a company with low turnover during an era of extraordinarily high stock market returns paved a golden highway for older generations to enjoy a predictable and safe career while padding their bank accounts with sizable checks and buying comfortable suburban homes.

Today, the climb-the-ladder approach is broken. The 1990's stock market boom, for example, had a probability of roughly 0.40 percent of occurring. In other words, don't expect to collect a nice pension by working at an employer for the next 30 years. Those days are over. In addition, employees who stay in companies longer than two years earn less than 50 percent of what routine job switchers make over the course of a lifetime.

Rather than acknowledge the brokenness of conventional wisdom, traditional college advisors have doubled down on it. The results have been disastrous for students.

Consider the extent to which parents will tolerate their children being absolutely miserable, if it means that their child will have "succeeded" at college. After a survey showed a rise in student psychological problems on campus, a retired college chairman emailed a colleague and asked, "Do you think parents at your school would rather their kid be depressed at Yale or happy at [the] University of Arizona?"

"My guess is 75 percent of the parents would rather see their kids depressed at Yale," the colleague quickly replied. "They figure that kids can straighten the emotional stuff out in [their] 20s, but no one can go back and get the Yale undergrad degree."

In summary, for students to unlock college success, they must understand that:
- Conventional wisdom—that is, the way people expect students to approach college and life in general—no longer provides meaningful results in today's economy. By itself, the "enroll-study-graduate"

method serves as a completely useless springboard and won't provide college students with an effective launching pad.

- Students who blindly follow the path of conventional wisdom are destined for underachievement, over-indebtedness, and unnecessary misery. Forces such as academic inflation, globalization, and soaring college costs will continue to devalue conventional wisdom's approach to college.

- Regrettably, despite these powerful forces, many college advisors have failed to see the perils of conventional wisdom. First, conventional wisdom worked in the past, so they expect it to keep working. Second, traditional college advisors played the college game decades ago, when the world was much different, blinding them to the new realities of the modern economy.

While all these pitfalls of conventional wisdom are true, what's also true is that learning has never been more accessible, experiences have never been more available, and opportunities have never been more valuable. We are living in a world of extremes. For those who reap, they reap in abundance. For those who flounder, they flounder longer. HACKing college helps students live a life of abundance, while avoiding the landmines scattered across the college landscape. Without further ado, let's start HACKing college!

SELF-AWARENESS

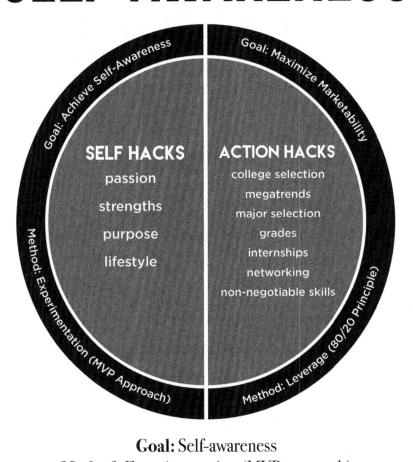

Goal: Self-awareness
Method: Experimentation (MVP approach)

Use experimentation to quickly, cheaply, and reliably develop self-awareness

Whoever best describes the problem is the one most likely to solve it.
—DAN ROAM, AUTHOR

Stop me if you've heard this story before (actually, just keep reading). A college student spends thousands of dollars on tuition, locks himself in the library for hours each week, attends every class, and generally commits years of his life in every respect imaginable. Then, upon graduation, the student discovers all the effort, money, and time failed to deliver a job he likes. *This can't happen.*

All too predictably, students without a clear college game plan are destined for difficulty. Take it from my sister, Andrea Winey (West Chester '12, Spanish):

> In middle school, I traveled to the Dominican Republic, where I saw so much poverty. That stirred within me a desire to help people in my career. That's why I majored in Spanish. Unfortunately, aside from teaching, there are not many job opportunities for Spanish majors. But I knew that I didn't want to teach Spanish. In fact, I didn't know what I wanted to do after college. I didn't have a college plan other than to graduate with a Spanish degree.
>
> Graduation was a real awakening. I had a Spanish degree but no job and lots of bills to pay. I didn't know what to do. So I interviewed with a temp agency. They placed me in a job where I process customer orders by entering the information into a computer—much like a secretary. I don't use my Spanish degree at all. I've come to hate my job. I hate sitting behind a desk all day.

A lack of college strategy caused Andrea to land a low-paying, unfulfilling job, despite her college degree.

The remainder of the Self-Awareness Cornerstone provides the fundamental principles students need to know in order to overcome this problem, determine *what* to do in college, and position themselves to take action.

Self-Awareness: The Solution

Until we see what we are, we cannot take steps to become what we should be.
—CHARLOTTE GILMAN, AMERICAN WRITER AND CIVIL RIGHTS ACTIVIST

So what's the solution to ensure that college students, much like Andrea, don't land a job they hate after graduation? *Self-awareness.* Simply put, self-awareness is the understanding of who you are and how you are similar to or different from others.

Self-awareness is so powerful that studies have found it serves as the strongest predictor of overall success. In other words, neither brains nor brawn can determine success as accurately as understanding *the extent* of your brains or brawn (or lack thereof). Peter Guber, co-owner of the Golden State Warriors basketball team, framed the importance of self-awareness like this:

In my four decades of experience as a leader and entrepreneur in diverse industries from entertainment to sports to new media to education, in the hierarchy of factors most important to career success, I would rank self-awareness as #1. I wish I knew this at age 22.

Despite the extraordinary benefits of self-awareness, today less than 30 percent of people are self-aware, meaning that the majority of individuals mistakenly believe that they possess certain personal characteristics that they actually don't. For example, 70 percent of high school seniors believe they have "above average" leadership skills, even though it's impossible, by definition, for more than 50 percent to be "above average." It's no surprise, then, that college students repeatedly wander aimlessly through college, much to their misfortune.

By developing self-awareness, students can simultaneously minimize the financial and economic disaster of discovering all-too-late that a particular major, industry, or even college altogether was a bad decision, while maximizing the opportunities to land in a lucrative, meaningful job.

How to Best Achieve Self-Awareness: Experimentation

Aim, fire, aim, fire, aim, fire.
—Reid Hoffman, co-founder of LinkedIn

Imagine if a professor tried to teach you how to ride a bicycle in the same way she teaches any other subject. Most likely, you would stay up late at night memorizing the names of various bike components. You would be marked down on tests—and lose self-confidence—for misspelling *derailleur*. Under this system, you might excel, or you might struggle. You would never ride a bike. That's a problem.

Similarly, in the college arena today, it's the absence of *doing* that causes students' difficulties. That's why students routinely find themselves trapped during college and after graduation. They never actually ventured out to see whether they found their job, industry, or career path enjoyable in the first place.

Fortunately, there is a different approach, one used by cutting-edge startup companies located in Silicon Valley. It's the process of launching an unfinished product, with the intention of receiving immediate feedback and tweaking to meet customer demands. Entrepreneurs call this the "Minimum Viable Product" (MVP) approach. The MVP approach can be effectively applied to people too. But because people aren't products, I call this process "experimentation."

In general, there are two ways to receive feedback from experimentation:

1. **The "Steering Wheel" Feedback Loop:** Responses that are instantaneous, cheap, and reliable. Consider how the feedback between the driver and steering wheel is so immediate and automatic that we often don't think about the many turns we take while we drive.

2. The "Rocket Ship" Feedback Loop: Responses that are delayed, expensive, and unpredictable. Consider how the feedback from launching a rocket ship first requires millions of dollars for construction, assembling a team, and conducting sophisticated calculations, all before the rocket ship makes it to the launching pad. It's only after years and millions of dollars that you discover if the launch is even successful.

To maximize the likelihood of a successful college career, students must embrace the Steering Wheel Feedback Loop. In doing so, students can easily and quickly correct errors in assumptions they may have made regarding their college careers. Using the Rocket Ship Feedback Loop, however, is like the college graduate who spends four years in school, graduates, and then works a few years in his desired field, only to discover he hates his job.

Each of the Self-HACKs within the Self-Awareness Cornerstone are designed to mirror the Steering Wheel Feedback Loop and provide students with personalized feedback as cheaply, quickly, and reliably as possible. The following section represents the three-step process involved in unlocking the magic of the Steering Wheel Feedback Loop, and provides a framework for how students can best use the Self-HACKs.

Step #1: Define Your Assumptions

Through the experimentation process, students play the role of scientists investigating themselves. And as a scientist, the first step to conducting an experiment is to create a hypothesis of what is expected to occur.

More specifically, for our purposes, you must define your assumptions in regard to your proposed college career track. Ask: *"What has to prove true in order for me to realistically expect that my proposed college track is a good one?"*

To get you started, here are some examples, which I've broken into two categories:

Success Related Assumptions
- **Work Style:** I assume that I prefer to work independently, not on teams.
- **Location Preference:** I assume that I prefer to work and live inside a city, not work and live in the country.
- **Analytical Style:** I assume that I perform best when I'm crunching numbers (quantitative analysis), not figuring out how a piece of a problem fits within the broader context (qualitative analysis).

Personal Fulfillment Related Assumptions
- **Compensation:** I assume that making a reasonable amount of money matters in my career.
- **Motivation:** I assume that working on something I care deeply about is important to me.
- **Lifestyle:** I assume that I prefer a high-pressure, well-compensated job, despite having little time off, compared to a more casual job with more personal flexibility.

For example, suppose you want to pursue accounting, a field that requires significant computation and independent work, while providing a generous salary. As a result, effective assumptions might be: "I assume that I'll be comfortable conducting advanced calculations," or "I assume that I'll enjoy working by myself."

If you're struggling to create assumptions, log onto LinkedIn (www.linkedin.com) and search the profiles of people who you think you'd like to become. For example, suppose you want to know more about people who majored in biomedical engineering in college. From the LinkedIn search, you'll see that most biomedical engineer graduates work at three employers: GE Healthcare, Medtronic, and Siemens Healthcare. Since you know where you'll likely end up, just reverse engineer the process. Now your assumptions could be, "I assume that I'll enjoy working at one of these three major corporations." If you still can't find the right people, use PayScale (bit.ly/degreeprofile) to discover typical salaries, job descriptions, and locations of hundreds of career paths.

Step #2: Test

Tell me and I forget; teach me and I may remember; involve me and I will learn.
—Xunzi, Confucian Philosopher

Every assumption from Step #1 must be tested. And I mean *every* assumption.

Perhaps the most effective way to test assumptions is by immersing yourself in your projected environment. Internships, job experiences, volunteering, and even gap years are several of the many ways to accomplish this. No matter the environment, students must get out of the library and into the real world.

Zach Clemens (James Madison '14, Computer Information Systems) demonstrates how just being out in the real world equipped him with the insight necessary to achieve success during and after college.

> During college, I interned at a local bank every Christmas and summer break. My internship wasn't really related to technology, which was the focus of my major. But I eventually moved over to the technology side.

> In general, my banking internships helped prepare me for Accenture, the consulting company where I now work. Just putting on a suit and tie, being in a professional environment, and working 40 hours a week showed me what I was getting into. Lifeguarding, for example, wouldn't have prepared me for that.

Despite only having recently graduated, Zach has accomplished much in his short career, mainly thanks to the experimentation he conducted during college. "I hit the ground running at Accenture," said Zach. "Ever since coming on board, I've worked face-to-face with clients, handled the backend affairs, and everything in between."

Similarly, Aaron Myers (Penn State '09, Psychology; Phila. College of Osteopathic Medicine '17, Clinical Psy.D.) explains how his work experience senior year of undergrad confirmed that he was actually on the right career track:

> I had an inclination of what I wanted to do. But what solidified it was not anything I did in school. Instead, it was my job senior year, when I worked at the local psychiatric hospital. The work experience did it for me. I could actually see the things we were talking about in class.

Experimentation can also be conducted from the comforts of your own home. Included in the Self HACKs are recommended resources, websites, and books that range from $15 to completely free, and can provide critical insights in rapid fashion.

Step #3: Draw Conclusions, Repeat the Cycle

A desk is a dangerous place from which to view the world.
—JOHN LE CARRE, AUTHOR

The final step in the experimentation process is to revisit your assumptions. In light of your testing from Step #2, which assumptions were true? Which were false?

For example, in our earlier accounting hypothetical, the assumptions were: "I assume that I'll be comfortable conducting advanced calculations," and "I assume that I'll enjoy working by myself." As part of your experimentation, suppose you interned at an accounting firm. Did your internship confirm these assumptions? If you worked independently, did you enjoy it, or did you want more teamwork? How easily were you able to complete the tasks assigned to you?

If your experiment confirmed your assumption, perhaps accounting is a fitting career track. If, however, the experiment invalidated your assumptions, there's a good chance it's time to head in a different direction.

The key to Step #3 is to not stop. After you draw your conclusion, repeat the whole cycle. This is why it's called a "feedback *loop*." Your whole college career should be one major loop that tests, retests, and then tests again the assumptions you've made along the way.

One final note: in Step #3, students frequently think of an outcome as "good" or "bad" depending on the end result. That's a mistake. Why? You don't know what's going to happen in Step #3 before you experiment. That's why you experiment in the first place. You can only make decisions based on the information you have in the moment. Instead, view the feedback from Step #3 as the ammunition necessary to re-tackle Step #1, but more informed than before. "Experiments are fact-finding missions that, over time, inch scientists toward greater understanding," said Ed Catmull, president of Pixar. "That means *any* outcome is a good outcome, because it yields new information."

RIVER GUIDE TURNS DENTIST: WHY REJECTING THE "LIFE IS LINEAR" BELIEF MATTERS

Many students, thanks to conventional wisdom, buy into a "life is linear" approach and focus on checking off "life milestones" in a predictable, orderly fashion. For example, a career services director at the University of Texas says that she finds many students, who majored in political science, decide to pursue law school simply because they think it's the logical next step.

Fortunately, Jack Ver Ploeg (New Hampshire '09, Political Science; New England '17, Dentistry) has rejected this "life is linear" narrative.

Jack's high school experience was like many students: filled with uncertainty. In fact, Jack debated even going to college. "After high school graduation, I was tired of tests and decided to take time off," explained Jack. "I heard about a 'Gap Year,' so I decided to join my sister and brother and ride our bicycles from Anchorage, Alaska down to Mexico."

When Jack returned, he decided to enroll in college, bringing with him an unconventional method of living life outside the box. In particular, Jack began a long series of experimentation, testing his career-related assumptions, which included working on a Montana ranch and as a river guide in Grand Teton National Park, despite majoring in Political Science, something much different.

While many conventional wisdom advocates are quick to label Jack's decisions as "childish" or "reckless," Jack disagrees. "I needed to try different things before I decided dentistry is what I want," said Jack, now on his way to running his bustling family dental practice. "When you get broad exposure to many things, it rounds you out. It has made me a better dentist."

Ultimately, Jack's success arose not *despite* this windy process but *because* of it. Most importantly, Jack's story shows that experimenting outside the box—even with seemingly irrelevant activities—can lead to self-awareness.

The Timing of Experimentation

Many college students want to know *when* experimentation should occur. The answer is that you should begin experimentation *now*, regardless of where you are in the college process. The sooner, the better. For the following five reasons, the ideal situation is to complete the majority of the experimentation process as close to Day 1 of freshman year as possible, allowing you to hit the campus ground running.

Reason #1: Early Self-Awareness Accelerates College Performance

Research shows that only one in five young people have a clear vision of what they want to accomplish in life. This lack of vision enhances a student's chances of wandering aimlessly throughout his or her college career.

"But Kyle," you object, "didn't you just tell me to reject the 'life is linear' approach? Didn't you just encourage me to experiment with things outside the box?" Yes, I did. But the difference is that I encouraged you to reject the "life is linear" belief so that you can *intentionally* experiment with certain activities. Intentionally experimenting, even in a wide array of activities, is much different than drifting through college with no plan at all.

Reason #2: You Have Time

When you are young, you are cash-poor, but time-rich. Your wallet might be empty but your weekends are pretty much free. That flips when you are older. After you graduate, suddenly you find your wallet is full (at least, sorta) and your weekends are crammed with activities. You might have money to spend but no time to do it.

Overbooked schedules limit experimentation, as it forces focus on the things right before you. Experimentation requires flexibility, exploration, and time. And these things are never more abundant than while you're young.

Reason #3: The Downside Is Small

Suppose you take a gap year, but it fails to develop the self-awareness you had hoped. What's the downside? You're out some cash and a little time—not a big deal. In fact, you walk away with memories to forever cherish. When you're young, the cost of experimentation going poorly is basically zero.

That changes over time. Family, bills, and other responsibilities increase risks if things go wrong, making experimentation more difficult.

Reason #4: Debt: The Surest Way to Prevent Experimentation

Who goeth a borrowing, Goeth a sorrowing.
—Thomas Tusser, English poet

Even if you are an experimentation pro, life after graduation will inevitably look much different. You'll want to experiment as a new college graduate, too.

Importantly, however, one thing can bring these precious experimentation opportunities to a screeching halt: debt. Debt is perhaps the most sure-fire way to predetermine what you must do after college graduation.

Not surprisingly, nearly 20 percent of college graduates with student loans eventually give up on their preferred line of work. With bills regularly rolling in, repayment must be made, forcing college graduates into a job, *any* job. Eventually, these college graduates become locked inside their less-than-ideal position or industry, simply because they cannot escape their massive student loans. That's why it's important to limit the amount of student loans you take on.

How $250,000 in Student Loans Restrict Brilliant Lawyer's Career Opportunities

My former law school classmate was one of the smartest people in our class. In only three short years after graduation, she landed a highly desirable job inside a prestigious U.S. government agency. However, as she explains, her crushing amount of student loans virtually locks her into that job, even if she wants to change course later:

> I have $250,000 in loans at 8 percent interest. I'm lucky I'm eligible for public service loan forgiveness if I don't go anywhere for another eight years. But my husband has another $250,000 in loans. He isn't so lucky...It's literally impossible to get out from under it, and we make comparatively high salaries.

In other words, my former classmate is forced to work inside the federal government for the next *eight* years of her life. That's enough time to go through college *twice*. Otherwise, as she states, she'll never be able to escape her crushing debt.

Fortunately for her, she actually likes her job. But imagine a different situation, where a student fails to experiment and is now locked inside a job he or she hates for nearly a decade. Without question, debt limits the amount of career options—and therefore opportunities—college graduates have.

Reason #5: Embrace Failure: You Can Afford to in College

I've missed more than 9,000 shots in my career. I've lost almost 300 games. Twenty-six times I've been trusted to take the game-winning shot and missed. I've failed over and over and over again in my life. And that is why I succeed.
—Michael Jordan, six-time NBA champion

Failure has been long viewed as a dirty word. Students, who receive an F on an exam, have "failed." Athletes who try out for the football team and get cut have "failed." It's no surprise that failure is often equated with "not good enough," "not smart enough," or "not capable enough." That's why students run from failure. But students who want to be successful *must* fail. I'm not talking about learning *in spite* of failure. I mean learning *because* of failure.

There is a method to failing successfully, and it begins with failing fast. Once you see something won't succeed, pull the plug immediately. Fast failures not only avoid wasting resources, they provide the fuel to make it through the experimentation process again and again—the essence of a Steering Wheel Feedback Loop—thereby increasing self-awareness.

Use these three steps to increase the likelihood of failing successfully:

- **Step #1. Log your failures:** write down what happened.

- **Step #2. Categorize your failures:** identify whether it was a screwup (a simple mistake), a weakness (something that happens over and over again), or a growth opportunity (something that doesn't happen often and is fixable).
- **Step #3. Identify growth insights:** ask these three questions: (i) "What is there to learn here?" (ii) "What went wrong?" and (iii) "What could be done differently next time?"

Finally, students who avoid failure in college actually set themselves up for more failure in the future, because they develop self-awareness too late. "Ironically, the more you risk failure—and actually fail—the greater your chances of success," said leadership guru, John Maxwell.

Warning: Do Not Do This

Things which matter most must never be at the mercy of things which matter least.
—GOETHE, GERMAN PHILOSOPHER

I know many students will be tempted to ignore the Self-HACKs and immediately jump into what is perceived as the more "practical" stuff within the Execution Cornerstone.

But with the increasing costs of getting college wrong, the Self-HACKs have never been more practical. Why? To succeed in college, students *must* first know *what* to do and *where* to start. That's exactly what the Self-HACKs explain.

HACKING TAKEAWAYS

- Millions of students wander aimlessly through college, wasting thousands of dollars and years of time.
- To solve this problem, students must develop "self-awareness," an understanding of who they are and how they are similar to or different from others.
- The best way to develop self-awareness is through "experimentation," a process of testing and re-testing assumptions every student makes about his or her own college track.

With a conceptual framework developed, it's time to dive into the step-by-step process of determining exactly *what* to do inside the college arena. As a result, let's explore the four Self-HACKs inside the Self-Awareness Cornerstone:

1. Passion
2. Strengths
3. Purpose
4. Lifestyle

SELF HACK # 1
Passion

Never follow your passion, but never be without it either

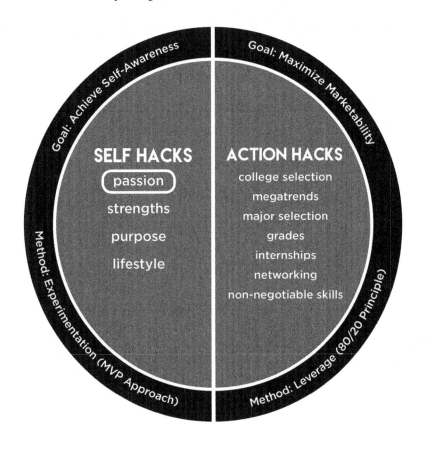

*The next time someone tells you to 'do what you love
no matter what,' ask to see their tax return.*
—AUSTIN KLEON, AUTHOR

I began my undergraduate career in the College of Education at Penn State. During my freshman year, however, I slowly began to realize that pursuing a major in secondary education was not a good fit for me. First, I found my education classes mildly interesting at best. I wanted to learn complex, thought-provoking ideas, not just better ways to teach high schoolers concepts I already knew. Second, I couldn't identify with many of my classmates. At no point did I meaningfully engage with a classmate where I left thinking, "Now this guy gets it." Something was missing.

No advice was more influential to me wanting to be a teacher than the same advice spoon-fed to millions of incoming college students: "follow your passions." This advice sounds great in theory. Just pursue something you love to do, right? What could go wrong?

It didn't take me long to discover that "follow your passion" was bad advice. In my college ignorance, I had assumed that by following my passion—even though I had no idea what my passion was—everything would turn out all right. It doesn't.

The Passion HACK will demonstrate how passion practically fits into the college equation, techniques for students to quickly find theirs, and how students can boost their college success as a result.

The Real Deal on Passion

It's hard to do a really good job on anything you don't think about in the shower.
—PAUL GRAHAM, Y COMBINATOR CO-FOUNDER

What does it mean to have "passion," anyway?

Passion is more than just an "interest" in something. For example, I have an "interest" in reading, but I would never want to actually be a professional reader, such as a copyeditor. That's because an "interest" is something you're excited or curious about, but not something that gives meaning to your life. "Are you going to go to your sweetie and say, 'Marry me! You're *interesting*,'" a TEDx speaker once asked. Umm...no. Instead, passion is a deep, emotional conviction that drives us to achieve our vision of something meaningful.

Passion is something every high achiever can identify within themselves. That means for those wanting superior college success, they must know their passion, too.

When asked the question, "What is the most important thing for a sixteen-year-old to do this summer vacation?" Peter Diamandis, co-founder of Singularity University, explained the importance of starting with passion:

> The single most important thing for a high school student, college student, even for anyone listening here...is understanding what his or her passion is....[I]f you know your passion at that age, you can start to really use that to drive where you go to college, what you learn in college, what you do in building companies.

Importantly, students who know their passion are able to work with *intensity* on what matters to them. And when you work with intensity, it means you can actually work fewer hours. It's the difference between going through the motions versus making an impact. Legendary basketball coach John Wooden explained that when you like what you do with all of your heart, it "ignites plain old work" and unlocks your fullest potential.

The story of Sarah Lucas (Penn State '10, Microbiology; Minnesota '19, Ph.D. Microbiology) demonstrates how passion can fuel a wildly successful career, both before and after graduation. Sarah is already a science superstar, and she isn't even finished with her education. Despite still being in school, Sarah has already authored four publications, spoke at the prestigious Mayo Clinic, and presented her work at the American Society for Microbiology. What's the secret to Sarah's success? As Sarah explains, passion:

> You can't be successful in this field unless you love it. I've seen people who aren't passionate switch majors or decide to go to medical school. If you don't love science, this career is going to be difficult for you. Undoable, I would say.

Unlike many others, Sarah absolutely loves what she does. In fact, she speaks about her career in almost a romantic way:

> I get paid to figure out the world, figure out how life works. I can sit and think about things that no one knows anything about. That's such a privilege. It's really an honor that society supports me in this career. These thoughts drive me. I couldn't imagine doing anything else with my life.

Sarah's story matches exactly what science tells us about the relationship between passion and success. Studies show that students who are driven by the internal satisfaction of the activity itself actually outperform students who are not. Not to mention, these same students have higher self-esteem, better relationships, and greater general well-being. The magic of passion isn't confined to college success—it can mean an overall better life.

As a student, do you feel the way Sarah does about your major, your industry, or what you're setting out to do in college? What do you love to do just for the sake of doing it? Just by knowing these answers, students can expect better grades, a better network, and a better career.

How to Identify Your Passion

Start with "Flow"

Working hard for something we don't care about is called stress.
Working hard for something we love is called passion.
—SIMON SINEK, AUTHOR

In just a few decades, human performance has grown faster and farther than at any other point in history.

For example, in 1960, a surfer rode a 25-foot wave (two-in-a-half stories high), considered the biggest wave ever caught at the time. Then, in 1996, a surfer caught a 35-foot wave (three-in-a-half stories high).

Fast forward to 2000. Laird Hamilton, an extreme surfer, found himself on the shores of Teahupoo, a beach in Tahiti. That day, Hamilton was told that the waves were so big that they were "unridable." "They said, 'We don't go out there when it's like this,'" recounts Hamilton.

Then Hamilton did the seemingly impossible and rode the famous "Millennium Wave," a 55-foot (over five stories high) tall monster. "It was like a dam bursting," recalls one surfer. It was the biggest wave ever ridden....until it wasn't. In 2011, Garrett McNamara caught a spectacular 78-foot goliath (nearly eight stories high) in Portugal, the biggest wave currently ever surfed. Today, surfers are looking to break the 100-foot mark.

"What does surfing have to do with college?" you ask. College, much like surfing, is about performance. It's about getting results. Surfers were able to ride waves as tall as buildings by getting inside a mental state called "flow."

"Flow" is the state in which people are so involved in an activity that nothing else seems to matter.

"Flow activities," or experiences enjoyed for their own sake, have specific qualities. On one hand, the activities are challenging enough that they do not lead to boredom, but are not overly challenging that they cause anxiousness. Spotting your flow activities is one of the key ways to supercharge your college success and ride a monster wave inside the classroom.

To identify flow activities, experts have developed the "flow test." Flow test participants are given a pager, set to beep ten times each day. After the pager goes off, the participants respond to several questions.

You can easily and cheaply replicate the flow test by simply setting your cell phone to ring several times a day over the course of a week. Every time your cell phone goes off, answer the following questions:

- **What are you doing?** Are you completely involved in what you're doing—that is, focused on your activity—or are you distracted and noticing the time passing?
- **How do you feel?** Are you experiencing a great inner clarity—that is, knowing what needs to be done and how well you are doing it—or are you unsure how to accomplish your current task?

- **What are you thinking about?** Are you believing that the activity is doable—that is, your skills are adequate to complete the task—or are you feeling a sense of boredom or anxiousness?
- **What is driving you?** Are you being driven by intrinsic motivation—that is, you find the process itself rewarding—or are you doing something because of external factors?

Ultimately, the flow test provides, in real time, accurate data that does not cost you a dime. That's why the flow test is one of my favorite ways to discover passion.

How Students Describe Flow

1. **Disregard for Grades:** Josh Taylor (Trevecca Nazarene '10, Mass Communications). For a radio class, I started creating commercials and doing promos. It was the only time in college I remember working on projects late into the night, not caring what my grade was, and having fun doing it.

2. **Disregard for Time:** Gret Glyer (Grove City '12, Entrepreneurship). During sophomore year I entered a business plan competition. I wrote two business plans and an elevator pitch. One of the projects was called "Grandma's phone," which turned a smartphone into a very basic interface. I poured myself into it, built teams around it. It took a lot of time away from my studies, but I didn't care. I loved it.

3. **Disregard for Money:** Hope Burke (Stanford '14, History and African Studies). After college, I enrolled in Teach for America. A lot of my friends went to work in investment banking. Very few Stanford graduates pursue public sector work. But, for the first time, I'm discussing things that matter. I talk about inequality. I talk about race. I value people and their stories.

In addition to the flow test, you can use the following three approaches to help identify flow activities, and therefore, your passion.

Approach #1: Look at Your Actions

> *Above all, to thine own self be true.*
> —WILLIAM SHAKESPEARE

It was 1976 and Steve Wozniak quit his 9-5 job and co-founded Apple Computers with Steve Jobs. Apple's success is no secret, going on to become the most valuable publicly traded company in the world.

In order to build revolutionary products, Wozniak had to be passionate about technology, and he was. Wozniak explains how looking at his actions helped identify his passion:

> I spent a long time in my life…just building little devices for fun. "For fun" is one of the key things. 'Cause that drives you to think, and think, and think, and make it better, and better, and better, than you ever would if you're doing it for a company. Build things at first for yourself—that you would want.

The secret to Wozniak's success was capitalizing on things he already was doing. And why was he already doing them? Because he loved it. By simply identifying how he preferred to spend time, Wozniak was able to identify his passion and build one of the most storied careers in the history of business.

Approach #2: In-House Tests

The man who is prepared has his battle half fought.
—MIGUEL DE CERVANTES, SPANISH AUTHOR

You can also discover your passion from the comfort of your own home. Here are three of my favorite in-house tests, which I've used to discover my passion.

Emotional Intelligence 2.0

Although *Emotional Intelligence 2.0* comes as a book, by accessing bit.ly/emointelligence, users can complete a 28-question survey, which took me less than seven minutes. The survey generates a customized report and provides feedback specific to your personality. I used the personalized report to confirm that I am a driven, type-A guy. This feedback was helpful in providing the confidence I needed to launch nuwaverly (bit.ly/nuwaverly) shortly after graduating law school, a website about investing.

Self-Tests Used by Millionaires

Ask these questions:

- *Ev Williams (Medium)*: "Would I want this to do well regardless of whether or not I profited?"
- *Seth Godin (Linchpin)*: "Am I willing to risk public humiliation for the sake of this thing succeeding?"
- *Elon Musk (SpaceX)*: "Could I fail repeatedly and not want to give up?"

The "Enjoyment" Exercise

On a sheet of paper, create three columns. At the top of each column write the following:

1. Activities I *really* enjoy doing
2. Activities I *don't* mind doing
3. Activities I *do not* enjoy doing

After you complete your columns, begin to brainstorm activities that fall under each column. Consider all types of activities, including academic, physical, social, and relational. Even consider activities that are seemingly irrelevant to your passion. For example, if you love hanging out with friends, write "hanging out with friends" under the "activities I *really enjoy*" column. Don't limit yourself. Write as many activities down as possible. You may want to complete this exercise over the course of a week or two, allowing for new activities to emerge.

After you listed activities under each column, focus your attention *only* on the "activities I really enjoy doing" column. Remember: you must be *passionate*. The "activities I *don't mind* doing" and "activities I *do not enjoy* doing" column cannot sufficiently fuel your inner drive.

Now that you are focusing solely on the "activities I really enjoy doing" column, try to identify any common themes. Ask yourself:

- What are the common settings of these activities?
- Who are the common people involved in these activities?
- What are the common emotions experienced in these activities?
- How can I apply the essence of what I like about these activities to various professions?

For example, if you *really enjoy* reading, writing, children, and helping others, you might conclude that your passion is to "help elementary school-aged children prepare to succeed as young adults."

Approach #3: Gap Year

Self-knowledge is best learned, not by contemplation, but by action. Strive to do your duty and you will soon discover of what stuff you are made.
—Goethe, German philosopher

In 2013, following my law school graduation, rather than immediately transitioning into the legal market, I took a brief sabbatical. Think of it as a shortened gap year. I ventured down to Guatemala to serve some of the most impoverished places in Latin America. The experience was heart wrenching. I observed individuals, who, needing to survive, rummaged through landfills in order to obtain anything of nominal value, including discarded scrap food. I observed legless beggars in the street, who could not depend on a government safety net to provide their next meal. I observed whole villages of houses built of nothing but flimsy tin, likely not strong enough to withstand a strong wind.

This experience awoke in me the sobering reality that millions of people still live in desperate poverty despite the great prosperity of the twenty-first century. Going home to the safety, comfort, and affluence of Washington, DC with a life purpose to work forty hours a week for the next forty years of my life in order to retire at 65 years old lost much of its appeal. These experiences have developed my self-awareness like I couldn't imagine.

For many students, taking a gap year outside of their hometown is not feasible. And that's ok. At its heart, a gap year is not so much about a location, but an experience. The entire goal of a gap year is to immerse yourself in a totally unfamiliar experience, something that pushes you. In particular, look for opportunities that will yield meaningful work experience or academic preparation for college. For those sticking around their hometown, this can be achieved by volunteering or working at places you otherwise wouldn't. To discover gap year opportunities, and to learn how to create an unbelievably affordable gap year, visit bit.ly/kylewineygapyear.

Getting Realistic: Follow Opportunity

If passion drives you, let reason hold the reins.
—Benjamin Franklin

Imagine being a math whizz. You can multiply four-digit numbers together in a second. Rocket science comes to you as easily as tying your shoes. Not surprisingly, math is your passion. Some might say math was your first true love. Here's the problem: the year is 1491.

In 1491, high-level math was not very important. Most likely, you would have spent your days tending the crops or fashioning a horseshoe as a blacksmith. Back then, people with technical skills, not academic abilities, were in high demand. People passionate about math weren't getting a job, no matter how great their abilities.

Now fast forward to today. How many companies are hiring blacksmiths? None. Demand for math wizards, however, has never been higher. They are almost guaranteed a job right out of college. Today, it significantly matters if students love math.

The point is that financial and economic realities matter in determining whether you should follow your passion. As discussed, passion is undeniably essential for success. But passion alone is not enough. Success requires both passion *and* opportunity. Otherwise, students end up like the unemployed math wiz in medieval times or the unemployed blacksmith in the modern economy. Keep these simple equations in mind:

Passion + No Opportunity = Hobby
Passion + Opportunity = Success

To demonstrate, consider the story of Peter von Kahle (Flagler '12, Communications). Peter always loved videography. As a kid, Peter played with his parents' camcorder, filming silly movies involving remote control cars. He's been hooked ever since.

Today, Peter owns and runs his own videography business (bit.ly/watchpvk), one that he founded at age 22. In a few short years, Peter has become wildly successful, filming the 2014 Super Bowl and regularly trekking deep into the Amazon Jungle to capture inspiring stories. Peter is great at what he does because he loves doing it.

The important part to Peter's story, however, is not that Peter loves videography. It's that Peter knows at the end of the day, he has bills to pay—no matter how passionate he is about his job—which he explains:

> I consider what I do a job in the sense that I use it to support myself. There are days when it feels like less than a hobby. Occasionally, I have to do things I don't want, such as wake up for 4:30am shoots, just to bring in money.

But Peter understands that only by following opportunity is he able to pursue his passion:

> A lot of people, especially my former classmates, failed at trying to do what I do. They just didn't know how to make money. They did everything for free. My high school teacher once told me, "Never do anything for free that you can get paid for." That's my approach to videography.

By keeping an eye on opportunity—and thus his paycheck—Peter is able to pursue his passion for videography.

Many college students today, however, completely neglect Peter's approach. They *only* follow their passion without any regard to whether their passion leads to opportunity. That's a mistake. Both passion *and* opportunity are needed for students to achieve success. Otherwise, following passion without opportunity is merely engaging in a hobby.

"But what if all my passions don't lead to opportunity?" you ask. Fortunately for you, that's not possible. The great thing about passion is that it actually *attracts* opportunity. Leadership expert John Maxell calls it "The Law of Magnetism." Even if your passion is not *initially* tied directly to opportunity, the mere fact that you are engaging an activity with passion will consequently *create* opportunities. Your job is to take advantage of the opportunity when it comes.

The 3 Common Mistakes Related to Passion

In addition to what we've already discussed, there are three more problems that commonly occur when students try to follow their passion.

Passion Problem #1: People Pleasing

> *I can't give you a surefire formula for success, but I can give*
> *you a formula for failure: try to please everybody all the time.*
> —HERBERT BAYARD SWOPE,
> FIRST RECIPIENT OF THE PULITZER PRIZE

You know the feeling. You want to be liked. Everyone does. When we are young, this pressure is called "peer pressure." When we are older, it is called "people pleasing." No matter the name, people of all ages do it.

Fortunately, many students have pushed back. One of them is Long Dam (Cal Poly '11, Engineering; Cal Poly '13, Engineering). Long works for an engineering company that designs and manufactures rockets delivering supplies to the International Space Station. Long notes the fulfillment he receives from doing what he loves, even though he initially encountered resistance from his family:

> My mother wanted me to be a doctor—just like the Asian stereotype. But I knew that I always wanted to work inside the aerospace industry and, in particular, space exploration. I always felt like I could make more money elsewhere, but I love what I do. If you find something you like, go for it. Don't choose something else because that's what people want you to be. In the end, it works out better.

Thankfully, by focusing on his passion, Long avoided wasted years, perhaps a lifetime even, engaged in a career he found unfulfilling.

Passion Problem #2: Envy

People-pleasing isn't the only force that removes focus from passion. Another common feeling is envy. Envy is the flip side to people pleasing. People pleasing says, "I must be liked *by* you to be happy." Envy says, "I must be *like you* to be happy."

You know what I mean. You want your classmate's smarts so you can score straight A's, too. You want to love engineering like your friend, so you can create the latest and greatest app. Even if you aren't envious of the people around you, social media makes it easier than ever to peek into the lives of others. As a result, it's easier now to want what others have, without even knowing these people.

If you let it, this comparison game will crush your passion. Instead of focusing on your inner fire, you will look outward to the things you feel that you should have but don't. It's a loser's mindset, because it focuses on deficiencies rather than opportunities.

One of the best ways to guard against envy is what legendary management guru Tom Peters calls a "to-don't" list. Many people have a "to-do" list. Your mom has probably made one for you at some point. But a "to-don't" list focuses on what you should *not* do, things that are best left untouched. And what are those things? Activities outside of your passion that fail to advance the things you really care about.

Passion Problem #3: Passion Only for "Success"

You cannot say to a Yalie, 'find your passion' [because] most of us do not know how. This is precisely how we arrived at Yale: by having a passion only for success.

—Yale student's email to professor

After I graduated from undergrad, I enrolled in law school. Why? Not because I always dreamed of being a lawyer. Instead, I wanted to be a "success." I thought success meant either becoming a doctor or a lawyer. I opted for the lawyer.

Millions of students like me pursue career tracks largely because they want to be a "success," even if it leads to a job they hate. For example, Patricia Lee (Georgetown '16, Government) describes a sad story of how many of her classmates follow "success" and not passion:

> So few of my classmates pursue their passions. A group of my friends majored in Pre-med during our freshman year because they were passionate about medicine. But when things got hard, they dropped out. Now they are working at banks just because they know they can make money. These people have accepted that they are going to be miserable for years.

This is such a common pattern: students, in the name of "success," exchange their passion for misery. They take a high-paying, soul-crushing job with the intention of working there for only a few years. "Don't worry," they say. "This is just for a few years. I'll pay off my student loans, get myself in a good financial position, then chase my real dreams."

This argument sounds great on the surface, but the problem is the follow-through is almost impossible. Inevitably, these students pay back their loans, but start living a lifestyle that requires a fat salary to support. They want to "keep up with the Jones's." "Just one more year…" they keep saying. "One more year" becomes five and then never.

Furthermore, studies show that people who only have a passion for success actually end up miserable. Why? Professor and motivational expert Edward Deci found that when people made "success" their goal, they actually started experiencing a decreased interest in whatever they were doing. In other words, success actually suppressed their desire to do the activity, even if the activity was something they enjoyed doing for years. Ultimately, taking a high-paying, soul-crushing job can be one of the biggest mistakes college graduates make.

Bringing It Full Circle

None, but people of strong passion are capable of rising to greatness.
—Honore Gabriel Riqueti, French Revolution leader

In the end, passion is necessary—but by itself is not enough—to supercharge college success. Something else is needed. That something else is job opportunities. When you fuse together both passion and opportunities, you've created the perfect mixture for launching a successful college career.

Before I wrap up, let me just add one more thing. "Passion" is very difficult to discover, particularly as a teenager or early twenty-something. But don't let that discourage you! After all, the benefits of knowing your passion are so high, you can't afford to dismiss it. Fortunately, through experimentation and the resources in this HACK, you can get closer to realizing what your true passion is, even if you don't fully get there before college graduation. At the very least, experimentation should give you an idea what you're *not* passionate about—and that's just as helpful in fashioning together a college career that is right for you.

Even if it takes a while, keep looking. Don't quit! One of the most moving things I've ever heard on this topic is from Steve Jobs, Apple's co-founder:

> Your work is going to fill a large part of your life, and the only way to be truly satisfied is to do what you believe is great work. And the only way to do great work is to love what you do. If you haven't found it yet, keep looking. Don't settle. As with all matters of the heart, you'll know when you find it. And, like any great relationship, it just gets better and better as the years roll on. So keep looking until you find it. Don't settle.

HACKING TAKEAWAYS

- To be successful, students must follow passion *and* opportunity.
- Students who follow passion without opportunity are merely engaged in a hobby.
- Don't confuse "passion" with "people pleasing," "envy," or a "passion for success."

SELF HACK #2
Strengths

Go all-in on your strengths, go all-out on your weaknesses

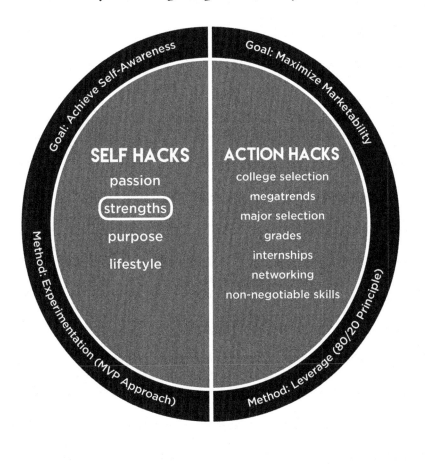

SELF HACKS
- passion
- strengths
- purpose
- lifestyle

ACTION HACKS
- college selection
- megatrends
- major selection
- grades
- internships
- networking
- non-negotiable skills

Goal: Achieve Self-Awareness

Goal: Maximize Marketability

Method: Experimentation (MVP Approach)

Method: Leverage (80/20 Principle)

Criticism has the power to do good when there is something that must be destroyed, dissolved or reduced, but it is capable only of harm when there is something to be built.
—CARL JUNG, PSYCHOLOGIST

Throughout college, and into much of my professional career, I continued to ponder the same question: should I invest more attention, time, and energy into improving on my weaknesses, thereby becoming more well-rounded, *or* should I ignore my weaknesses and double down on my strengths, making me more one dimensional? Throughout my college career, everyone said that I must choose the first option and concentrate on my weaknesses. Then I found out why.

Consider the following hypothetical. You begin a conversation with your friend after your friend receives the following grades. Which of these grades would you spend the most time discussing?

- "A" in English
- "A" in social studies
- "C" in biology
- "F" in algebra

If you answered "algebra," you are among the *super*-majority of people. In fact, according to a Gallup survey, 77 percent of individuals chose to focus on the F in algebra, while only 6 percent on the A in English, and 1 percent on the A in social studies.

What does this mean? It means that people are *obsessed* with focusing on an individual's weaknesses, not strengths.

Regrettably, this weakness mania is not specific to a particular culture, country, or race. It's everywhere. Gallup found that all types of respondents— American, British, French, Canadian, Japanese, Chinese, young and old, rich and poor, highly educated and the less so—they answered the same: weaknesses, not strengths, deserve the most attention.

"But, Kyle," you object, "F's lead to failing out of school. Why shouldn't you focus on the F?"

Obviously, the "F" in algebra deserves some attention. But the question Gallup put forth was phrased quite carefully: "Which of these grades would you spend the most time *discussing*?" And that's precisely the problem. Teachers, faculty, family, and friends spend way too much time harping on a student's weaknesses, rather than building upon a student's strengths. That needs to change. And changing your perspective can unlock serious results in college.

The Strengths HACK shows how playing to your strengths can lead to over-sized results and reduce the stress arising from compensating for your weaknesses.

Failure to Admit Our Own Weaknesses Creates More Failure

If at first you don't succeed, try again. Then quit. There is
no point making a fool of yourself.
—W.C. FIELDS, COMEDIAN

Consider the embarrassingly bad performances conducted on *American Idol,* the television show where contestants sing onstage in hopes of winning a coveted album deal. These contestants, despite their awful voice, perform with the utmost confidence. They close their eyes, flail their hands, and shimmy their hips. They are animated, enthusiastic, and determined to win.

In one episode, a male contestant performed Whitney Houston's "I Want to Dance with Somebody." After about fifteen seconds, Simon, *American Idol's* notoriously blunt judge, interjected with the following observations:

> Last year I described someone as being the worst singer in America. I think you're possibly the worst singer in the world based on that performance. And I'm absolutely serious. I've never, ever heard anything like that in my life. Ever.

The contestant looked as if Simon had just shot his dog. He was shocked. He was in disbelief. He was mortified. "How could Simon say this?" the contestant's facial reactions said.

What is perhaps the biggest surprise is that the contestant allowed Simon's criticism to be a surprise at all. Anyone capable of hearing knew this guy had some of the worst vocals around.

Unfortunately, traditional college advisors, using their traditional approaches, produce students like the *American Idol* contestant. Advisors believe if a student works harder, even if that student doesn't have the natural skills, he can do anything and be anything he wants. Teachers believe that a student, who is poor in math can be the next Nobel Prize winner if only she spent more time on homework. Parents believe that their child, who is bad in writing, can win the next Pulitzer Prize, if only he spends more time on his essays. This nonsensical approach is precisely why many students stumble through college and flounder as professionals. No one has told them they aren't any good at what they do.

So why do we flee from our strengths and obsess over our weaknesses? We are afraid.

We are terrified at not being good at something, so we do everything possible to cover up weaknesses. We work longer hours. We ratchet up the intensity. Of course, none of this ever works.

By overcoming the fear of failure, you can achieve much more in college than you ever hoped. But you have to first realize that success isn't about being good at everything. You are going to be bad at things—*many* things. And that's perfectly okay. Take it from Gary Vaynerchuk, the guy who turned his family wine business into a $60 million company:

You need to bet on your strengths and don't [care] about what you suck at. Way too many people in this room are going to spend the next thirty to forty years of their lives trying to "check the boxes" of the things that they're not as good at. And you're going to waste [loads] of time…Once you believe [in your strengths], go directly all chips, all in…The truth is, if you want to be an anomaly, you got to act like one.

If you want to achieve more in college, the first step is accepting that you cannot be great in all subjects or occupations. The sooner you get comfortable with this reality, the sooner you can create a better college career. And once you do, the sky is the limit. Let's look at some people who have done just that.

Using Strengths to Accomplish More and Do Less

You're going to get an education—that's nice. But if you don't use your gift, that education will only take you so far. I know a lot of people that got degrees that they ain't even using. It's your gift.
—STEVE HARVEY, COMEDIAN

The highest-level performers know that they can't be anything they want to be. So they don't even try. Take Usain Bolt, for example, the "fastest man in the world," having set a world record in the 100-meter dash in 9.58 seconds. Bolt, living up to his last name, can sprint up to 23 miles per hour. This feat has led many to speculate that Bolt can run a mile in less than the illustrious 4-minute mark. But when Ricky Simms, Bolt's trainer, was asked this question, Simms responded, "Usain has never run a mile."

To some, it may seem ridiculous that the fastest man in the world has never run a mile. But, as all runners know, running distance and running sprints are much, much different. Bolt specializes in sprints, not distance. So he doesn't even try to become great at distance running. *You* might even be able to run a mile faster than Bolt. But I bet all the money in my wallet (ok, that's not much), you can't run 100 meters faster than Bolt.

So what does this mean for college students? Dave Nossavage (Misericordia '10, Math; Villanova '14 Statistics) explains:

> In college, I focused on developing my math skills. I accepted that meant being bad in classes I was required to take but never going to use in the real world, such as Zoology. I can't believe I had to take Zoology! Anyway, I figured I could afford to get bad grades in those classes because I offset them with my good math grades.

Rather than working really hard to "succeed" in the classes where Dave didn't naturally excel in, he just threw in the towel. He didn't care how he did in those classes. In fact, he hardly tried. Is that reckless? Not at all. Listen to how Dave landed his sweet job as a data scientist at a fast-growing startup company:

There's no shortage of opportunities for graduates who are interested in math. Where I work now, no one ever looked at my resume. All they cared about is the kind of individual I am. Am I a hard worker? Do I have experience? Do I have a track record for success outside of the classroom? No one cares how I did in Zoology.

Did you get that? *No one cares how Dave did in classes that tested his weaknesses.* Well, actually, some people might have cared. His Zoology professor likely cared. His parents probably cared. But the ones who ultimately matter—the employers—didn't care one bit.

To jump on the same path to success, students must double-down on the classes in which they excel and ignore the others. In doing so, students can study less, while, at the same time, putting themselves in a better chance to win.

How to Identify Your Strengths

Most people think they know what they are good at. They are usually wrong....
And yet, a person can perform only from strength.
—Peter Drucker, founder of
modern business management

By now, hopefully you realize that a strengths-based college approach is the only smart college approach out there. But to capitalize on your strengths, you first need to know what they are. Here's how you can quickly find out.

Step #1: Where Do You Naturally Excel?

I'm no genius. I'm smart in spots—but I stay around those spots.
—Thomas Watson, IBM founder

Nature or Nurture? That's a common question that most people—and particularly, the most successful people—want to know. Is our intelligence fixed and therefore cannot be increased, as the Nature crowd believes? Or can practice and effort grow our intellect, as the Nurture crowd believes? Who is right?

As it turns out, our intelligence—and therefore our strengths—are both a product of Nature *and* Nurture. "It's not either-or," said Stanford psychologist Carol Dweck. Instead, modern research makes clear that our strengths are a function of our efforts *and* our natural abilities, so both are important to achieving college success.

But HACKing college isn't meant to show you all of the ingredients involved with college success. It's to help identify the few elements that rocket you toward success faster and with less effort. Therefore, what we really need to know is the answer to the following question: do our efforts *or* our natural abilities have a bigger *impact* on our success?

Research has given us an answer. Our natural abilities—those things that we cannot acquire through learning or practice—affect our success more than the work we invest. In other words, although Nature and Nurture are both key, Nature is *more* important. That's why playing to your strengths is absolutely critical.

In many ways, this is just common sense. If you're not naturally athletic, there's no reason to think that a 7-day per week training program is going to make you a great soccer player.

To help you identify your strengths, I recommend the following tools:

- *StrengthsFinders 2.0* (bit.ly/strgthfinder). More than a book, in less than 20 minutes, this resource produces a personalized report that shows you where your strengths and weakness lie. My results indicate that one of my strengths is "Learner," which means that my drive to be informed motivates me to master certain subjects. Because of my Learner strength, the report recognizes that I thrive in situations where I have the opportunity to demonstrate my knowledge and talents—insight that would have helped me chart a college career.

- *StandOut* (bit.ly/stndt). Similar to *StrengthsFinders*, this book also produces a personalized report in less than 20 minutes. *StandOut* is different in that it guides you through specific scenarios, so you don't need a lick of self-awareness to begin. My *StandOut* assessment indicated that I was a "startup specialist," someone who hates structure and bureaucracy, and someone who enjoys working independently and with highly competent people. Had I known this earlier in college, I would have reconsidered starting out as an education major, saving me time and money.

- *My Next Move* (bit.ly/nextmv). Sponsored by the U.S. Department of Labor, this tool takes 10 minutes and uses questions to help connect you with specific careers that account for your strengths, interests, and time you're willing to invest in your education. One of the career tracks the report recommended I pursue is becoming a lawyer, something I eventually became.

- DiSC (bit.ly/trdisc). A DiSC assessment provides a personalized report into how you respond to conflict, what motivates you, what causes you stress, and how you solve problems. Some websites charge $250 for this service. Use this link provided to access a *free* DiSC assessment report thanks to leadership guru Tony Robbins. The test took me less than 15 minutes. My report said, "You're an excellent team player," feedback I could have used in college to seek out a major that was more collaborative.

The purpose of these resources is to determine your strengths, not to anoint you with them. Remember, your strengths are already inside of you. You were born with them. Use these tools to find reoccurring patterns of thought, feeling, and behavior—known as "themes"—which indicate the presence of a strength.

Knowing your personal themes also has another benefit: it identifies college tracks that are *not* best suited for you. By knowing more about your strengths, you can start investing earlier in areas that fit, and avoid areas that play to your weaknesses, saving you time, money, and stress.

USING GRADES TO CONFIRM YOUR STRENGTHS

Alex Rekas (NoVA C.C. '07, Math; James Madison '10 Studio Art) finished high school as an average student. "I graduated high school with a 3.0 GPA," said Alex. "I applied to colleges my senior year but didn't have the grades to get into a lot of places."

After high school, Alex enrolled at a small in-state college, but began to struggle almost immediately. "My first semester I had a 1.70 GPA," Alex said. "My second semester I had a 2.30 GPA. I finished my freshman year with a 2.10 GPA. I eventually left that school and went to a community college."

But the same struggles followed Alex to community college. "I started community college with the intention of getting my associates degree in engineering," explained Alex. "But my first year wasn't great. I had a 2.50 GPA. I wasn't enjoying my classes, but I was sticking with it, because I thought I'd eventually transfer into a 4-year college and pursue engineering."

Eventually, Alex graduated from community college with a degree in Mathematics. After graduation, Alex wanted a bachelor's degree at a 4-year university in something more aligned with his strengths. "I realized I wanted to do industrial design," explained Alex. "I composed an art portfolio and was admitted."

Once Alex began taking his art classes at James Madison, he realized he had finally found his place. "I began scoring much higher grades and actually enjoying my classes," Alex said. "All of this reaffirmed that I didn't know what I wanted to do up until that point in my life. Once I started doing well in these classes, I felt like that's where I was supposed to be."

Alex had finally found his place in the world as a functional artist—a long way from where he began as an aspiring engineer. The classroom struggles Alex experienced early in his college career demonstrated that he had yet to find his strengths. Once Alex began excelling in art and design classes, however, Alex knew that he had identified his strengths. You too should use your classroom experiences as a feedback mechanism for identifying your own strengths.

Step #2: What Are You Better At Than Others?

If you don't have a competitive advantage, don't compete.
—JACK WELCH, FORMER CEO OF GENERAL ELECTRIC

Having a strength isn't just about being naturally good at something. Many people are good at things. That was Step #1. Playing to your strengths is also about being better at something than other people—that's your *competitive advantage.*

Let's circle back to Dave Nossavage (Misericordia '10, Math; Villanova '13 Statistics) and listen to him explain how knowing his competitive advantage helped identify his strengths.

> When I think back to school, nine out of ten kids hated math. But ever since I was a kid, I've been good at math. It always came naturally to me. I enjoy the problem solving aspect of it. When I got homework, it was easy. I always wanted to learn more.

I know what many of you are thinking, "This guy is crazy—he actually likes math?!" But when people give you that reaction, and you're actually talented at whatever it is, that's when you know you've found your competitive advantage. In fact, that's how Dave found his. "I was good at math and everyone else hated it," Dave said. "Since I knew I could make a career out of math, I knew it was for me."

At college, you'll find that many students are good at what they do. But the key is to follow what you are good at *compared* to everyone else.

"But what if I'm average to everyone in every way imaginable?" you object. "Then I can never have a competitive advantage." Fortunately, however, that's impossible. Everyone has unique personal experiences, distinctive thoughts, and a story unlike anyone else. It's your job to discover how these things give you an edge over others.

HOW GRADUATE TURNED YOUTUBE SENSATION WITH 75+ MILLION VIEWS

Josh Taylor (Trevecca Nazarene '10, Mass Communications) realized early on he was a masterful storyteller with talent beyond his classmates. "Not to brag, but I sensed that I was the best student in my Radio class," Josh said. Knowing his own strengths, Josh spent his early college years doing nothing but perfecting his craft. "I completed four years worth of my specialized communication courses in my first two years at college," Josh said. "I hated taking Gen-Eds—I was so bored."

Even though Josh was still early into college, his talents landed him a *live* radio show in Nashville—for two years! "The interviewer was so impressed with my college work that he decided to bring me on board," Josh said. "I broadcasted all across the city. It was a blast."

As graduation neared, Josh looked for the next step. "I enjoyed radio, but I knew I couldn't do it forever," Josh said. "Unless you enjoy sitting alone in a basement and playing a song 100 times, you need something else."

Playing to his natural storytelling abilities, Josh took a job at a TV station his senior year, but he never quit his radio job. "I hosted a radio show, worked a full-time job at the TV station, and took a full course load of classes," Josh said. "I did my homework while I played music at the radio station." Now that's going all in on your strengths!

A short while after graduation, Josh used his strength as a masterful storyteller and launched the YouTube show *Messy Mondays*. "About six months later, we had a video go viral," Josh said. "I soon quit my job to do YouTube full-time. It's basically the most fun thing ever." Today, Josh runs *Blimey Cow* (bit.ly/blimey-cow), a YouTube channel with over 75 million views and 450,000 subscribers. That's the power of a harnessing your competitive advantage.

Step #3: Avoid the "Jordan Illusion"

> *You cannot be anything you want to be but you*
> *can be a lot more of who you are already.*
> —Tom Rath, author

Inevitably, difficulties will strike. Maybe you get roughed up by an exam. Maybe you fail to lock down that internship. Whatever it is, sooner or later, you'll find yourself questioning your strengths.

It's during these times that students are faced with a critical question: "Do I put my head down and try harder, or do I concede that I am not meant to be doing this?" Working harder when you should stop is a waste of time. But not working harder when you should *not* stop is a missed opportunity.

How can you know the difference?

Consider the story of Michael Jordan. Jordan's basketball career famously began for what did *not* happen. As a high school sophomore, Jordan failed to make the varsity team at Laney High School in Wilmington, North Carolina. Laney's high school coach opted for the height of a 6-foot-7-inch giant rather than the underwhelming 5-foot-9-inch Jordan. Jordan would later recall, "It was embarrassing not making the team. They posted the roster and it was there for a long, long time without my name on it."

In response, Jordan trained like a man possessed. Ruby Smith, a physical education teacher at Laney recalls:

> I normally get to school between 7:00am and 7:30am. Michael would be at school before I would. Every time I'd come in and open these doors, I'd hear the basketball. Fall, wintertime, summertime. Most mornings I had to run Michael out of the gym.

In essence, Jordan's rejection from his high school varsity team was his motivation to build one of the most storied careers in the history of professional sports.

College students may draw inspiration from Jordan's story and believe that "hard work can propel me to success tomorrow, even if I lack the talent necessary today." But that's not really the moral of Jordan's story.

The truth is that Jordan was *not* an incompetent basketball player, even as a high school sophomore. During his sophomore year, Jordan played junior varsity and produced several 40-point games. In Jordan's junior year, he scored 35 points during his first varsity game. Jordan was so good as a high school player that, the University of North Carolina—one of the best college basketball schools in America—had already targeted him as a priority recruit before his senior season.

Jordan's countless hours in the gym didn't take a clumsy goon from chump to champ. Basketball was already Jordan's natural strength. His basketball abilities simply needed to be refined, sharpened, and battle-tested.

The story of Michael Jordan demonstrates that without some preexisting talent—something off of which you can build—success will always evade you. You will be like the horrific contestants on *American Idol* rather than the feel-good story of Michael Jordan. In order to maximize your strengths, there must be underlying talent. No amount of hard work can replicate that.

HACKING TAKEAWAYS

- Winners *only* do what they are good at and don't even try to improve upon their weaknesses.
- Focus on your natural strengths *and* your competitive advantage.
- Avoid believing that hard work can turn a weakness into a strength, something known as the "Jordan Illusion."

SELF HACK #3
Purpose

Find your *"Why?"*

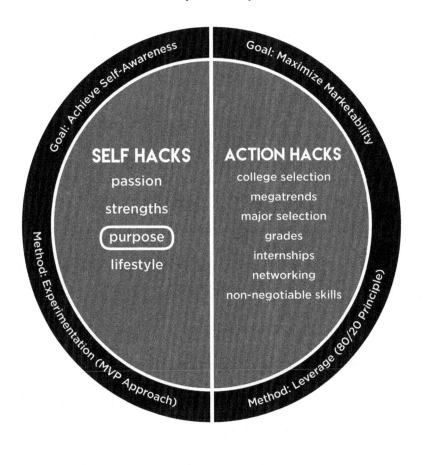

Goal: Achieve Self-Awareness

Goal: Maximize Marketability

SELF HACKS
passion
strengths
purpose
lifestyle

ACTION HACKS
college selection
megatrends
major selection
grades
internships
networking
non-negotiable skills

Method: Experimentation (MVP Approach)

Method: Leverage (80/20 Principle)

I went for the jugular question.
—Arno Penzias, Nobel Laureate in Physics

It was my third year of law school. I was supposed to be in class. I wasn't. Instead, I was in the library reading *The Purpose Driven Life* by Rick Warren, something much, much different than *Trusts & Estates*, the class I was skipping.

To many, skipping class seems completely reckless, especially to conventional wisdom advocates. But I had a different concern. I had no idea *how* I wanted to live my life or *why* it mattered. My family had modeled a set of values, but were those *my* values, I wondered? Or did I just live under them because that's what my family expected? Did it even matter? I didn't know.

To answer these questions, I relied on something I learned in college known as the "5 Whys," an analytical process pioneered by Toyota and responsible for its rebirth during the 1950s. Whenever Toyota encountered a problem, Toyota workers asked "Why?" five times in order to get to the heart of things. "Go directly to the source and keep asking, 'Why?'" Taiichi Ohno, former Toyota vice president explained. Consider this example from Toyota:

1. **"Why did the robot stop?"** The circuit has overloaded, causing a fuse to blow.
2. **"Why is the circuit overloaded?"** There was insufficient lubrication on the bearings, so they locked up.
3. **"Why was there insufficient lubrication on the bearings?"** The oil pump on the robot is not circulating sufficient oil.
4. **"Why is the pump not circulating sufficient oil?"** The pump intake is clogged with metal shavings.
5. **"Why is the intake clogged with metal shavings?"** Because there is no filter on the pump.

The 5 Whys helped Toyota workers dig past what initially appeared to be the problem (circuit overload) and hone in on the real problem (filter-less pumps).

I used the same 5 Whys approach for my personal dilemma. I first began asking myself why class was important. After all, I had been going to class nearly all of my life but had never really stopped to think why it mattered. Here were my 5 Whys:

1. **"Why is class important?"** So I can learn.
2. **"Why is learning important?"** So I can get good grades on my final exam.
3. **"Why are good grades on my final exam important?"** So I can get a good job.
4. **"Why is a good job important?"** So I can launch a successful career.
5. **"Why is launching a successful career important?"** Hmm....

I didn't know how to answer Question #5. Was a successful career supposed to be all about me? My paycheck, my job title, my prestige? Or was a successful career about serving other people and making a difference in the world? Maybe a combination of both? I wasn't sure.

Most concerning, I couldn't believe this was the first time I had ever thought to ask these questions. I had been so busy in life taking classes that I had never stopped to ask why they mattered in the first place. But when I actually stopped to think, I felt like a fool for failing to ask earlier. It seemed like such an obvious question. I mean, it was foundational to everything I was doing.

Eventually, I came to understand that my use of the 5 Whys addressed a simple, profound, and universal question: *"What is my purpose?"* In other words, "What am I doing here?" That's when I plunged myself into answering this question.

The Purpose HACK contains the answers I found, the reasons why it matters, and the ways it can make your college career (and life) infinitely better.

What is "Purpose," Anyway?

The purpose of life is to contribute in some way to making things better.
—ROBERT F. KENNEDY

Before diving in, let's be clear with what I mean by "purpose." One of the best descriptions I've encountered is from leadership guru Tony Robbins:

> [Purpose is] whenever you have…a mission that's larger than yourself—whether it be your children, whether it be your business, whether it be a non-profit focus—I don't care what it is. Something that is…more than just you.

To further expand upon this definition, Stanford professor and purpose expert William Damon has highlighted two common characteristics of purpose:

- **Purpose is More Than a Goal:** Purpose is a goal of sorts, but it is more far-reaching and more stable than common lower-level goals such as "to have a good time tonight," "to find a parking place in town," "to buy an inexpensive pair of shoes that look nice," or "to pass that chemistry test."

- **Purpose Goes Beyond Personal Meaning:** Purpose may play a part in one's personal search for meaning, but it goes beyond personal meaning and therefore is not strictly synonymous with it. Purpose reaches out to the world beyond the self. It implies a desire to make a difference in the world, perhaps to contribute something to others, or create something new.

In short, purpose is an "ultimate concern." It is the final answer to the question of "Why?" Why am I doing this? Why does it matter? My ultimate concern was exactly what motivated me to skip my *Trusts & Estates* class and think about life at a deeper level inside of the library.

There are two common mistakes people make when thinking about purpose. The first mistake concerns happiness. "The only way for us to have long-term happiness," explains Tony Robbins, "is to live by our highest ideals, to consistently act in accordance with what we believe our life is truly about." In other words, purpose leads to happiness, not the other way around.

The second common mistake with purpose concerns passion. Unlike purpose, passion is a play on your own desires. It's like saying, "I love to do it, because I love to do it." But purpose is something different. Purpose arises because of its effect on *others*. Purpose starts on the outside but then fuels a fire on the inside.

Finally, purpose can arise outside of college and a career. For example, one of my personal heroes is my late great-grandmother, who died at the age of 104. She never attended college, never held an official job, and never got her driver's license. Yet she had purpose in supporting her family and serving her local community—all of which she did spectacularly. But because this book is about college, from here on out, I'll assume that you're going to find your purpose within your career, even though there are other ways.

Why Purpose Leads to Outperformance

If you count the time I'm in the office, it's probably no more than 50-60 hours a week. But if you count all the time I'm focused on our mission, that's basically my whole life.
—Mark Zuckerberg, founder of Facebook

Elon Musk, founder of SpaceX, Tesla Motors, and SolarCity, understands that the key to success is linking what we do to purpose. "I didn't go into the rocket business, the car business, or the solar business thinking this is a great opportunity," said Musk. "I just thought, in order to make a difference, something needed to be done; I wanted to have an impact."

Clearly, being purpose-driven is important for achieving Elon Musk-like results. But purpose is also important for achieving extraordinary fulfillment. For example, in 2006, Warren Buffett, widely considered the most successful investor in the world, vowed to donate more than 99 percent of his wealth to philanthropy during his lifetime. "I couldn't be happier with that decision," remarked a glowing Buffett. Even though this money represents the fortune of a small country, giving, not hoarding, brings Buffet fulfillment.

Let's take a closer look at purpose in action within the context of a recent college graduate. Consider the amazing story of Gret Glyer (Grove City '12, Entrepreneurship), someone who found his purpose at an early age. This self-discovery has fueled a lifetime of achievement, even though Gret graduated college merely five years ago. Before we get to all of Gret's achievements, listen to Gret explain how a purpose-less life left him miserable, even though he was great at it:

> After college graduation, I started working 60+ hours a week for one of the largest car rental companies in the country. I started in customer service but got promoted in only six months, the fastest of any customer service rep in the history of the company. In a few short months, I managed a multi-million dollar company. But I couldn't get behind the mission. In my job, "the customer was always right," even if they threw a fit and acted like a child. It was my job to appease them simply because they had money. Catering to temper-tantrum throwing customers is soul sucking. I hated it.

Despite Gret's extraordinary performance, he hated what he did. So Gret did something radical. Here's how Gret explains it:

> After working at the car rental company, I moved to Malawi, one of the poorest countries in Africa. When I arrived, I knew that I had found my place. For example, on Fridays I would visit this remote village. One day, I was tasked with helping out a group of ten young boys. The people in charge gave me five pieces of paper and five crayons. But there were ten boys and only five pieces of paper and five crayons. So I decided to break the group into five pairs, giving one boy a crayon and the other boy a paper. I watched them color together with so much enjoyment. Then it hit me: there are so many poor people that I can actually do something about it. I slowly began to realize that my heart is for those in extreme poverty.

Gret has traded in a conventional career for a life of purpose. And the results are incredible. Today, Gret, at the age of 26, has achieved the following:

- Raised $150,000+ in venture capital to found and launch DonorSee (bit.ly/DonorSee), an app that allows donors to send money to people and see the impact it has made;
- Crowdfunded $100,000+ for the construction of the Girls Shine Academy (bit.ly/GirlsShine), an all-girls school located in Malawi;
- Founded HOWMs (bit.ly/HOWMs), a nonprofit dedicated to building homes in impoverished African villages; and
- Created his own podcast (bit.ly/BadMissionaryPodcast) and You-Tube channel (bit.ly/BadMissionaryYouTube) to raise awareness for the needs of Africans.

Just like Elon Musk and Warren Buffett, Gret has used tremendous service to fuel his success. In other words, Gret has found his purpose.

Not only has Gret accomplished at the age of 26 what others hope to accomplish in a lifetime, Gret lives a life filled with abundant joy and happiness. "Someone once apologized to me for asking how the construction of the all-girls school was going because he didn't want to talk about my 'work,'" said Gret. "But I love this stuff! I usually wake up at 5am just to check my email because I'm excited to see what's on deck for the day."

Unfortunately, many students think they don't have time to discover their purpose. They are too busy studying, hanging out with friends, or just relaxing. However, Harvard professor Clayton Christenson explains why he encourages all of his students to put purpose before school:

> I promise my students that if they take the time to figure out their life's purpose, they'll look back on it as the most important thing they will ever have discovered…In the long run, clarity about purpose will trump knowledge of activity-based costing, balanced scorecards, core competence, disruptive innovation, the four Ps, the five forces, and other key business theories we teach at Harvard.

Here's a professor who gets it. Here is also a professor who understands why I skipped *Trusts & Estates* to read *The Purpose Driven Life*. It's not reckless. It's practical.

REPLICATE HABITS OF TOP PERFORMERS: DRAFT YOUR OWN MISSION STATEMENT

One of the best ways to make your own purpose clear is to draft a personal mission statement—similar to these extraordinarily success people:

1. **Denise Morrison, CEO of Campbell Soup Company.** "To serve as a leader, live a balanced life, and apply ethical principles to make a significant difference."

2. **Oprah Winfrey, The Oprah Winfrey Network.** "To be a teacher. And to be known for inspiring my students to be more than they thought they could be."

3. **Sir Richard Branson, Founder of The Virgin Group.** "To have fun in my journey through life and learn from my mistakes."

4. **Joel Manby, CEO of Herschend Family Entertainment.** "To love God and love others."

A personal mission statement focuses on what you want to be (character) and what you want to do (achievements) based on certain values. To draft your own free personal mission statement, visit bit.ly/makemissionstatement.

The Science Behind Purpose and Outperformance

The world makes way for the person who knows where he is going.
—Ralph Waldo Emerson, essayist

Traditionally, people thought things like money, prestige, and promotion—things commonly considered "rewards"—motivated people to work hard in pursuit of a "good job." This belief took hold during the Industrial Age, an era during the early 1900s where work was primarily mechanical and uncreative in nature. Best selling author, Daniel Pink, explains why rewards were effective for Industrial Age style work:

> Rewards, by their very nature, narrow our focus. That's helpful when there's a clear path to a solution. They help us stare ahead and race faster…For routine tasks, which aren't very interesting and don't demand much creative thinking, rewards can provide a small motivational booster shot.

But times today are different. Jobs in the 21st century are more complex, requiring workers to develop creative solutions and operate independently with little supervision. As a result, a playbook different from pursuing fame and fortune is needed.

Yet students continue to play under the old, broken system. Scientists found that when people use this Industrial model in the 21st century workplace, it lowers motivation, lowers creativity, and decreases performance—things necessary to thrive in the modern economy. Not surprisingly, today only 38 percent of workers believe that they are part of something meaningful, a warning as to where following conventional wisdom will lead students.

Fortunately, there is an alternative. As Pink describes, the solution is built on findings that scientists and researchers have time and time again made:

> The science shows that the secret to high performance isn't our biological drive (our survival needs) or our reward-and-punishment drive, but our third drive—our deep-seated desire to direct our own lives, to extend and expand our abilities, and to fill our life with purpose.

In other words, purpose is the answer. The research shows why. Researchers have found that people motivated by purpose have "greater conceptual understanding, better grades, enhanced persistence at school and in sporting activities, higher productivity, less burnout, and greater levels of psychological well-being." That's a lot of reasons to be purpose-driven.

How to Find Your Purpose

"Would you tell me please, which way I ought to go from here?"
"That depends a good deal on where you want to get to," said the Cat
"I don't much care where..." said Alice.
"Then it doesn't matter which way you go," said the Cat
—ALICE'S ADVENTURES IN WONDERLAND, 1865

With so many reasons to be purpose-driven, you would think that everyone would know their purpose. But they don't. Today, only one in five people between the ages of twelve and twenty-six have a clear vision of where they want to go, what they want to accomplish in life, and why.

However, it's not that students *completely* lack purpose. It's just that their view on purpose is muddled. Rather than clarity, students merely have vague aspirations. That's why researchers have called them "drifting dreamers," students "with high ambitions, but no clear life plans for reaching them."

Use the following three scientifically proven steps to stop drifting in its tracks and find your purpose.

Step #1: Use Experiences to Find Your *Why?*

Forget about will power. It's time for why-power.
—DARREN HARDY, PUBLISHER OF SUCCESS MAGAZINE

In 2000, the Oscar award-winning movie *Erin Brockovich*, starring Julia Roberts, was released. The movie captures the true story of Erin Brockovich, an unemployed single mother, who becomes a legal assistant and almost single-handedly brings down a California power company accused of polluting a city's water supply. With her risqué clothes and rough demeanor, no one takes Brockovich seriously. However, Brockovich's discoveries helped spearhead one of the biggest class action lawsuits in American history against a multi-billion dollar corporation.

Prior to becoming a legal assistant, Erin Brockovich never dreamed of saving lives as a clean water advocate. It just happened. Similarly, those who have led revolutionary movements—Mahatma Gandhi, Martin Luther King, Jr., and the Dalai Lama—did so in response to what they saw going on around them. They weren't groomed or trained to tackle these issues.

Many people think that their purpose is "delivered" to them. But it wasn't for these great leaders. It won't be for you. Instead, both experience and experts demonstrate that purpose *emerges* largely from our unique experiences, opportunities, and challenges. In other words, finding your purpose is about *discovering* meaning from the very things in front of you. I call this process *"Finding Your Why?"*

Let's circle back to Gret's story and learn how he found his *Why?* from an earlier experience:

In 9th grade, I went to Africa on a safari. I remember seeing so many poor people, many of whom lived in shacks. There are billions of people who live on a dollar a day and millions of people who don't have access to clean drinking water. I just kept thinking, "Should we care about this? Isn't this the right thing to do?"

As a teenager, Gret saw poverty firsthand. He witnessed the living conditions. He observed the disease. These were personal experiences for Gret. Gret saw, touched, and tasted poverty. Through an experience—that is, an African safari—Gret found his *Why?*

Like Gret, you too need to have experiences to find your *Why?* Unlike Gret, however, your experiences don't need to be African safaris. In fact, meaningful experiences can occur in your everyday environment. Take a look at the following story.

HOW A PROFESSIONAL HOCKEY PLAYER FOUND HIS *WHY?* IN A POLICE CAR

Josh Watson (Rochester Institute of Technology '13, Marketing) launched his professional hockey career when most of us were still learning algebra. By tenth grade, Josh transferred out of public high school and into a prep school designed to groom hockey players for the NHL. "My whole life I wanted to play professional hockey," Josh said. Josh quickly emerged as one of America's best hockey talents. At age 17, Josh played on Team USA, and won a gold medal for the U-17 team.

After high school, Josh moved to Vancouver to play hockey in a Canadian league. Within a year, Josh was recruited by RIT, one of the premier colleges for hockey. "Once I got into college," Josh said, "I wanted to turn pro."

Shortly after graduation, Josh was signed by an NHL minor league team. "My first game was on New Year's Eve," said Josh. "And we won! It was so cool." But Josh's fate changed after the win. Josh endured a series of trades, cuts, and uncertainty. Eventually, Josh retired from professional hockey at the age of 22, forty years before most of us will retire from anything.

In light of his retirement, Josh began to look for a new career path. It was then that he remembered an exhilarating experience he shared with a friend shortly after graduating from college. "I had a buddy who was a police officer," explained Josh. "One day, my buddy let me go out on patrol with him. I watched him arrest someone. It was such a rush!" Based on that experience, Josh decided to become a police officer. "Being a police officer is all about teamwork, something I loved about hockey but grew to miss after I retired," said Josh.

Today, Josh works as a police officer outside of Washington, D.C. It didn't take long for Josh to know that he found his *Why?* as a police officer. "I recently helped arrest a guy who was illegally carrying a gun in public, and the gun was concealed. Getting a gun off the street is so meaningful. Who knows what that guy would have used the gun for. That's potentially saving a life. In the end, there's always going to be criminals, but that day, I made a difference."

One experience—that is, riding on patrol with his buddy, who was a police officer—helped Josh discover his *Why?* That's it—just one ride. Truly, the threshold for finding your *Why?* is not as daunting as you think. But you need to get out and start having experiences.

Step #2: Pursue a Worthwhile Goal

For, in the end, it is impossible to have a great life unless it is a meaningful life. And it is very difficult to have a meaningful life without meaningful work.
—JIM COLLINS, BUSINESS CONSULTANT

Finding Your Why? can be overwhelming. Many students don't know where to start. The idea seems too confusing, too abstract.

Fortunately, research has indicated that students frequently found their *Why?* by asking, "What is something important in the world that can be corrected or improved?" In other words, pursuing something important—that is, a worthwhile goal—is at the heart of Step #2. Worthwhile goals can be anything that makes valued contributions to the world. For example, scientists are dedicated to discovering natural truths, and artists are dedicated to creating new forms of beauty.

Frequently, these worthwhile goals take the form of helping people. That's exactly what Aaron Myers (Penn State '09, Psychology; Phila. College of Osteopathic Medicine '17, Clinical Psy.D.) has done as a psychologist:

> Working in the mental health field allows me to connect with people. So many people don't have access to quality medical treatment. Many of those people don't have a voice, either. Many rape victims, for example, are blamed for being raped. From my experiences, however, these victims are simply ashamed. Using my platform in the medical field motivates me to be a great clinician. I want these people to know that professionals like me truly care about them. It's nice to have a nice car or a big house, but it's really about the relationships.

What is the worthwhile goal Aaron pursues? Providing quality healthcare, giving people a voice, showing people that they matter. At the end of the day, for Aaron, it's all about people. People are his *Why?*

Another common example of a worthwhile goal is doing something that serves a higher cause. That's the story of Long Dam (Cal Poly '11, Engineering; Cal Poly '13, Engineering), whose work supports the International Space Station:

> My work as an aerospace engineer helps support the forefront of the space industry. I play a small part in pushing science and research forward for the next chapter of human civilization. Everyday, my work is part of a bigger picture. That's why I love what I do.

What is the worthwhile goal Long pursues? Innovating, creating new frontiers, and opening up new opportunities for society. At the end of the day, for Long, it's all about the meaning beyond the job. A higher cause is his *Why?*

Ultimately, *Finding Your Why?* requires the pursuit of a worthwhile goal, one that typically helps people or advances a higher cause. That's why purpose-driven people are some of the most successful people in the world. It's not about them. It's about others. In an almost backwards way, it's only by first serving others that people achieve their own success. It's as if success found them.

Step #3: Surround Yourself with People that Support Your Purpose

Tell me with whom you consort and I will tell you who you are.
—GOETHE, GERMAN PHILOSOPHER

Once you discover your *Why?* (Step #1) and your *Why?* is built on a worthwhile goal (Step #2), it's time to accelerate. That acceleration takes the form of surrounding yourself with a social support system where you can thrive in pursuing your *Why?* You need friends, classmates, mentors, and other like-minded folks to help you achieve what you've set out to achieve.

Many people believe that their *Why?* is deeply individualistic and therefore originates with them. But research establishes that social groups command an extraordinary influence over our *Why?* It's as if we unconsciously think, "Those people over there are doing something terrifically worthwhile."

That's the story of Siree Allers (University of Texas '11, Geography, Arabic; George Washington '16, Intern'l Affairs). Early in life, Siree traveled extensively around the world. Siree's travel experiences, combined with her interest in the Middle East, compelled her to begin surrounding herself with like-minded people. The desire to understand the cultures and societies of the Middle East at a human level was, as Siree says, "A seed that was planted at an early age."

Siree continued to water that seed by surrounding herself with people who shared the same values, even before entering college. "In high school, I joined a group that supported Amnesty International," said Siree, a global organization that campaigns for human rights. Even back in high school, Siree was building out a network to support her *Why?*

In the years between undergrad and graduate school, Siree began working at the U.S. Embassy in Baghdad, Iraq. While there, Siree worked with some of the most persecuted, war-torn victims of conflict in the world. Similar to high school, Siree once again surrounded herself with like-minded people. "There was this one trainer," explains Siree, "who cast the refugee resettlement program I was working on in a very humanitarian way. That training helped me realize that my work just wasn't about recording information; it was about helping people heal."

Ultimately, for Siree, human rights and refugee issues were her *Why?* Starting as early as high school, Siree began to build a community of people around her *Why?* which helped Siree land one of the most prized jobs in her field.

The bottom line is that to fully unleash our Purpose, we need to be surrounded by people who support and encourage us. The common problem for college students, however, is that once they've found their *Why?*, they soon discover their friends don't share the same values. It's important for students who've found their *Why?* to seek out new social groups who are working toward the same outcome.

Visualizing Your Funeral to Focus on Your Purpose...Really

Start with the end in mind.
—Stephen Covey, author

College will try to pull you in a million different directions. And it will, if you let it. Thankfully, you can use your purpose to fight against these pressures. One of the best tools I've discovered to facilitating radical focus is to imagine my own funeral. Yes, a funeral. I know it sounds morbid, but envisioning my own death is actually very helpful. I got the idea from a Stanford commencement speech given by Steve Jobs, co-founder of Apple, who explains the value of this exercise:

> When I was 17, I read a quote that went something like, "If you live each day as if it were your last, some day you will most certainly be right." It made an impression on me, and since then for the past 33 years, I've looked in the mirror every morning and asked myself, "If today were the last day of my life would I want to do what I'm about to do today?" And whenever the answer has been "no" for too many days in a row, I know I need to change something. Remembering that I'll be dead soon is the most important tool I've ever encountered to help me make the big choices in life. Because almost everything...falls away in the face of death, leaving only what is truly important. Remembering that you are going to die is the best way I know to avoid the trap of thinking you have something to lose.

When you realize that you only have a finite time on this earth, suddenly you stop sweating the small stuff. An overdue library book does not distract you. Failing a quiz worth five percent of your class grade doesn't, either.

To make this exercise most effective, visualize your funeral and answer the following questions:

1. Who is attending my funeral?
2. What are they saying?
3. What are the emotions in the room?
4. How are people interacting with my family and friends?
5. In what town, city, or country is the funeral located?

Be sure to visualize in as much detail as possible, with as much emotion as possible. This "funeral exercise" is perhaps the best way for students to plunge into the process of *Finding Your Why?* and focus on the big things in life—those that lead to both greater achievement and greater fulfillment.

HACKING TAKEAWAYS

- Purpose is an "ultimate concern" and is something greater than you.
- People who link their career with purpose are more effective, sucessful, and fulfilled than those who don't.
- To discover your purpose, start with *Finding Your Why?*, move to pursuing a worthwhile goal, and conclude by surrounding yourself with like-minded people.

SELF HACK #4
Lifestyle

Lifestyle design first, college planning second

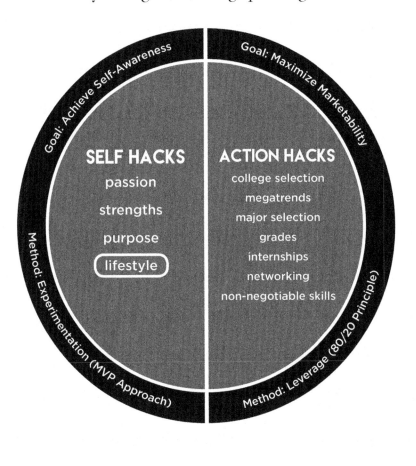

Goal: Achieve Self-Awareness

Goal: Maximize Marketability

SELF HACKS
passion
strengths
purpose
lifestyle

ACTION HACKS
college selection
megatrends
major selection
grades
internships
networking
non-negotiable skills

Method: Experimentation (MVP Approach)

Method: Leverage (80/20 Principle)

Lifestyle design should come before career selection.
—TIM FERRISS, AUTHOR

During the final semester of my sophomore year, I transferred out of the College of Education and into the College of Business. At the time, I couldn't exactly explain why, but I knew that money was (and still is) important to me. I remember trying to explain my reasoning to people. I said things like I wanted to "do more than just teach" and "I have too much drive to be confined to a classroom."

In listening to my own explanations, I felt like a greedy 20-year old. A young sell-out. "You're exchanging money for the opportunity to impact the lives of the next generation," people said.

But looking back, I understand what I was *trying* to say. I wasn't trying to say teaching is unimportant. It is important—that's why I wanted to be a teacher in the first place. Instead, I was trying to say that *I didn't want to make a teacher's salary.* Only after enrolling in college did I discover that by choosing my major, I was choosing my career, which meant that I was choosing my *lifestyle.*

But no one ever told me the importance of lifestyle. They were too focused on having me choose a career path first, *then* leaving it up to me to squeeze out a lifestyle around whatever salary I would later make. As I discovered too late, the order of this decision-making process is backwards.

Your career path, including your college career, goes hand-in-hand with your future lifestyle. You can't separate the two. In fact, the lifestyle you want after college *determines* the choices you should make in college. I didn't want to be a teacher, because I didn't want a salary where $6 Starbucks lattes threaten my monthly budget. Does that make me greedy? No. It's just how I want to live my life.

Whatever career path you ultimately choose—and whatever steps you take in college to achieve it—you need to think about your future lifestyle *now.*

Lifestyle Design: Is It "All About the Benjamins" or "Saving the World?"

[Students]agonize: Between making money and doing something of lasting social value. Between challenging their intellects and exercising their creative impulses....With a decision as important as this, they struggle to find the reasons that make one choice stand out above all the others.
—BARRY SCHWARTZ, PROFESSOR

Like me, one of the most common struggles a student faces at college is whether to pursue some greater cause (e.g. teaching), or pursue money, fame, and achievement, (e.g. Wall Street), or something in between. Where to even start?

Not surprisingly, how students answer this question heavily influences their lifestyle. Career paths resembling Wall Street jobs predictably lead to relatively more work and less flexibility, but relatively fatter paychecks and more prestige. I call focusing on these job qualities as "objective outcomes," because things like money and prestige can be measured. Conversely, career paths resembling teaching jobs predictably lead to relatively less work and more flexibility, but relatively slimmer paychecks and less prestige. I call focusing on these job qualities as "subjective outcomes," because things like fulfillment and satisfaction are things only students can value for themselves.

Typically, a tradeoff occurs between Wall Street and Save-the-World type career paths. For example, it's difficult to find a job that pays like a Wall Street hedge fund manager, but offers summer vacation like a public school teacher. But it's also difficult to find jobs that are as fulfilling as a public school teacher, but offer cash bonuses like, well, Wall Street hedge fund managers. Whether rightly or wrongly, students must make their lifestyle decisions within the framework of this reality.

Money Matters, But Only Up to a Point

Wealth is the ability to fully experience life.
—Henry David Thoreau, philosopher

In 2013, I went on a mission trip to Guatemala and witnessed some horrific poverty. One day, I encountered a lady on the street selling Chiclets, the bubble gum, for two cents a pack. On average, she made $2 a day. On this $2-per day budget, she supported her family of seven—all of whom lived with her in the same small house.

During our conversation, this woman told me how her daughter had recently fallen and broken her leg. The break was so bad that the daughter's bone poked through her skin. *The daughter's broken leg was sticking out of her body.* Obviously, this would upset any mother. But this lady had an even deeper concern: she couldn't afford to take her daughter to the hospital. You think money mattered to this family? Absolutely.

No matter what lifestyle you choose, you need enough money to cover your basic needs. You need enough money to treat a broken leg sticking out of your body. But more than that, you also need to *feel* like you can provide for your basic needs in the future. You need to feel a sense of, "I can pay my bills"—both today and tomorrow.

How much money is that? Depending on the lifestyle chosen, the amount can vary, but research shows that wellbeing does not generally increase for household incomes in excess of $75,000. In other words, it appears that $75,000 is enough money for people to generally provide for themselves, and feel like they can provide for the future. (Note: for students with a massive amount of student loans, your minimum salary must be well over $75,000, which limits your career options and is one more reason to avoid major debt.)

Importantly, once you take care of your finances at a basic level, more money has little effect on your overall happiness. The richest Americans, those earning more than $10 million annually, reported levels of personal happiness only slightly greater than the office staff and blue-collar workers they employ. That's why, despite being the richest country in the world, the United States barely squeaks inside the top-20 happiest countries in the world, trailing behind the likes of Mexico and Austria.

Ultimately, being poor makes people miserable, but being rich does not, on average, improve a person's wellbeing, either. Money matters—*really matters*—but only up to a point. To see if your college track is likely to lead to a $75,000 a year salary, check out bit.ly/findsalary.

SURPRISE! A MILLIONAIRE LIFESTYLE DOESN'T REQUIRE A MILLION DOLLARS

Many students pursue particular careers, not because they love them, but largely because they want a paycheck capable of supporting a millionaire lifestyle, even if it comes at great physical costs. For example, a year after I graduated law school, my former classmate confessed that, although she was making $160,000 (as a 26-year-old!) working at a premier law firm, she was so stressed that her eyelashes began falling out!

When I asked why she didn't quit, my friend explained that she needed to stay and become a partner in the firm (making $300,000+), and earn enough money to support her desired high-class lifestyle. In other words, my friend believed that living a millionaire lifestyle required a million dollars.

In a similar situation to my high-class friend, world traveler, Rolf Potts, recalls watching the 1987 iconic movie *Wall Street* starring Charlie Sheen, in amazement. In *Wall Street*, Charlie contemplates leaving the corporate grind, buying a motorcycle, and driving all the way across China. But to do this, Charlie thinks he needs a boatload of cash. Potts explains why Charlie's belief is just plain wrong:

> When I first saw this scene...I nearly fell out of my seat in astonishment. After all, Charlie Sheen, or anyone else, could work for eight months as a toilet cleaner and have enough money to ride a motorcycle across China. Even if they didn't yet have their own motorcycle, another couple months of scrubbing toilets would earn them enough to buy one when they got to China. The thing is, most Americans probably wouldn't find this movie scene odd.

In other words, according to Potts, living like a millionaire doesn't require a million dollars. That's what my friend was missing. She wanted to live a fancy lifestyle and thought she needed $300,000 a year to do it. But as Potts observed, doing things we commonly associate with millionaires, such as world travel, requires much less money than we typically think—something to keep in mind when designing your own lifestyle.

The Icing on the Cake

Make your lives extraordinary.
—DEAD POETS' SOCIETY, 1989

After taking care of your financial needs at a basic level, lifestyle design is completely up to you. Like me, some students target objective outcomes, such as money, prestige, and awards. Other students, however, target subjective outcomes, such as fulfillment and satisfaction. Let's take a look at students who have done both.

When he arrived at college, Justin Muthler (Misericordia '10, Education) didn't set out to become a millionaire. Justin explains:

> I knew that I'd rather go to work, do my thing, then come home. I like having a job that when I clock out, I'm able to do the things I'm passionate about. When I chose to become a teacher, I knew that I was going to have weekends, holidays, and summers off. I like that.

When thinking about lifestyle design, Justin focused on schedule flexibility in order to allow time for things he loves—a subjective outcome.

Today, as a public school teacher, Justin lives out the lifestyle he had envisioned early in college. Because the school day wraps up around 3:00pm, Justin has plenty of time in the evenings to do what he is most passionate about: coaching tennis. Justin coaches both the high school men and women's tennis team in his school district, and previously coached Division III tennis at Misericordia University, where he won Coach of the Year. "I love to coach," said Justin. "Teaching allows me to do just that."

Not only has lifestyle design allowed Justin to accomplish much in his short professional career, it also provides Justin the space necessary to engage in activities he loves outside of work, mainly hunting. "Every Saturday, I'm able to do what I love," explained Justin, referring to never having to work a weekend.

In essence, Justin pursued subjective outcomes by targeting a career with maximum schedule flexibility so that he could focus on things he loves: coaching and hunting. Majoring in education was simply the avenue to his preferred lifestyle. It's safe to say that, regardless of whether it's the week or weekend, Justin is doing what he loves. It's all thanks to the teaching lifestyle.

But lifestyle design is unique for everyone. Similar to me, Kevin Arbogast (Akron '09, Finance) chose a different target in college: bigger paychecks, an objective outcome. "Once I quit baseball in high school," Kevin explains, "my dad told me to go out and get a job." That's exactly what Kevin did. In fact, Kevin got *three* jobs. "I worked three jobs because I love being busy," said Kevin. "Plus, to be honest, I love making money."

When Kevin entered college, he knew one thing for sure: a lifestyle of living paycheck-to-paycheck was not a future he wanted. "I just love being able to do what I want with my friends and family," said Kevin. "I wanted a job that affords me the financial ability to do fun things whenever they come up."

With these lifestyle preferences in mind, Kevin explored engineering and nursing, two majors that lead to some of the best job prospects. Eventually, however, Kevin switched into finance. "I've always been interested in investing," said Kevin, "and given what I wanted out of college, finance made sense."

After graduation, Kevin quickly found the lifestyle he set out for. Since receiving his diploma, Kevin has worked as a financial advisor and now co-manages more than $60 million for over 90 clients. Most people would give their left arm to accomplish what Kevin has. And, yet, it took Kevin only a few years. How? Lifestyle design. Early into the college game, Kevin had a good understanding of what college paths helped and harmed crafting the lifestyle he wanted. "I wouldn't change a single thing I've done in the past six years," said Kevin.

Ultimately, lifestyle design is your choice. Justin focused on subjective outcomes with his college career, such as schedule flexibility, trading off objective outcomes, such as higher paychecks. Kevin chose objective outcomes with his college career, such as higher paychecks, trading off subjective outcomes, like schedule flexibility.

Are you more like Justin or Kevin? To help you in your own lifestyle design process, ask yourself these three questions:

1. **What is Your Ideal Day?** Do you like your day to be structured or not? Busy or less so?
2. **What is Your Ideal Work?** Who are you working with? What are you doing?
3. **What is Your Relationship with the World?** What are your ideal experiences? When was the last time you experienced something amazing?

Discovering how to best design a lifestyle right for you can be challenging. Sometimes it can be surprising. But for students to excel in college, they must approach lifestyle design as one of the first items to conquer at college.

HACKING TAKEAWAYS

- Your desired lifestyle determines how to play the college game, not the other way around.
- After making $75,000, personal happiness no longer increases. As a result, lifestyles built on earning more than $75,000 for the sake of personal fulfillment are destined for disappointment.
- Whatever lifestyle you choose, choose a great one.

This concludes the Self-Awareness Cornerstone. Here were the highlights:

The two big picture concepts:

Goal:	Achieve self-awareness
Method:	Experimentation (MVP approach)

The individual HACKs:

Self HACK #1: *Passion* – never follow your passion, but never be without it, either

Self HACK #2: *Strengths* – go all-in on your strengths, go all-out on your weaknesses

Self HACK #3: *Purpose* – find your *Why?*

Self HACK #4: *Lifestyle* – lifestyle design first, college planning second

After reading through each of the Self HACKs, and spending time on their exercises, you, the student, should have developed a better understanding of *what* to do at college—a foundational first step to launching a successful college career.

The next section, the Execution Cornerstone, provides the conceptual framework to make sense of the Action HACKs. Each Action HACK provides the step-by-step process to help students maximize their marketability. Ultimately, the Execution Cornerstone, with its accompanying Action HACKs, helps students determine how to do the items tailored to their specific interests as revealed in the Self Awareness Cornerstone, thereby, supercharging the chance of scoring their dream job faster and with less effort than ever before.

EXECUTION

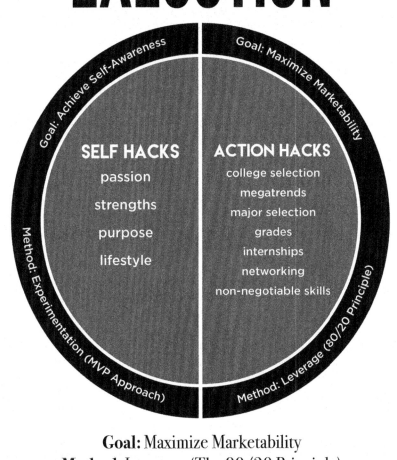

Goal: Maximize Marketability
Method: Leverage (The 80/20 Principle)

*Focus on the 20 percent of things that matter most
from an employer's perspective, ignore the 80 percent of
things that don't*

*Give me a lever long enough and a fulcrum on which to place it, and
I shall move the world.*
—ARCHIMEDES, GREEK MATHEMATICIAN

I saw it all the time. In fact, I did it, too. Students, in the name of "getting ahead" and "working hard," fully invested themselves in all things related to college. These students engaged in intense study sessions, immediately after which they hustled to a group meeting, immediately after which they hustled to finish homework. Enjoying life squeezed somewhere in between.

Why did I do this, and why do so many other students continue to do this? *We believe that all activities in college have equal value.*

Here's what I found: they don't. In fact, it's scientifically proven.

To demonstrate, let's look at the timeline of the richest people in world history. While several of history's wealthiest are sprinkled across the centuries, many of these fat cats appear during a specific period in history: the American Industrial Revolution. In other words, throughout all of history, a disproportionally small amount of history's richest comes from a single generation born in a single country during a single point in time. Talk about imbalance.

Wealth is not the only imbalance in life. Research shows that a small amount of people are responsible for a high amount of productivity, a small amount of computer code is responsible for executing a large amount of operations, and a small amount of city blocks are home to a large amount of marriage license recipients. Imbalance is everywhere.

How can this be?

"Leverage" is the idea that a disproportionately large amount of outcomes are predictably concentrated in a disproportionately small amount of inputs. There is a law of leverage—as true as any law of gravity—called "The 80/20 Principle." The 80/20 Principle asserts that a minority of things—usually 20 percent—leads to most of the results—usually 80 percent. The imbalance may be 65/35, 70/30, 80/20, or any number in between. The critical concept behind The 80/20 Principle is that there *is* an imbalance in cause and effect, regardless of the exact ratio.

Unfortunately, many college students believe that working hard at one thing is just as important as working hard at another. However, college students who ditch this belief and use leverage can free up so much time and accomplish what others can't. As a result, the secret is to know where the high-leverage points are inside the college arena.

Each of the Action HACKs inside the Execution Cornerstone represents one of the few areas that largely determine a student's overall college success. Simply by tackling these activities—and only these activities—students can maximize their marketability in the least amount of time, energy, and resources possible. Self-Awareness taught you *what* to do, leverage teaches you *how* to do it.

Students must note that while embracing leverage and The 80/20 Principle may save you a ton of time, it's not a license to slack off—at least not completely. Even though The 80/20 Principle substantially cuts down on the amount of work you must do, students must effectively perform the remaining work. In other words, you must do the 20 percent of the important things with 100 percent effort.

Before diving into the Action HACKs, it's first important to understand some basic concepts relating to why each Action HACK was selected, why it works, and how it can change your life.

Why College Success Does Not Go to the "Smartest" Student

The customer's perception is your reality.
—KATE ZABRISKIE, PRESIDENT OF BUSINESS TRAINING WORKS

I used to naïvely think that college success meant being the smartest in the class. It does not.

What does it mean to be the "smartest" in your class, anyway? Some might answer scoring the highest grades. But if that's true, why do students with lower GPAs continue to beat out students with higher GPAs for jobs? Remember my story with my fraternity brother? That's exactly what he did.

The answer might surprise you. College success has less to do with being the best than you may think. In reality, college success is about being *perceived* as the best. In their classic *The 22 Immutable Laws of Marketing,* Al Ries and Jack Trout describe how worse products (think lesser performing students) can beat out better products (think better performing students) in the marketplace:

> Many people think marketing is a battle of products. In the long run, they figure, the best product will win. It's an illusion. There is no objective reality. There are no facts. There are no best products. All that exists in the world of marketing are perceptions in the minds of the customer or prospect. The perception is the reality. Everything else is an illusion.

Despite what everyone else says, there are no "smartest" students. There are no "best" students. There are simply students, period. Each of these students has a specific story to tell and experiences to share. Some of them have higher GPAs, some of them have more internships, and some of them have better networks. But none of these things makes the student "smarter" than anyone else. If it did, employers would only hire students with the highest GPAs. But they don't.

So if being the "smartest" isn't the key to college success, then what is? As Ries and Trout said, it's all about *perception*. Recall that the purpose of college is to land a job. That's the endgame. As a result, what matters at college is how employers *perceive* your ability to provide value to their company, not whether you're the "smartest" candidate.

Ultimately, each of the Action HACKs are designed to send the clearest, loudest, and most effective signal to employers—a signal that demonstrates why you're the most qualified candidate for the job.

The Rise of the Personal Brand: How Perception Matters

Those who tell the stories rule the world.
—AMERICAN INDIAN PROVERB

Right now, many of you may be thinking, "Ok, Kyle, so I have to be *perceived* as smart, capable, and determined in the eyes of employers. I get it."

No you don't…not yet.

You think that the goal is to simply have employers positively perceive the skills listed on your resume, which then is supposed to make them think, "Yeah, I think this graduate is capable of performing this job." That was how the world worked in 1990. Today, the perception runs deeper, the scope broader. Today, the game is all about *personal branding*. With the right personal brand, you can launch your college career into the stratosphere.

Self-branding expert, Tom Peters, says it like this:

> Regardless of age, regardless of position, regardless of the business we happen to be in, all of us need to understand the importance of branding. We are CEOs of our own companies: Me Inc. To be in business today, our most important job is to be head marketer for the brand called You.

Previously, your college experience—everything from your major, to the organizations you join, to the college itself—largely defined your personal brand. Saying "I am a Penn State graduate" told companies, customers, and people in general enough about you and the value you were capable of providing.

Today, however, expectations are changing. People want to know even more about you. They want to know what your values are. They want to know if and how you serve in the community. They want to know the way in which you treat other people. In short, today your brand is perceived holistically, not simply through the lens of your college experience.

Importantly, personal branding alters the way in which companies hire employees. Studies have found that we are increasingly living in a world where people will have their own brands and sell their skills to those who need them. As a result, you need to develop these in-demand skills and your individual brand *now*.

In order to develop a personal brand, you must tell a story. But not just any story. *Your story*. You need to talk about how your unique life experiences shaped your goals, your ambition. You need to highlight your internships, job experiences, and classroom projects in a way that weaves together a personal narrative. Most of all, your story must be authentic and true. "If you're going to be a brand, you've got to become relentlessly focused on what you do that adds value, that you're proud of, and most important, that you can shamelessly take credit for," said Tom Peters. That's why I started *HACKiversity* with a section called "My Story."

To help you begin creating a personal brand, start by answering these questions:

- Why did you major in X?
- How did you choose Y university?
- What motivated you to pursue the internship at Z company?

Ultimately, by graduation, students must come away with an engaging, concise story that highlights their abilities, skills, and experiences. "Shaping a career narrative is like building your own brand, and you need to be able to sell it to potential employers," says college expert Jeffrey Selingo. "Not only must you be an ideal candidate—you have to show them that you are." That's why personal branding has become *the* way for students to maximize their marketability, and therefore, their job prospects.

The following three concepts apply throughout the Action HACKs and can supercharge a personal brand. Think of them as sort of "universal HACKs."

Concept #1: Going Narrow and Deep (Niche) is Better than Wide and Shallow (Following the Crowd)

If you cannot do great things, do small things in a great way.
—Napoleon Hill, author

Imagine you have a heart attack (I hope you haven't). Ten days from now, you are scheduled for heart surgery. Who do you want as your surgeon? The best surgeon, right? You're not going to take chances by opting for anything less than the best.

That's how employers are now approaching the hiring process. They don't want just anyone. They want the best. It's too expensive to train someone, get them up to speed, to later find out the newly hired person can't perform. So employers cherry pick the best college students available.

When I say "best," most likely you picture a student with the highest GPA, best internships, and most connections. But, as we discussed earlier, being the "best" is not actually about being the "best:" it's about being *perceived* as the best.

But there's a wrinkle to this game that I have yet to mention...until now. Today, nearly everyone believes that college students must compete against each other to climb the same ladder and reach the same top. But students don't. Here's the greatest news: right now—yes, this very second—it's easier than ever for college students to be perceived as the best. Marketing expert Seth Godin explains:

> The mass market is dying. There is no longer one best song or one best kind of coffee. Now there are a million micromarkets, but each micromarket still has a best... More places to win.

Everything now has a subcategory, creating many more ladders, and thus many more tops for students to mount. Winning inside these "micromarkets" is what I like to call "winning niche."

A good example of personal branding and winning niche is the story of my cousin, Adam Winey (Penn State '17, Engineering). Most notably, Adam doesn't have the highest GPA in his class. By focusing on traditional resume line items—including school, major, and GPA—Adam may not appear extraordinary. But that's a mistake.

Adam has built a personal brand around one of the most niche activities: archery—you know, bow and arrows. Here are a few lines from Adam's resume: (1) achieved All-American as part of the Penn State Archery Team, (2) interned at the U.S. Department of Agriculture, Natural Resource Conservation Service, (3) built and designed his own archery bow in spare time, and (4) spent countless hours archery hunting in the woods.

These are all things employers previously considered of little value. Until now. Think about what all these things say about Adam:

- **He Has Deep Knowledge.** Adam's engineering degree enables him to understand the mechanics of how an archery bow functions. More importantly, Adam applies this knowledge in a practical sense by building and designing his own archery bows. Considering he's an All-American, Adam knows first-hand how an optimal archery bow operates or should operate.
- **He Fits the Part.** By hunting, Adam walks the walk. As a result, Adam fits the customer profile of someone to whom an archery company aims to sell its product. You think that's valuable insight to an employer? You bet.
- **He Brings the Full Package.** Adam not only brings with him a deep understanding of archery and hunting, he also brings a deep understanding of the hunter's habitat: the wilderness. As part of his internship with the Department of Agriculture, Adam worked to preserve land for the wild game he hunts.

Each year, thousands of students graduate with an engineering degree from Penn State, but there will be only one archery master. Adam's personal brand is *the* archery guy. There's no one else like him.

Before wrapping up the section, there's something else students must know about why it's important to win niche. *It's easier.* Reid Hoffman, co-founder of LinkedIn, says it like this:

> If you try to be the best at everything and better than everyone…you'll be the best at nothing and better than no one. Instead, compete in local contests—local not just in terms of geography but also in terms of industry segment and skill set.

Stop competing with everyone inside your major, even everyone at your college. Instead, start trimming your specialty down to where there's not much competition at all. Then, develop a personal brand around that specialty. Stop trying to do it all. Win niche.

Concept #2: The Magic of Integration

There is no such thing as work-life balance.
Everything worth fighting for unbalances your life.
—ALAIN DE BOTTON, AUTHOR

Imagine that one night you go over to your friend's house for dinner. While there, your friend says, "You know what will make you study better? Potato chips! If you're not eating potato chips before you study, you're doing it wrong."

At the same party, another person comes up to you and says, "You know what will make you study better? Rice cakes! Research shows that rice cakes are low-calorie and stimulate brain activity. You gotta have rice cakes to study."

Hearing that same advice, another person chimes in and says, "You know what will make you study better? Ice cream! I have so much more success if I eat ice cream before I study."

Again, another person comes up to you at the party and says, "Celery. You've got to get into celery."

By the end of the night, you have all this great advice from your friend and your friend's friends. Who are you supposed to listen to? You're not sure. So you go to the grocery store and buy potato chips, rice cakes, ice cream, and celery—every thing that was recommended. You want to cover all of your bases.

This is a simple metaphor called the "Celery Test," and it demonstrates that anyone looking at you from the outside has no idea what you stand for, what you believe, or what you are doing. You have potato chips and ice cream, which are unhealthy snacks. Does that mean you just want to stuff your face with junk food while you study? But if that's true, why did you buy rice cakes and celery, which are healthier snacks? Maybe you are health conscious, but then again, maybe you aren't. It's hard to tell.

The Celery Test represents a common mistake made by many college students: obscuring their personal brand by engaging in many unrelated college activities. For example, imagine a college student who participates in drama club, is a computer science major, and serves as his fraternity's president. What's the common connection? I have no idea, and neither does anyone else. That's a problem.

Fortunately, there's a way to not only fix the problem of the Celery Test, but also to maximize the effect of your personal brand faster than ever. How? Through a concept known as *integration*. Integration is the process of combining as much of your life as possible—including both inside and outside the classroom—into overlapping, related activities.

To get a better sense of how you can best integrate your college career, let's learn from Julia Robertson (Auburn '13, Public Relations).

Julia's college career began with a bit of turbulence. "I wanted to major in film," explained Julia, "but I realized that Auburn's Film program was geared more around established media." Instead, Julia wanted a major that led to working at a non-profit organization, where she could showcase people doing great work in the community. After searching for the right major, Julia eventually declared a major in public relations.

Shortly thereafter, Julia began integrating her life—academic, personal, and professional—which created spectacular success, leading to her rise as a YouTube sensation. In less than *three* years after graduation, Julia has accumulated over 2.5 million views on her YouTube channel, Julia Robertson (bit.ly/ JulesoftheSouth). Here's her journey:

- **The Beginning.** Senior year of college, Julia launched a YouTube channel for fun, integrating her free-time activities with her major. "At first, I didn't really know what to do, so I just made funny videos, like what it meant to be from the South," explained Julia. "The video was so bad that I now have it set to private. But it was a start!"

- **Fast Results.** After graduation, a public relations company offered Julia a job, mainly because they liked that she had launched her own YouTube channel. In other words, *Julia got a job through integration.*

- **World Traveler.** After college graduation, but before working at the public relations company, Julia set out to accomplish something amazing: travel around the world. Over the course of four months, Julia visited twenty countries, all the while harnessing the power of integration. "I started a travel vlog," Julia said. Julia recorded her entire journey and uploaded the content to her YouTube channel—the same YouTube channel that landed Julia a job months before. This move would soon pay dividends.

- **Job Promotion.** Once Julia returned home from her four-month trip, she began working at the public relations company. But because of her world travel, Julia had become much more valuable, as she had documented and showcased the entire experience. Julia's improved skillset caught the eye of Adventures in Missions (bit.ly/adventuresinmissions), an established non-profit organization. They offered her a job, which she accepted. Can you imagine traveling the world and getting a job out of it? Sign me up! That's integration at work.

- **Sharpening Skills.** While working at Adventures in Missions, Julia creates and designs YouTube videos. In other words, Julia gets paid to learn skills at work, which allow her to enhance her personal projects. It's a virtuous process, meaning Julia is winning in both her professional and personal lives *at the same time.* Again, that's the magic of integration.

- **Society Contribution.** Today, thanks to her integrated life, Julia is making waves on a global scale "Ultimately, I want to make short films to tell the stories of people doing incredible work in foreign countries," said Julia, "but mainly those who can't afford to tell their own. I want to help these people secure funding for what they do." Who are these people? Those who run orphanages in Africa. Those who help homeless in Asia. Amazing.

Julia's story demonstrates that extraordinary success and personal fulfillment is possible through integration. To see how integrated your life is currently, and to learn how to further integrate your life, visit bit.ly/my4circles. To see what is most important in your life, and thus where integration should start, visit bit.ly/integrationnow. I've used both to help me integrate my life.

Concept #3: Using the Internet to Brand You Inc.

I'm not a businessman. I'm a business, man!
—JAY Z

There are many ways to brand yourself, but I highly recommend using technology, because once you post something online, millions of people gain access without you having to do any additional work. Here are some simple tools to get you started:

TOOLS AND TRICKS TO PERSONAL BRANDING

>**Social Media – the Free and Easiest Way to Brand Yourself**

- **LinkedIn (www.linkedin.com)**

  Start here. There are more than 40 million students and recent college graduates on LinkedIn, making them the fastest growing demographic. Over 98 percent of recruiters use LinkedIn and over 94 percent of them have successfully hired candidates through the platform.

  To construct an effective profile, start by completing the summary field and highlight three to four of your biggest achievements. Be sure to use numbers to demonstrate your abilities as much as possible. Below the summary field, provide as many links, documents, and multimedia pieces as you can. It's always best to show, not tell, your abilities. Also, change your default LinkedIn URL to your name (e.g. www.linkedin.com/in/kylewiney); otherwise, you'll have something hard to remember, such as www.linkedin.com/in/20101902. The most leveraged technique is to use a professional headshot. Employers don't care if you are 18 or 68–they want to see professionalism. For the most ambitious students wanting to expand their personal brand, post articles, mainly on Tuesdays through Thursdays at 5pm to 6pm, when people are most active.

- **YouTube (www.youtube.com)**

  To make your brand more personable, move on to YouTube. Within the first 15 seconds of your videos, mention your channel's name and why you do what you do.

- **Twitter (www.twitter.com)**

  While Facebook is (at least for now) purely personal and LinkedIn is purely professional, Twitter is caught in the middle. Many companies—especially newer and trendier companies—want to see your Tweets. Adopt the 60/20/20 Rule: 60 percent of tweets to subjects inside your career track, 20 percent to professional issues in general, 20 percent to other personal items. To get a 48 percent bump in retweets, use a picture. To maximize exposure, tweet Mondays through Thursdays at 1pm to 3pm.

> **Automate and Batch-Schedule Your Social Media Posts**

- **Hootsuite (www.hootsuite.com)**

  Schedule content, monitor posts, and respond to comments across LinkedIn, Twitter, YouTube, and more.

- **Buffer (www.buffer.com)**

  Batch-schedule all of your social media posts across LinkedIn, Twitter, YouTube, and more. Buffer even suggests stories to share.

- **TweetDeck (www.tweetdeck.twitter.com)**

  A stand-alone application to monitor and schedule tweets. Most hardcore Twitter users swear by this.

> **Review and Enhance Your Online Presence**

- **BrandYourself (www.brandyourself.com)**

  Today, every student has *two* resumes: the piece of paper given to employers and whatever appears after Googling their name, something every employer now does. BrandYourself reviews the results that Google produces and allows students to decide whether to delete or keep links, including social media posts. I used BrandYourself to delete a college picture uploaded to Facebook that showed someone puking in the background. No one needs to see that. Do the same.

- **PhotoFeeler (www.photofeeler.com)**

  Unsure whether your LinkedIn headshot makes you appear competent or stuffy? Choose a photo and receive feedback from complete strangers on how you come across.

> **Cost-Effective Legal Services and Company Formation**

- **LegalZoom (www.legalzoom.com)**

  I'm a lawyer. We are expensive. Typically, I charge $300 per hour, while some of my friends charge $600 per hour. These costs don't bode well for students seeking to build a personal brand by founding their own business or non-profit–something I highly recommend. Thankfully, LegalZoom offers legal services for a fraction of the price and has serviced over 3.6 million customers.

> **Show Off Your Projects**

- **Behance (www.behance.net)**

  One of the best online platforms for college creatives to showcase their work, as every thirty days, projects are viewed nearly 65 million times.

HACKing Takeaways

- College success does not go to the "smartest" student but rather to the student employers *perceive* to be most capable of providing value to the company.
- The 80/20 Principle demonstrates that most things in college *do not matter*. Instead, virtually all of the value of college is locked inside a small amount of activities.
- To become successful, college students must weave together their entire college experience into an easily digestible story to share with employers–the essence of personal branding.

After covering these fundamental principles, it's time to dive into the Action HACKs—those few, selectively chosen action-items that maximize a student's marketability. As a result, let's explore the seven Action HACKs inside the Execution Cornerstone:

1. College Selection,
2. Megatrends,
3. Major Selection,
4. Grades,
5. Internships,
6. Networking, and
7. Non-Negotiable Skills.

Action HACK #1
College Selection

Go elite, but if not elite, seek value

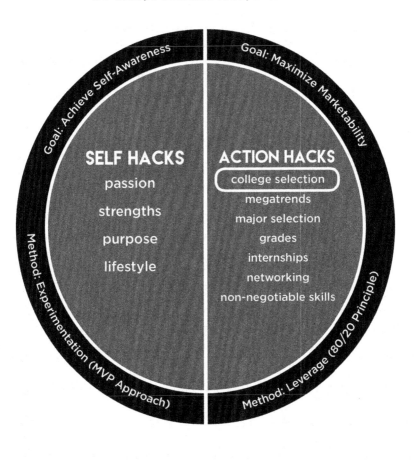

Goal: Achieve Self-Awareness

Goal: Maximize Marketability

SELF HACKS
passion
strengths
purpose
lifestyle

ACTION HACKS
college selection
megatrends
major selection
grades
internships
networking
non-negotiable skills

Method: Experimentation (MVP Approach)

Method: Leverage (80/20 Principle)

[F]amilies, sending their kids to college is a huge investment, and they are making that decision with almost no information as to whether it will pay off or bankrupt them.
—Peter Cappelli, professor

"Kyle, you can graduate with *no debt!*" my parents exclaimed, urging me to take the free ride. "Why wouldn't you choose that option?" That was 2010, the year when I received a full-scholarship to the University of Baltimore Law School.

I, however, had my mind set on another law school: George Mason. At the time, George Mason was ranked close to the coveted top-20 law schools in America. The University of Baltimore, however, was considered a "Tier 3" law school—academic code for "you don't deserve a number." However, George Mason didn't offer me a scholarship. I would have to pay full price.

My decision boiled down to the following: (i) attend George Mason, the more prestigious school, but go into serious debt, or (ii) attend Baltimore, the significantly less prestigious school, but graduate with no debt. It was a $100,000+ decision. How many of those do you have in your life? Unfortunately, I blew mine.

To help make my decision, I bought all of the popular college books out there. Mr. Responsibility, right? Too bad none of them helped.

All of the books did the same thing: ranked colleges from "best" to "worst." These rankings, however, didn't tell me anything meaningful. They simply told me that George Mason was a "better" school because George Mason ranked higher than Baltimore. But a second grader knows that. Instead, I wanted to know whether it was *worth* paying $100,000+ to attend a school ranked 24 compared to paying $0 for a school not even ranked. None of these books helped me answer that question.

Without anywhere to turn for good advice, I relied on my gut. Here's what I thought: Go to the best school possible, because graduates from better schools earn more money. Then, pay off whatever loans I have with my bigger paychecks from my better job, a process that would take two to three years…I thought. That's why I decided to enroll in George Mason. When I graduated, I had $140,000+ in debt. Four years later, I'm on track to pay it off by age 45 (that's with accelerated payments).

My entire rationale for choosing George Mason hung on one major assumption: I would land a job paying $160,000 right out of law school. After all, that's the salary George Mason advertised that its incoming students should expect to make.

While I was in law school, however, the bottom fell out of the legal market. This was basically the second time I graduated into some of the toughest economic times. Except for the most elite students, law firms were not hiring new attorneys. They only wanted seasoned veterans.

My dreams of making $160,000 upon graduation vaporized. In fact, I didn't even make $60,000 in my first job. Many of my classmates were un-employed for one, even two years, following graduation with $100,000+ in student loans to repay. To my parents, my financial problems reaffirmed their belief that I should have taken the scholarship at Baltimore.

After playing the college game for so long and living out its consequences in the workforce, I've come to see that both my parents and I were partially right—and partially wrong—about how to choose colleges. For reasons that we'll see, my parents actually had the right answer (take the scholarship), but for the wrong reason (always attend the cheapest school). I had the wrong answer (attend George Mason), but for the right reasons (elite colleges are incredibly valuable).

Elite Colleges: Life is Good on Top

Getting into an elite college is harder than ever. But once you're in, the way things work today, all you need to do, to a significant extent, is just show up.
—WILLIAM DERESIEWICZ, PROFESSOR

Today, the value of college is a story of extremes. On one end of the spectrum are what I call the "Elite Colleges." Think of the Ivy-League schools (e.g. Harvard, Yale), the west-coast powerhouses (e.g. Stanford, Caltech), and the other brand names scattered throughout the country (e.g. M.I.T., Duke). In essence, the Elite Colleges are the top 20 colleges in America. Only about 1 percent of graduates come from Elite Colleges. Then there is every other college, what I call the "General Colleges."

As The 80/20 Principle would predict, virtually all the value of a college degree is locked away inside a small amount of colleges. Where? Elite Colleges. That's why "Going Elite" is so, so powerful. Here are the four reasons why you should Go Elite, if given the chance, no matter the cost.

Reason #1: Better Job Opportunities

The number one rule in duck hunting is to go where the ducks are.
—JASE ROBERTSON, DUCK DYNASTY

Growing up, I used to wrestle with Cory Briggs (Harvard '14, Sociology) on my backyard trampoline. He was my next-door neighbor. Like me, Cory grew up in a small town without filthy rich parents. But listen to him explain how attending Harvard changed his life:

> The name itself gets you an interview. Dropping the 'H-bomb' is a thing. Your resume goes to the top of the pile. Actually, it goes on a separate pile. Every major company conducts on-campus interviews at Harvard, such as Apple, Google, Amazon, JP-Morgan. To land a job, you don't have to impress anyone during the interview—you just have to not disappoint. And that makes

all the difference. One interviewer told me once, "You are here right now because of where you went to school." Going to Harvard was easily the biggest game-changing decision of my life. There is really no downside.

By simply graduating from an Elite College, doors now swing wide open for Cory. He receives radically different treatment than everyone else. Job opportunities come to him, simply because of the Harvard name.

Not only do doors swing wide open for students going through the traditional hiring route, there's a valuable backdoor that opens, too. Simply because of the name, Elite College graduates gain access to high-powered individuals, who are otherwise unavailable. These are the multi-millionaires, the people who own 100 businesses, the people who, with one phone call, can change your life. "Just by going to Harvard I've golfed with the CEO of one of the biggest Fortune 500 companies," explained Cory. "The Harvard name equals instant credibility."

Reports reflect exactly what Cory experienced. Since 1972, the returns of attending an Elite College have been rising. When projecting the lifetime difference in earnings between Elite and General College graduates, Elite College graduates earn *several million dollars more* than the General College graduate. Consider the massive implications: because graduating from an Elite College generates millions of dollars more over a lifetime, students should attend Elite Colleges, even if it means paying a few thousand dollars in extra tuition or foregoing scholarships elsewhere.

THE POWER OF A NAME: WHY ELITE COLLEGE GRADUATES DON'T NEED *SHARK TANK*

Shortly after college graduation, David Levit (Princeton '10, Public Policy) founded his own startup company. Like all startup companies, David quickly encountered a problem: he needed outside investment to grow his business.

For many, raising a hundred thousand dollars, or even tens of thousand dollars, is nearly impossible. It's too risky for a bank to lend to a broke twenty-something. There is the possibility, however, of "venture capitalists," investors willing to place bets on risky businesses, just like on the hit television show, *Shark Tank*. But venture capitalists are generally impossible to reach. They are too busy, too insulated, and too important to be bothered. That is, unless you graduated from an Elite College.

David explains how his alma mater opened doors with venture capitalists. "I primarily landed my meetings with venture capitalists through the Princeton network," David said. "At almost all venture capital firms, there's at least one Princeton alum. I reached out to the top ten venture capital firms and received a response from almost all of them. The Princeton's network is definitely impressive."

Think about that: because of the Princeton name, David, held conversations where hundreds of thousands of dollars were at stake. Many college students are happy just to have an interview where a summer internship is at stake. That's the advantage of an Elite College.

Reason #2: More Career Options, Regardless of Major

No one in HR ever got fired for hiring a Harvard kid.
—JEFF HUNTER, HUMAN RESOURCES EXPERT

For those keeping score at home, you'll notice that Cory Briggs (Harvard '14, Sociology) graduated with a Sociology degree, one of the majors in the least demand. But when you graduate from the likes of Harvard, different rules apply to you. Cory easily leveraged his Sociology degree from Harvard and now works at a premier commercial real estate investment fund in Washington, D.C. With a degree from an Elite College, students experience lower barriers to enter a job and fewer restrictions in transferring between jobs. That means graduates from Elite Colleges have a greater ability to job hop until they find something that perfectly fits their tastes.

Reason #3: Better Classmates

Pick out associates whose behavior is better
than yours and you will drift in that direction.
—WARREN BUFFETT, INVESTOR AND PHILANTHROPIST

Facebook started out with a brilliant founding team. Mark Zuckerberg, Facebook's co-founder, scored a perfect SAT exam. Eduardo Saverin, Facebook's other co-founder, made $300,000 in a summer making bets on heating oil. It wasn't a coincidence that two geniuses partnered to create one of the world's most successful companies. In some sense, by merely being in the same vicinity as other highly qualified students, it was inevitable. Going Elite is like immersing yourself in a fishbowl of talent.

It's no surprise that Elite Colleges have the best students. But what is surprising is just how lopsided the talent pool is. Among Elite Colleges, 90 percent of all students scored in their high school's top 10 percent. With so many college all-stars, finding opportunities, such as creating the next Facebook, or connecting with someone on the fast track to success in corporate America, is almost unavoidable.

Reason #4: Cheaper Price Tag...Seriously

Another reason to attend Elite Colleges—as if you need another—is the overly generous scholarships. Studies show that graduates from Elite Colleges carry less than 40 percent in student loans compared with graduates from General Colleges, and more than half of all Ivy League students graduate without *any* type of student loan. In other words, not only are Elite

Colleges offering elite degrees, but they are doing so at extraordinarily cheap prices, providing even more value.

In summary, if given the opportunity, students should enroll in Elite Colleges no matter the price tag and no matter the scholarships offered elsewhere. Elite Colleges offer students better job opportunities, more career flexibility, smarter classmates, and, very likely, cheaper tuition. With all these advantages, it's no surprise that graduates from Elite Colleges make millions of dollars more than graduates from General Colleges. "The Harvard brand name will continue to be a cash cow for a lifetime," said Cory Briggs (Harvard '14, Sociology).

General Colleges: The Non-Elites

Give me six hours to chop down a tree and I will spend the first four sharpening the axe. —ABRAHAM LINCOLN

General Colleges, where 99 percent of students go, are those colleges not included in the Elite Colleges. That means the majority of students will need a different playbook than the simple go-at-all-costs approach for the Elite College students. But it's first important to understand three principles that explain how General Colleges compare to each other, thereby setting the foundation for HACKing opportunities.

General College Principle #1: Little Difference in Prestige

"Kyle, I want you to meet Jennifer, one of your fellow summer interns," said a judge at the courthouse, where I was clerking. "Jennifer attends the John Marshall School of Law."

"What is *she* doing here?" I immediately thought. That reaction had nothing to do with Jennifer personally, but everything to do with her law school's reputation. You see, the John Marshall School is a Tier 3 law school. I passed on my free ride at the University of Baltimore, a Tier 3 school, and paid $100,000+ to attend George Mason, just so I could land jobs unreachable to Tier 3 law students. But here was Jennifer—a Tier 3 law school student—with the same internship.

As I discovered too late, Jennifer could compete with students from higher ranked law schools because *most employers don't care about school reputation.* In fact, employers have repeatedly said that college reputation is one of the *least* important considerations in making hiring decisions, finishing below internships, jobs, volunteering, and other extracurriculars.

Do you understand just how significant this is? It means that—*in regard to General Colleges*—paying more money to attend a higher ranked college offers little payback. This is exactly the reason why I blew my decision when I paid $100,000+ to attend George Mason, rather than take the free ride to the University of Baltimore. I mistakenly thought that George Mason was an Elite College. After all, at the time, George Mason was ranked 24, only four spots removed from the coveted top 20.

But four spots makes a huge difference. Think about it like this: whether a school is an Elite or General College is like whether you catch a homerun ball from your favorite baseball player. Either you do or don't—those are the only two options. It doesn't matter if you were close to catching the ball but some over-zealous 50-year old snatched it out of your hands. At the end of the day, you don't have a homerun ball.

It didn't matter how *close* George Mason was to being considered an Elite College. Bottom line, it wasn't. That's all that matters.

General College Principle #2: Little Tradeoff in Program Quality

When I attended George Mason Law School, nearly every professor held *multiple* degrees from Ivy League schools. One even clerked for William Rehnquist, former chief justice to the U.S. Supreme Court. Another served in the George Bush administration.

These professors are not exceptions. Great professors are everywhere, even at lesser-ranked General Colleges. Why? With 1.5 million professors in the U.S., they far outnumber the needs of just Elite Colleges, which means accomplished professors are making their homes at General Colleges, too. As a result, General College rankings don't necessarily dictate the quality of their academic programs.

General College Principle #3: Where Not to Go

Although I just provided two principles that demonstrated little difference in prestige and quality among General Colleges, there are *three* exceptions to this rule: (1) non-accredited colleges, (2) "unheard of" colleges, and (3) online colleges. Let's tackle these in turn.

Limitation #1: Non-Accredited Colleges

Allen Nichols (University of Colorado '10, Engineering; University of Colorado '11 Engineering) has had an incredibly successful college career, interning at three of the major engineering firms in the country and graduating with a 3.80 GPA. Allen's college success followed him into the workplace, where he now leads a team of fourteen people and oversees projects generating $20 million in revenue a year. Today, because of his rapid success, Allen runs his company's internship program and makes the hiring decisions for his team.

"The first thing I look for is a degree from an accredited college," explained Allen. "If they don't have an accredited degree, I don't even read further," he said, referring to his position as the hiring manager. "I value having a '*real*' degree." According to Allen, "real" degrees only come from "accredited colleges." "Accredited Colleges" are colleges overseen by a third-party organization charged with assessing colleges' quality. In general, if a student can receive federal student aid from the school, it is accredited. To ensure accreditation, visit the U.S. Department of Education (bit.ly/4-yearaccreditation) or, for online programs, visit Guide to Online Schools (bit.ly/onlineaccreditation).

Limitation #2: "Unheard of" Colleges

The second limitation concerns a college no one has heard of, no matter how inexpensive. It's just not worth it. Why? One-third of all employers will consider a school they've never heard of as a *negative* factor in the hiring decision. It's like getting penalized for something that is supposed to be an asset. In fact, studies show that no matter the person making the hiring decision—including HR, a manager, or an executive—graduating from an unknown college is the *least* effective way to land a job relative to any other type of college, especially in the media or communications industry. That's why students shouldn't go bottom fishing during the college selection process.

Limitation #3: Online Colleges

Finally, avoid an online degree. I'm not talking about degrees obtained online from a traditional, 4-year university. I mean avoid schools that are purely online, such as the University of Phoenix. Employers have even said that online degrees are "undesirable." In fact, when compared against all other college types (e.g. private, public, regional), employers rated online colleges as the *least* desirable, particularly inside the science and technology industries.

With these three General College Principles in mind, it's time to start HACKing General Colleges.

HACKing The General College Selection Process

Don't count the things you do. Count the things that count.
—Zig Ziglar, life coach and motivational guru

With no significant difference across General Colleges (except as mentioned in Principle #3), students can focus on one critical component of the college selection process: *value*. Remember, the sole purpose of college is to score a job. That means colleges that routinely channel students into higher-paying, higher-quality jobs at a cheaper price should be preferred over those that don't. That's why HACKing General Colleges is all about "seeking value."

Today, seeking value has never been more important, because colleges now offer such wildly different value. Studies show that a whopping one in four colleges offer a *negative* return on investment, meaning that the best route forward for those students is to simply drop out.

Fortunately, these tools help students seek value more effectively and quicker than ever before. The following resources are among the best available and include some of my favorites:

- *The Economist* (bit.ly/economistvalueadded) and **The Brookings Institution** (bit.ly/brookingsvalueadded) offer a free visual tool that compares the salary of the college's graduates to the salary the same graduates would have earned if they had attended a different college—a process known as the "value-added" approach and my personal favorite.

- **PayScale** (bit.ly/payscalevalue) compares the value of colleges based on graduate earnings from millions of users and ranks the best return on investment for nearly every college.
- **College Scorecard** (bit.ly/collegescorecardgov) is the U.S. Department of Education's database, where students can sort colleges based on graduate salaries, graduation rates, and annual cost.

The FAQs:

Ask me no questions, and I'll tell you no fibs.
—OLIVER GOLDSMITH, NOVELIST

Students routinely bump into the same questions regarding the college selection process. Instead of leaving students left to solve these questions on their own, this section provides help. Below are the three most common questions.

FAQ #1: Should I Go to a Better Out-of-State College or a Worse In-State College (a college rankings question)?

Many students wrestle with the decision of going out-of-state to a higher-ranked college or staying in-state at a lower-ranked college. Sarah Lucas (Penn State '10 Microbiology; Minnesota '19 Ph.D. Microbiology) explains how she encountered this exact situation:

> As a high schooler, I debated between going out-of-state to Penn State or staying in-state and attending Virginia Tech. On one hand, Penn State had a great chemistry program, which emphasized undergraduate research—something really important. Plus, I wanted the excitement of going away. Virginia Tech had a great program, too, but not as good. On the other hand, Penn State cost $20,000 more a year. I ultimately chose Penn State.

Sarah's choice is very common: choose the higher-ranked college, at any cost. But is going out-of-state to a "better" school really worth it? Sarah explains why it's not:

> I don't think an 18-year-old has a great idea of how debt affects your life. Debt won't necessarily hamper your future success, but success comes much, much easier without debt. I didn't think about that when I went to Penn State. Even though I had a great time and got a great education, if I had to do it again, I would definitely not pay an additional $20,000 a year. I would have gone in-state to Virginia Tech and saved the money, even if I got less research experience.

As Sarah's story demonstrates, unless you have a *really* good reason, it makes little sense to pay more money for a higher ranked General College. Debt is a really big deal, and students can save tens of thousands of dollars just by following Sarah's advice. Attending an in-state college, even a lower ranked one, is perhaps the easiest way to save thousands of dollars on tuition.

FAQ #2: Should I Go to A More Expensive College that I Love or A Less Expensive College that I Only Sorta Love (a college cost question)?

Frequently, students fall in love with a particular college. "I can totally see myself here!" they say. The college also happens to be one of the most expensive.

Andrea Lucas (South Carolina '10, Public Relations, English), Sarah's twin sister, explains how she paid more money to follow her heart:

> As a senior in high school, I knew I wanted to go to a big school, especially one with great football. Most of the in-state schools didn't appeal to me, so I went out-of-state to South Carolina. Once the recession hit in 2007, however, my parents told me that I had to pay half of my tuition unless I transferred to an in-state school. I was conflicted because South Carolina was starting to be my second home. Ultimately I made the decision to stay at South Carolina and pay half of the tuition through student loans.

As college students often do, they choose with their heart, not their head. That's what Andrea did. But now, with graduation years behind her, Andrea has a much different perspective:

> Unfortunately, no one explained how student loans would affect my life post-college. I ended up graduating with $60,000 in debt and a job that paid a third of that. I've had to sacrifice many things in my twenties as a consequence—buying a house, affording a vacation, traveling to friends' weddings. I've even had to say no to graduate school.

So would Andrea make the same decision again? She explains why she wouldn't:

> I love my alma mater, but, I know that if I had gone to another school for a lower price, I would have loved it there as well. If I had been better informed of the toll debt takes on a person's life, I would have made a different decision.

You may be like Andrea and absolutely fall in love with a school. Perhaps you go there right now. But the question is not whether you love your school. The question is *how much are you willing to pay to love your school?* How much is that love worth to you?

That brings us to the question of student loans. Today, like Andrea, nearly everyone graduates with debt. For the Class of 2016, the average student graduated with $37,172 in student loans.

What's worse, today, nearly $417 billion in student loans—roughly 39 percent of all student loans ($68 billion)—are in deferment, meaning students are unable to make repayment. At more than 1,000 colleges, at least half of students defaulted or failed to pay down debt within seven years of grating.

So how should students pay for college? Not take on *any* debt? Not quite.

While there is no clear answer, studies have found that the most successful college graduates have below $10,000 in student loans. These are the students who start fast and quickly climb up the career ladder.

But there's another reason to limit debt to $10,000. When debt obligations exceed that amount, suddenly salary—not fit, happiness, or career advancement—becomes the driving decision in choosing a job. This pressure has crushed the dreams of many. Nearly 20 percent of all college graduates with student loans eventually give up on their preferred line of work because of the pressures to make ends meet. No matter the General College, you should be very reluctant to take on more than $10,000 in student loans. For a great student loan calculator, visit FinAid (bit.ly/finaidcalculator).

FAQ #3: Should I Attend a Higher Ranked *Private* College or a Lower Ranked *Public* College (a college type question)?

Frequently, students choose to pay more to attend private colleges because they believe private colleges have more prestige than public colleges. But is that true?

The answer is no. "We do not find that students who attend colleges with higher average tuition costs tend to earn higher income years later," found researchers. Without higher paychecks to offset higher tuition rates, students should prefer cheaper public colleges over more expensive private colleges.

But there's even more reason to pick a public college. Studies show that, out of all the types of General Colleges, employers love major public colleges the most, because graduates "are often the most prepared and well-rounded academically, and companies have found they fit well into their corporate cultures."

Among the top five employer-preferred colleges are Penn State, Texas A&M, Illinois, Purdue, and Arizona State. Notice that these colleges are not the top place winners in the *U.S. News* rankings. Penn State is #47 and Texas A&M is #63, for example. But who cares what *U.S. News* says? Getting a great job after graduation is what matters. Here's the bottom line: if you don't get into an Elite College, you can get an edge by attending a major public university.

WHY IT RARELY MAKES SENSE TO ATTEND A LIBERAL ARTS COLLEGE

In *There Is Life After College,* author Jeffrey Selingo interviewed a recruiter of Proctor & Gamble, one of the biggest companies in the world, who said that employers actually have a bias *against* students from liberal arts schools. "We still expect our new hires to hit the ground running," said the recruiter, "and small liberal arts schools tend to prepare people for grad school"—suggesting that liberal arts graduates aren't prepared for the workplace.

Studies show that employers across the country feel similarly to the P&G recruiter, such that employers actually prefer liberal arts college *least* when compared to major public colleges, private colleges, and regional colleges. This is especially true for science and technology majors.

Liberal arts graduates confirm this bias. Jessica Straus (Davidson '07, English) graduated from Davidson, a top 10 liberal arts schools in the country. Nevertheless, Jessica said, "[Graduating from Davidson] didn't prepare me at all for the real world."

Ultimately, unless there is a very, *very* good reason to attend a liberal arts school, don't. They cost too much money and employers don't prefer them. That sounds like a bad investment to me.

Bonus Nuggets

But wait, there's more!
—RON POPEIL, FOUNDER OF RONCO AND PROMOTER OF SHOWTIME ROTISSERIE

Still can't decide what school to choose? Let me show you three additional ways to HACK the college selection process. Here are three "bonus nuggets," filled with experiences and insight to help you choose.

Bonus Nugget #1: Community Colleges

Go to the cheapest school possible to get your freshman and maybe sophomore classes. —MARK CUBAN, OWNER OF DALLAS MAVERICKS

With tuition at all-time highs, students are desperately trying to save money. One of the best ways to do this is to complete your general education requirements at the cheapest college possible. Then, after racking up two years worth of cheap credits, you transfer to a brand-name school and receive a brand-name degree.

That's precisely what Matt Nuar did: (N. Va. Community College '15; Virginia Tech '17, Chemical Engineering):

Community college is not just good: it's better than what people pay for. I had better professors and smaller class sizes. I saved a third in tuition just by doing my first two years at community college.

After two years, I transferred. I knew that big schools make employers want to recruit there, and I wanted an engineering job. All my credits transferred over. I would highly recommend community college to anyone.

Not only is the cost savings huge, community college also offers a back door into some of the best schools in your state. Many community colleges partner with in-state public colleges, where students who obtain an associates degree at the community college are virtually *guaranteed* admission into the state school. "Once you get your associates degree," said Matt Nuar, "admission into the 4-year college is almost automatic."

For example, consider that Virginia residents, simply by going to a Virginia community college, are virtually guaranteed admission into the University of Virginia, which ranks as the 26th best college in the country. That's landing a degree from a great college for a fraction of the cost, headache, and stress.

One of the biggest surprises I came across while researching for this book was how many students who attended community college raved about it. In fact, some graduates with whom I spoke actually *regretted* not going to community college before enrolling into a traditional 4-year college. "I wish I would have knocked out my prereqs at community college," Dave Nossavage (Misericordia '10 Math; Villanova '14 Statistics) confessed. "I would have saved so much money."

COMMUNITY COLLEGE: AN EXPERIMENTATION HEAVEN

The soaring costs of tuition create problems for students relying on their college courses to expose them to different subjects in the hopes of increasing their self-awareness. In one semester alone, students can spend tens of thousands of dollars in tuition. These financial pressures force many students, against their wishes, to prematurely select a college track.

The magnitude of these financial forces, however, doesn't exist in community colleges. As a result, students at community college are able to experiment—and thus develop self-awareness—for a fraction of the cost. Johnfrank Dieguez (Miami Dade College, '05 Undeclared; University of Miami '08, Communications) explains his experiences:

> In community college, I didn't know what to do with my career, but because the costs were so low, I could experiment. I

---

studied everything from music to business to psychology. This showed me so much about myself. Plus, when I graduated, I didn't have any student loans.

After graduating from community college, Johnfrank used his newfound self-awareness—which took $0 in student loans to acquire—to pursue something he loved: journalism and studio art. Consequently, Johnfrank enrolled in the University of Miami, where he flourished.

"My experience at Miami was incredible," Johnfrank described. "I worked with a great team of creatives, did photo shoots for the National Park Service and Miami football games, and traveled internationally."

These experiences helped Johnfrank develop practical skills, and therefore set the stage for extraordinary success after college graduation.

"Today, I produce and edit videos that help so many people," explained Johnfrank. "I consider my biggest success so far producing a five-video campaign, something my team donated, which ultimately raised $60,000 for an orphanage in India." Many of Johnfrank's videos (www.justjohnfrank.com) have received over 100,000 views on YouTube and continue to inspire people.

Ultimately, the cheap rates at community college provided Johnfrank the ability to experiment—the essence of a Steering Wheel Feedback Loop—and develop self-awareness for a fraction of the cost compared to a typical four-year university.

Bonus Nugget #2: Location, Location, Location

Toto, I have a feeling we're not in Kansas anymore.
—THE WIZARD OF OZ, 1939

There are three benefits location can offer: (1) local employers recognize and prefer local colleges, (2) cities have a huge advantage, and (3) staying put after graduation keeps your network intact.

Benefit #1: Local Employers Prefer Local Colleges

Let me state something that may not be obvious to all: if you want to work in New York, it doesn't make sense to attend college in Mississippi. Location matters.

Yet I see students making this mistake all the time. "I'm thinking about going to school in California," one Virginia high schooler told me. "Where do you want to work after college?" I asked. "I don't know," the student responded. "Maybe back home in Virginia or somewhere down South." Big mistake.

To demonstrate, after college, Matt Syme (Texas Christian University '10, Broadcast Journalism) found himself trying to break into the

Washington, DC job market—a place a long way from Texas, where he attended college. Not surprisingly, Matt faced some early difficulties doing it. "I came to DC blind," Matt said. "It took time to develop my network, to talk with local businesses."

Matt explains why he faced so much difficulty:

TCU is very much a Texas entity. Most of the students are from Texas. While the TCU name carries a lot of weight in Texas, it doesn't around the country. It's not that the pedigree is bad; it's just unknown. Interviewers often say, "I know the football team, but I don't know much beyond that."

Leveraging a college reputation located far away from where you're trying to work is an exceptionally hard hurdle to overcome.

But for as much as distant colleges are a disadvantage, local colleges are a huge advantage. Employers love them. These "regional schools" can be so powerful that some reports indicate that employers only slightly prefer Elite Colleges to these regional, General Colleges—a huge testament to their marketability. This is especially true for employers in the government and non-profit arena. And, when it comes to competing against General Colleges with a nationwide reputation (e.g. Michigan), regional schools have an almost identical affect on the hiring process. To help find the best regional school for you, visit College Measures (bit.ly/collegemeasures).

Benefit #2: The Advantage of Cities

Increasingly, job opportunities, and even entire industries, are tied to cities. For example, if you want to work in entertainment, you should move to Los Angeles, not Buffalo. If you want to work in energy, you should move to Texas, not Connecticut. If you want to work in technology, you should move to San Francisco, not Cleveland. In order to find out which city is best for you, use the "University Finder" tool under LinkedIn (www.linkedin.com), enter your major and the region of the country where you want to attend college, and view the popular campuses and employers for that particular career field.

There's one final reason why cities are incredibly advantageous: a *lack* of competition. For example, George Mason, where I attended law school, is located across the river from Washington, DC. Unlike the 20,000 to 40,000 interns who flock to DC each summer, because of my location, I was able to work in DC throughout the school year. As a result, I scored an internship at the prestigious U.S. Small Business Administration during my final fall semester, in part due to the reduced competition.

To help you find the cities where most recent grads are flocking, use the College Destinations Index (bit.ly/destinationsindex).

Benefit #3: Keeping Your Network Intact

One of the biggest HACKs to college is developing your network *during* college (covered in more detail in Action HACK #6). Most of your connections will be local, which makes sense, because these are the people you will most often see. But the minute you graduate and move 3,000 miles away from your connection base, you lose years' worth of relationships. That's why, unless you go to an Elite College where the college name is recognized nationwide, you should attend a college near where you plan to work after graduation.

Bonus Nugget #3: Scholarships

No matter which General College you've chosen, you can always use a few extra bucks to offset the inevitably high price tag. The easiest way to directly offset the high cost of college is to secure scholarships. Traditionally, sifting through the thousands of available scholarships made finding the right scholarship more trouble than it was worth, even for those scholarships valued at $1,000. Fortunately, Scholly (bit.ly/collegescholly) has made that problem much more bearable. Scholly has helped students win over $35 million in scholarships. Use it to drive down your college price tag even further!

Transferring Colleges

If you don't like something, change it.
—Maya Angelou, American poet and civil rights activist

Many students are going to have read the College Selection HACK *after* they enrolled into a particular college. For many of these students, they will regret the college they chose, or believe that a better college fit exists elsewhere. They will not be alone. Studies show that more than one-third of students transfer colleges, and of those who do, 45 percent decide to transfer more than once.

When thinking about transferring, however, it only makes sense to do so in light of the principles as laid out in the College Selection HACK, as well as the Self-HACKs. For example, transferring between General Colleges just to move up a slot or two in the rankings is likely not worth the hassle. But if you attend a General College and have an opportunity to transfer into Harvard, you'd need a very good reason *not* to do that. Ultimately, the College Selection HACK is not just for those prospective college freshman, it's for anyone who has their foot, or will have their foot, on a college campus.

It's the Student that Ultimately Matters

The golden touch is possessed not by the Ivy League College, but by its students.
—SHANE HUNT, HARVARD PH.D

HACKing college by graduating from an Elite College can no doubt supercharge your success…at least as an early graduate. But over the course of a lifetime, the rapid success that Elite College graduates have begins to level off when compared against a hard-working graduate from a General College. "It's the person, not the place, that matters," stated *The New York Times*, reporting researchers' findings.

That's great news for the 99 percent of students who don't graduate from Elite Colleges. It means that hard working graduates from virtually any college—over the course of a career—can compete with graduates from an Elite College.

Studies have also found that the strongest predictor of lifetime success is the best school that rejected your college application. In other words, over a lifetime, getting rejected from Harvard is just as valuable as graduating from Harvard. "Students who apply to schools for the ambitious are ambitious enough to do well just about anywhere," said one college researcher.

But this book is about HACKing college, after all. And I don't want students to have to wait 30 years to achieve the amount of success that can be had in three. That's why I wrote the College Selection HACK. But just know that if things don't go as planned, you can still achieve elite-level success later.

HACKING TAKEAWAYS

- No matter the costs, attend an Elite College, if given the opportunity. Why? "I don't consider myself extremely intelligent," said Hope Burke (Stanford '14, History and African Studies). "But when I tell people I went to Stanford, they say, 'Wow, you must be a genius!' People's reactions are so over-the-top."
- If an Elite College is not an option, "seek value:" choose a General College with the lowest tuition rates and best employment prospects, mindful that name recognition and accreditation still matter.
- For General College students, keep student loans below $10,000. For Elite College students, taking on student loans in excess of $10,000 is more acceptable.

ACTION HACK #2

Megatrends

Ride the waves of the next megatrends

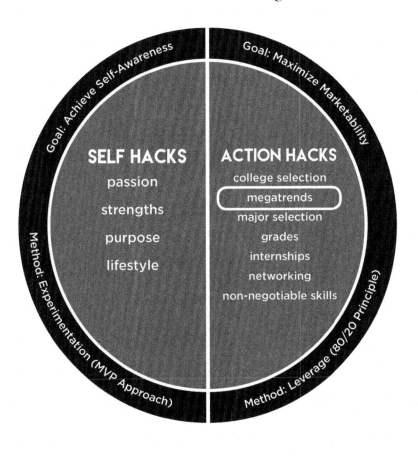

SELF HACKS
passion
strengths
purpose
lifestyle

ACTION HACKS
college selection
megatrends
major selection
grades
internships
networking
non-negotiable skills

Goal: Achieve Self-Awareness

Goal: Maximize Marketability

Method: Experimentation (MVP Approach)

Method: Leverage (80/20 Principle)

It's not enough to be great at what you do. You have to catch at least one really big wave and ride it all the way in to shore.
—Eric Schmidt, former Google CEO

During senior year, as part of a business class, I attended an on-campus conference that discussed "megatrends," multi-billion dollar economic revolutions that promised to change the technological, business, and social landscapes for years to come. The speaker asserted that students who wanted to supercharge their college success merely needed to focus their studies inside a megatrend. As someone looking for an edge, the speaker's hopeful message excited me.

My excitement, however, quickly waned in light of one simple reality: I had failed to position my college career in front of a megatrend. Plus, as a senior, I had little time left to adjust.

Looking back, I realized that even if I had known about megatrends, I likely wouldn't have paid much attention, anyway. I believed that just by graduating college, I had roughly the same opportunity to score a job as my classmates, no matter their major, and no matter their industry. It was simply a matter of merit, I thought, believing that the best students from each major would be employed equally across campus. Turns out I was wrong.

To demonstrate the power of a megatrend, during my senior year, I watched companies scoop up classmates positioned in front of megatrends, even students with mediocre grades and spotty class attendance. Students outside of megatrends, however, faced far more difficulty finding a job.

Today, there are many megatrends on the horizon. With more money sloshing around in the economy than ever before, and with technology rapidly accelerating, we are on the verge of more blockbuster revolutions. Ray Kurzweil, a futurist and chief engineer at Google, predicts that 20,000 years of progress as we know it will be crammed into the next 100 years. In true 80/20 fashion, these multi-billion dollar megatrends are concentrated in a few, particular areas. The Megatrend HACK identifies five megatrends as well as specific career opportunities inside each megatrend.

Since you likely won't be interested in every megatrend, feel free to skip to the megatrends sections of interest. It is also important to note that for some students, none of the following five megatrends will have much appeal. Deciding to refrain from pursuing a megatrend is not necessarily a bad decision, particularly for those guided by the Self-HACKs. However, extraordinary success occurs more easily and quickly inside of a megatrend.

Before showing you where the next megatrends are, however, let's cover three basic principles that explain how megatrends fit into the college arena, how we can spot a megatrend, and why embracing a megatrend should be one of the first things a college student does.

The 3 Megatrend Principles: Setting the Stage

Principle #1: How Riding Megatrends Differs from Typical College Approaches

The problem with college is that there's a tendency to mistake preparation for productivity. —SHIA LABEUOF, ACTOR

Throughout the 1990's Mark Cuban, current owner of the Dallas Mavericks, worked on launching his second major company, Broadcast.com, an online media company. Then, in 1999, at the height of the Internet bonanza, Cuban sold Broadcast.com to Yahoo! for $5.7 billion, one of the biggest deals in tech history at the time. With the deal finished, Cuban entered what he likes to call the "BBC:" the billionaire boys club.

Most importantly, Cuban didn't enter the BBC simply thanks to his expertise. For example, imagine if Cuban had been an expert in, say, making horse and buggy whips. No one ever would have heard of him, because today no one is concerned about horse and buggy whips.

Unfortunately, colleges today only focus on helping students follow a pathway that leads to becoming an expert. Colleges never ask if that pathway leads to becoming an expert in something as useless as horse and buggy whips, or something as in demand as computer programming. In essence, colleges only focus on *preparing* students for a career—even if that career is something entirely useless in the current economy. Not surprisingly, 50 percent of college students today are underemployed.

What students need to be successful, both in college and career, is preparation *and* positioning. That's exactly the moral to the story of Mark Cuban. Cuban's computer expertise *prepared* him to build amazing technology, but his *positioning* as a computer expert inside the Internet megatrend caused his expertise to translate into huge success. That's why riding a megatrend is about being both prepared *and* positioned. College focuses on preparation. The Megatrend HACK focuses on positioning.

Principle #2: How to Predict Megatrends

Ability is of little account without opportunity.
—NAPOLEON BONAPARTE

Positioning requires prediction, and prediction can be a tricky task. Fortunately, there are many stories of people who have ridden megatrends to unparalleled heights. One of them is billionaire founder of Amazon, Jeff Bezos. Bezos has prescribed the exact formula for how to identify the next megatrend:

> I always get the question, "What's going to change in the next ten years?" And that is a very interesting question. It's a common one. I almost never get the question, "What's *not* going to change in the next ten years?" And I submit to you that that second question is actually the more important of the

two, because you can build a business strategy around the things that are stable in time…It's impossible to imagine a future ten years from now where a customer comes up and says, "Jeff, I love Amazon; I just wish the prices were a little higher."

According to Bezos, the magic to spotting the next megatrend is to identify things that will *not* change ten years from today. Once students know where those things are, they can begin creating a college career positioned to ride those megatrends. As a result, each of the opportunities identified in the Megatrend HACK reflect economic forces that will *not* change in the next ten years.

Principle #3: How to Prioritize Seeking Megatrends at College

We work in occupation silos. Once you're in that silo, it's almost impossible to move across to a different one without getting an education in that occupation.
—ANTHONY CARNEVALE, DIRECTOR OF GEORGETOWN CENTER ON EDUCATION AND THE WORKFORCE

Unfortunately, many students jump right into picking a major, targeting a company, or dreaming about graduate school. That's a mistake. Former Google CEO Eric Schmidt explains why:

> When people are right out of school, they tend to prioritize company first, then job, then industry. But at this point in their career that is exactly the wrong order. The right industry is paramount, because while you will likely switch companies several times in your career, it is much harder to switch industries. Think of the industry as the place you surf…and the company as the wave you catch. You always want to be in the place with the biggest and best waves.

In other words, for students, picking an industry must be one of the *first* decisions they make in college. If they choose the wrong company, they can leverage experiences gained and easily switch into a new company within the same industry. However, if students choose the wrong industry, those same skills won't transfer into a new industry as well. Even worse, if students choose to remain inside a collapsing industry, their career opportunities will be severely diminished. That's why the Megatrends HACK is one of the first inside the Execution Cornerstone, and notably, comes before the Major Selection HACK (Action HACK #3).

The 5 Megatrends: Let's Ride Some Waves

The world's biggest problems are now the world's biggest business opportunities.
—PETER DIAMANDIS, CO-FOUNDER OF SINGULARITY UNIVERSITY

With the stage set, let's dig into the next five megatrends, those multi-billion dollar opportunities capable of changing your life.

Megatrend #1: The Demographic Megatrend

What's Not Going to Change in the Next 10 Years?: An aging, more populated world that demands a higher quality of life

On November 29, 1899, Emma Morano was born in Italy. You've probably never heard of her. As of November 2016, at the age of 116, Morano is the oldest person in the world. What's her secret? A daily glass of homemade brandy.

Morano represents a category of people known as "centenarians," people who reach the age of 100 or more. While Marano's age may seem exceptional, that's about to change.

Right now, there is a one in three chance of people in developed countries living to 100. People are simply living longer. Today, sixty is the new forty while eighty is the new sixty. Populations—especially in the West, Japan, and China—are aging so quickly that the number of people over the age of 60 will more than double between 2010 and 2030. By 2030, the world's population of people over the age of 65 will be one billion. That's a lot of old people!

Not only is life expectancy growing, so is the world population in general. Within the next minute, the global population will increase by 145 people. By 2030, more than 1.2 billion additional people will have been born. That's the equivalent to the entire population of China being born in the next decade. Can you imagine these billions of older people saying, "I just hope I don't live much longer," or "My hip hurts; I hope there's no treatment available." Of course not. These people are going to want a better, longer life. Welcome to the Demographic Megatrend!

Demographic Megatrend Opportunities

Healthcare Services: A surge in nurses, doctors, medical technicians, and many others will be needed to provide healthcare for more people, especially those who are aging. "We are going to be short 100,000 doctors in the U.S. alone by 2020," explains Peter Diamandis." The same shortage exists internationally, too. In total, the World Health Organization estimates a global shortage of 4.3 million healthcare workers. This spike in healthcare services will also include a demand for professionals to care for the elderly, such as at retirement home workers, and provide end-of-life treatment, such as Hospice care.

Synthetic Biology: Have you ever wanted to own a glow-in-the-dark cat? Now you can (watch at bit.ly/glowinthedarkcats). It's the magic of synthetic biology, a field that rearranges DNA to produce particular biological characteristics. Today, many companies are experimenting with our genetic code on a microscopic level in order to push medicine, and even agriculture, forward. For example, recently, Synthetic Genomics, a leading medical research company, announced an initiative to develop pigs with lungs that are compatible for transplantation into humans. By 2020, the market for synthetic biology is projected to be $38.7 billion.

Personalized Medicine: Medicine is going microscopic. Human Longevity is a company paving the way. It has created a giant private database of DNA and medical records. With a detailed view of our DNA, doctors can more accurately predict diseases we are likely to contract. It's like a "physical on steroids," says Dr. J. Craig Venter, founder of Human Longevity. Today, you can receive a personalized genetic report from 23andMe (bit. ly/23dnatest) for as little as $199. This is only the tip of the iceberg. In 2015, President Obama announced a $215 million investment in what could eventually be a "decade-long, billion-dollar initiative" to develop "precision medicines."

Financial Services: AARP, which is an organization for retired people, recently published a study declaring that we are entering a "Longevity Economy," a period where Americans over the age of 50 will own approximately $7.1 trillion in wealth. That number is expected to increase to more than $13.5 trillion by 2032. All that money must be managed by someone. That someone could be you.

Ultimately, the Demographic Megatrend will provide billions of dollars of opportunities—most certainly including healthcare and age-related services—but will also touch any industry looking at life on a microscopic level.

Megatrend #2: The Digital Megatrend

What's Not Going to Change in the Next 10 Years?: People demanding products when, where, and how they want them

Technology is no longer an individual sector. According to Cisco, "All businesses, including healthcare, agricultural, industrial, and manufacturing, are now digital businesses." This transformation has happened with warp speed. Consider that it took the telephone 76 years to reach half the U.S. population. The smartphone did that in less than a decade.

Can you imagine a customer saying, "I wish I had to wait longer to place my order," or "Hopefully, the product will not be perfectly tailored to my needs." Of course not. That's why many experts believe that such forces will add $2.2 trillion in opportunities by 2025 alone. Welcome to the Digital Megatrend!

Digital Megatrend Opportunities

Sensors: Smartphones and tablets are everywhere—all seven billion of them—and every smart device contains sensors. That's almost one smart device for every single person on the planet. To demonstrate just how widespread sensors have become, in 2015, there were 35.9 million square meters of sensors, or enough to cover half of Manhattan. Applications include Google's autonomous driving cars, ShotSpotter's urban gunfire detection system, and General Electric's engines. All of this demand translates into one thing: jobs. By 2023, Stanford predicts the sensor industry will represent a multi-*trillion* dollar industry—or 5 percent of global GDP—generating a total of approximately 55 million new direct and indirect jobs. To put that into perspective, consider that the U.S. created only 1.3 million jobs in the last *ten* years. Booyah!

Networks: By 2020, the number of Internet-connected devices is expected to explode to 50 billion, making the "Internet of Things"—the process of connecting devices to the Internet—a $1.9 trillion industry. For perspective, the size of the *entire* U.S. economy is $1.5 trillion. Imagine everyone in America going to work for a full year to do nothing but buy and sell network devices. Talk about opportunity! But it gets better. "I predict [the Internet of Things] will be five to ten times more impactful in one decade than the whole Internet to-date," forecasts John Chambers, chairman of Cisco Systems.

Artificial Intelligence and Robotics: In 2013, Amazon set the drone world ablaze when it announced its entry into the drone market. Then, in 2015, Walmart applied for permission to begin testing drones for home delivery, curbside pickup, and checking warehouse inventories. Not to be outdone, Google X hopes to launch its drone service by 2017, aiming to deliver customer packages within 30 minutes.

Drone technology is just a slice of a much bigger pie. Robots and artificial intelligence are capable of eerily human-like activities, such as writing poetry, creating trendy furniture, and serving as a human receptionist. With so much money at stake, experts have said, "Robotics is the fastest growing industry in the world, poised to become the largest in the next decade."

Cybersecurity: In 2013, the retailer Target was hacked during the holiday season. Hackers (not to be confused with the good kind of HACKers) accessed the financial information of more than 40 million customers. The damage to Target was enormous, losing billions of dollars in market value and its CEO Gregg Steinhafel, after 30 years of employment. To illustrate the seriousness of cyber attacks across the globe, James Clapper, former director of national intelligence, warned Congress that cyber attacks pose a greater long-term threat to national security than terrorism. That's why by 2020, the cyber security market will reach nearly $170 billion, with an annual growth rate of 9.8 percent. "If any college student asked me what career would most assure 50 years of steady, well-paying employment," said Alec Ross, former advisor to the Secretary of State, "I would respond, 'Cybersecurity.'"

Big Data: Data is everywhere. Eric Schmidt, former CEO of Google, stated that every two days we create as much information as we did from the dawn of civilization up until 2003. There is so much data that it's actually a problem. An Oxford study found, "Companies are drowning in the sea of information."

But not for much longer. "Big Data," sophisticated predictive analytics, is solving the problem. All companies are moving toward Big Data, even those you wouldn't think. For example, right now, basketball teams use

Big Data to determine whether to double-team a three-point shooter or to protect close-range jump shots. Companies have fallen so much in love with Big Data that Schmidt has said, "The sexiest jobs in the Internet Century will involve statistics, and not just in a parallel geeky world." Michael Dell, founder of Dell computers, said, "I think this is where the next trillion dollars comes from for our customers and for our industry."

Mobile Technologies: Today, over 75 percent of the global population has access to a mobile phone. In some countries, more people have access to a mobile phone than a bank account, electricity, or clean water. Several reports have showcased poor Chinese farmers using their limited money to buy cell phones at the expense of accessing running water or indoor toilets. As a result, consumer spending via mobile is projected to increase from $204 billion in 2014 to $626 billion in 2018—accounting for almost half of all e-commerce sales. The mobile trend is so big that, according to an Oxford study, mobile technologies are more likely to help business than "any other technology," opening opportunities in app development, telecommunications, and much, much more.

Cloud Computing: Software is expensive, so companies are increasingly turning toward "cloud computing"—services that are provided over the Internet and are paid for on an as-needed basis. "I can be a small business that can suddenly serve 20 or 30 million customers all around the world," says Ashish Agrawal, a product manager at Adobe. What's more, cloud computing allows companies and individual entrepreneurs to enter new markets quickly while slashing overhead costs. Experts predict that the public cloud services will balloon to a $141 billion industry by 2019. Go get your head in the clouds!

3-D Printing: Ever see *Iron Man 2?* Parts of the suits were 3-D printed, a process where physical items are built layer-by-layer, similar to how an inkjet printer lays down ink. What's more, computers are now able to add layers of plastic, metal, glass, leather, and even chocolate to create 3-D objects. Want an internal organ? 3-D printers have begun printing them, too. 3-D printing has been called a "Walmart in your home" for its on-demand ability to provide perfect customization. Of course, all this is creating massive opportunities inside a global manufacturing market valued at over $10 trillion.

Ultimately, the Digital Megatrend will provide a host of billion dollar opportunities—and even *trillion* dollar opportunities—for students, which will mainly involve disciplines in science, technology, engineering, and math.

Megatrend #3: The Resources Megatrend

What's Not Going to Change in the Next 10 Years?: More people demanding a higher standard of living, further straining natural resources

We know that the world population is increasing (Megatrend #1). But so are its bank accounts. By 2022, more people will be middle class than poor—an amazing feat. In 2014 alone, an expansion in global wealth created 920,000 new millionaires. With these added riches comes the desire—and ability—for a better life.

In particular, the comforts of climate control, automobiles, and clean drinking water are now becoming a reality for millions around the globe. Do you think the newfound middle class are going to say, "I really hate that my house is at a constant 72 degrees now," or "I wish that I had to walk 20 miles to the store rather than drive my car"? Of course not. They are going to want the same lifestyle you and I enjoy. And with their newfound cash, they will be able to buy it.

This new demand will further strain an already-stretched global ecosystem. Additional raw materials must be brought to market. New infrastructure must be deployed to bring the production of more resources online. Importantly, the world must create ways to satisfy all this demand without destroying the planet in the process. All this spells serious opportunity. Welcome to the Resources Megatrend!

Resources Megatrend Opportunities

Renewable Energy: Fossil fuels—oil, gas, and coal—have served as the workhorse of the global economy...until now. Over 200 countries vowed to reduce net carbon emissions to zero by 2050. By 2030, the share of electricity generated by renewable energy could reach 50 percent. Furthermore, experts say that annual spending on energy efficiencies must increase from $130 billion today to $550 billion by 2035. Solve the world's energy crisis, while riding one massive megatrend!

Food and Water: Experts suggest that there must be a 50 percent increase in food supply to feed a more demanding population, and by 2030, nearly half the global population may face water scarcity. "If nothing is done, we will run out of water faster than we will run out of oil," said Peter Brabeck-Letmathe, Chairman of Nestle. If you're thirsty for success and hungry for opportunity (see what I did there?), immerse yourself in an industry that's trying to figure out how to feed and hydrate billions of people.

Climate Change: Between 1950 and 2010, the Earth's average surface temperature rose at a rate six times higher than from 1890 to 1950. This radical temperature change has significantly altered weather patterns. The United Nations forecasts that the number of people in large cities who are exposed to cyclonic winds, earthquakes, and flooding will more than double between 2000 and 2050. As a result, countries are racing to rebuild their dated infrastructure to protect against extreme weather conditions. The cost of adapting to climate change for developing countries will be $70 billion to $100 billion *per year* through 2050. Sink your teeth into this opportunity!

Ultimately, the Resources Megatrend will provide multi-billion dollar opportunities as a result of increasing resource consumption, resource scarcity, and climate change—forces that will continue to exist for decades.

Megatrend #4: The Urbanization Megatrend

What's Not Going to Change in the Next 10 Years?: People wanting to be located close to jobs and opportunities

Where do you plan to live after graduation? If I had to guess, it's not in Smalltown, U.S.A. It's most likely in a city, a mindset exactly like millions of people across the world.

By 2030, almost two-thirds of the world's population will reside in cities, a 50 percent increase from 2013. As a result, *trillions* of dollars of opportunities are now moving into some of the world's biggest urban areas, particularly in developed countries. Welcome to the Urbanization Megatrend!

Urbanization Megatrend Opportunities

Housing and Urban Development: In 2016, the median house in San Francisco cost $1.2 million. With so much demand, getting prices back down in San Francisco to rates found in 1995 (about half of current costs) would require building 30 percent more houses. But San Francisco is no exception. Cities all across the nation, including Minneapolis, Washington, DC, and New York are having similar problems. To keep pace with urbanization, $41 trillion—nearly four times the size of China's economy—must be invested by 2030. All of this spells opportunities for those looking to build, develop, and move people into city houses, including housing developers, city planners, surveyors, real estate lawyers, real estate agents, and engineers.

Poverty: Not everyone, however, will benefit from rapid urbanization. Right now, one billion people—nearly one in seven people in the world—live inside city slums. That number could spike to two billion by 2030 if not addressed quickly. This means that more people will demand social services. Professions like social workers, mental health experts, and homeless service providers will be needed to assist more and more at-risk people living inside city limits.

Immigration: In the wake of increasing urbanization, many of these city newcomers will be immigrants looking for new opportunities. To accommodate this influx and ensure it's conducted safely and humanely, serious opportunities will exist for immigration lawyers and customs and border control services.

Ultimately, the Urbanization Megatrend will witness the movement of hundreds of millions of people, bringing with it, several hundred million dollar opportunities.

Megatrend #5: The "Rise of the Individual" Megatrend

What's Not Going to Change in the Next 10 Years?: People wanting more empowerment, control over their lives

During the summer of 2006, I received my much-awaited college email address. Not because I wanted a sleeker looking one (Hotmail worked just fine), but rather I couldn't wait to sign up for the newest and hottest online service: Facebook, which required a college email to register.

Once on Facebook, I realized *I had a voice*. Although my realization is no longer new to those in the developed world, billions of people, including the 60 percent of people currently offline (approximately 4 billion people), will soon experience what I did years ago.

Today, there is a new space race of sorts—a competition to see who can provide global Internet coverage at the cheapest rates to the most people. Google, Facebook, and billionaires Elon Musk, Richard Branson, and Paul Jacobs are each developing separate projects to blanket the Earth's atmosphere with balloons, satellites, or aircraft to provide affordable global Internet access. By 2030, half of the world will have Internet connection. The Internet's expansion will empower individuals like never before.

Can you imagine someone saying, "I don't want an Internet connection?" or "I don't want to be in better control of my life?" Of course not. This technological boom will empower individuals in a historic way. Welcome to the "Rise of the Individual" Megatrend!

"Rise of the Individual" Megatrend Opportunities

Social Media: Today, Facebook has 1.59 billion users, who watch 100 million hours of video per day and create 123 million events per year—serious growth for a company around less than a decade. Of course, Facebook isn't the only winner inside the social media arena. In 2012, roughly twelve people built Instagram in less than two years, and then sold it for $1 billion dollars, despite the fact that the company wasn't even profitable. Groupon, seen as a relatively new company, has over 50 million subscribers. Why are these companies so successful? Because social media is on fire. Right now, there are more likes per day on Facebook than Google searches.

Entrepreneurship: Intuit, the Silicon Valley-based software company, estimated that by 2020 more than 40 percent of the American workforce would be made up of "contingent workers," workers hired on an as-needed basis, such as freelancers. That's why around 70 percent of Millennials view themselves as entrepreneurs. For those entrepreneurs with a great idea, financing has never been more accessible. In 2025, crowdfunding will rise to $96 billion, making virtually any good idea capable of receiving financial backing. There has never been a better time to be an entrepreneur.

China: Opportunities inside the "Rise of the Individual" Megatrend are not just about the *who* but also about the *where*. These forces will empower millions, mostly in the East and particularly China. Just to keep up with its population boom, reports indicate that China must add $1 trillion to $2.2 trillion per year to its economy—basically the entire annual output of India. "Companies will need a new playbook to capture the coming wave of growth," concluded the Boston Consulting Group, one of the premier advisory firms in the world. As a result, those who know and understand Chinese culture, and who can effectively communicate to Chinese people, will enjoy major success. To see a list of other breakout countries, visit bit.ly/megatrendcountries.

The Rise of the Individual Megatrend will witness the empowerment of individuals at a historical level, creating multi-billion dollar opportunities and providing billions of people with a platform upon which they can succeed.

Ultimately, riding a megatrend is one of the biggest HACKs inside the college arena. Although pursuing an industry outside of a megatrend is not necessarily a bad idea (especially if the Self-HACKs suggest so), students who position their college careers in front of one of these five megatrends expose themselves to massive economic trends, thrusting their marketability to stratospheric levels.

HACKING TAKEAWAYS

- To achieve success, college students must be both prepared *and* positioned within the current economy.
- College students can identify megatrends by asking, "What's not going to change in the next ten years?"
- Megatrend positioning is one of the first things students must do inside the college arena, even before selecting a major.

ACTION HACK #3
Major Selection

Select "Skills Ready" Majors

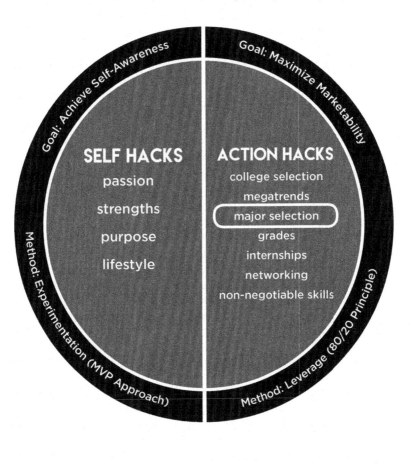

Goal: Achieve Self-Awareness

Goal: Maximize Marketability

SELF HACKS

passion

strengths

purpose

lifestyle

ACTION HACKS

college selection

megatrends

major selection

grades

internships

networking

non-negotiable skills

Method: Experimentation (MVP Approach)

Method: Leverage (80/20 Principle)

The difficulty lies not so much in developing new ideas as in escaping from the olds ones. —JOHN MAYNARD KEYNES, ECONOMIST

When I transferred from the College of Education to the College of Business, Penn State required me to declare a major. The problem was, although I knew I wanted to pursue business generally, I didn't know much about any of the business majors specifically.

The little I knew came from a few friends who were already business majors. During our conversations, they described Marketing as a "people-focused" major. I knew that I liked people, so I thought marketing might be a good fit. Largely based on this advice, I declared marketing as my major. Ironically, as we'll see in this HACK, I selected a major that didn't maximize my marketability.

Nevertheless, at least I generally knew what I wanted and consequently obtained a business degree. However, students without a general direction are destined for serious trouble, which is compounded by the dizzying array of majors awaiting them. For example, Michigan State offers more than 150 majors, Central Florida offers over 200 majors, and Arizona State offers a whopping 350 majors! Just imagine if you double major or add a minor. You have to sift through literally thousands of possibilities. With so many options, students are desperate for expert counsel—much like I was.

Not surprisingly, 80 percent of all students change their major at least once, and the average college student changes his or her major at least *three* times over a college career. Even still, nearly a third of all college graduates wish they had picked a different major.

Fortunately, The 80/20 Principle can help us sort through all the noise. In reality, there are several key majors that hold most of the value inside the college arena, and many majors that provide virtually no value at all.

The Major Selection HACK identifies the most valuable majors, highlights the duds, and explains how knowing the difference can make all the difference. But first, we need to understand how *not* to approach the major selection process.

The 3 Common Major Selection Mistakes

We made too many wrong mistakes.
—YOGI BERRA, PROFESSIONAL BASEBALL CATCHER, MANAGER, AND COACH

Below are the three common mistakes students make when approaching the major selection process. Knowing how *not* to select a major greatly enhances a students chances of selecting the right major.

Mistake #1: Ultra Specific Majors

Many students try to gain an edge by transforming into the perfect candidate. "I'll give those employers *exactly* what they want!" they say. Consider just how specialized some majors are:

- Bakery Science (Kansas State)
- Turf and Turfgrass Management (Ohio State and Purdue University)
- Fire Protection Engineering (Oklahoma State)
- Economic Crime Investigation (Utica College)

Supposedly, these majors train students to bake the best muffin, cut the perfect blade of grass, put out a fire in record time, or lock away criminals with ease. Because of the extraordinary focus, I call these majors "Ultra Specific" majors.

Ultra Specific majors seem utterly practical. What employer would turn away a college graduate with such practical skills?

The answer: many. By selecting an Ultra Specific major, students unnecessarily expose themselves to the ups and downs of a specific job inside a specific industry. Imagine a student early in college selecting a major based on wanting an ultra-specific job, but by graduation, discovers that the job has been automated, sent overseas, or simply unwanted. Uh oh. The prospects are so bleak that graduates with degrees no longer needed in the marketplace often face *higher* unemployment rates than graduates with a high school diploma only. By selecting a major with the intention of becoming a perfect candidate, students actually do the exact opposite.

Mistake #2: Liberal Arts Majors

Many students opt for the other extreme. "I want to be able to work anywhere, doing anything!" they say. "I want to keep my options open!"

Perhaps the most popular way for students to cast their nets as wide as possible is to select a liberal arts major, such as English, history, philosophy, or communications. For liberal arts majors, the idea is about breadth, not depth.

So what's the problem? For starters, liberal arts graduates have a hard time finding work. In fact, graduates who majored in the arts and psychology have nearly *twice* the unemployment rate compared to those who majored in other more technical fields.

For those liberal arts majors who manage to find jobs, the pay is typically low. For example, the average liberal arts graduate entering the workforce makes a meager $29,000, only $1,000 more than the average high school graduate. What's more, some liberal arts majors, such as fine arts, start off earning as little as $20,000, which is well below the salary of an average recent high school graduate.

All is not lost, however. Some liberal arts graduates win. Meet Stewart Butterfield, a multi-millionaire, cofounder, and CEO of Slack Technologies, a communications company. Butterfield is also the proud holder of an undergraduate and master's degree in philosophy and raves about the benefits of his liberal arts education:

Studying philosophy taught me two things. I learned how to write really clearly…And…I learned about the ways that everyone believes something is true…until they realized it wasn't true.

But here's what I didn't tell you about Butterfield: he graduated from an Elite College, two of them to be exact. For undergrad, Butterfield attended Canada's prestigious University of Victoria. For his master's degree, Butterfield attended Cambridge in England, one of the best universities in the world.

Butterfield having attended an Elite College is deeply significant. "You generally don't see people majoring in Philosophy, or other 'soft' majors, except in top schools," says a PayScale director, a company that collects data on student salaries. Why? A *Washington Post* report explains: "Elite Liberal Arts graduates don't merely tend to see a healthy bump in salary after a decade in the work force—they tend to see the most significant bumps, period." In other words, a liberal arts degree can thrust you into the same arena of success as Butterfield, but only if you graduated from an Elite College like Butterfield. Otherwise, liberal arts graduates find themselves lagging in both job prospects and compensation.

GRADUATE SCHOOL: WHEN A LIBERAL ARTS DEGREE REQUIRES MORE

Many students, finding their career prospects lacking (often liberal arts graduates), turn to graduate school in hopes of a marketability boost. But does graduate school, particularly for liberal arts students, enhance marketability?

Adelina Longoria (University of Houston '03, Psychology; Oklahoma State '08, PhD Psychology) is a walking one-stop-shop for graduate school advice. In addition to getting her PhD, Adelina has worked as a professor, meaning she knows how graduate school operates from both sides of the desk, and for many premier companies. If that's not enough, Adelina once sang for the President of the United States!

Adelina explains how, to achieve success in her field, a PhD was necessary:

> A psychology degree by itself is not all that marketable to employers. The problem is that the degree only provides a general introduction into the material. At most universities, there is no specialization—and therefore no practical skills developed—until graduate school.

For some students, waiting to develop practical skills in graduate school is not a problem, mainly those who know the *exact* career they want. That's Adelina's story. "Ever since middle school, I knew I wanted to be a psychologist," said Adelina.

Many other students, however, are less sure. It's this uncertainty that can wreak havoc. Why? Graduate school is like doubling down on your college career, and more debt and more time is the ante. As a result, getting graduate school wrong is like getting two college careers wrong at once.

But graduate school gets even more complicated, as it no longer guarantees a sure ticket to success. Adelina explains:

> A lot of people think they need a masters or a PhD to get ahead. I don't necessarily agree. If you're just relying on a graduate degree to be the only backing you have, you're going to come up short.

Reports reflect exactly what Adelina says. In nearly every field, a college graduate with at least three years of experience will out-earn students freshly out of graduate school. Furthermore, recently 59 percent of graduates with a masters degree remained underemployed, demonstrating that a graduate degree does not necessarily produce better job prospects.

Graduate school, then, is not so much a pipeline into a dream job, but rather the price for the *opportunity* for a dream job. That's why students who choose a major that requires a graduate degree to be marketable, such as liberal arts majors, must be doubly sure that their major is the right fit. To see which majors require a complimentary graduate degree, visit bit.ly/gradschoolmajors.

Unless students graduate from an Elite College, liberal arts majors aren't very marketable except when they are accompanied by a graduate degree. Even then, however, because of graduate schools' rising costs and decreasing marketability, students must be doubly sure of their college track. Ultimately, so many things have to go right for a liberal arts degree to make sense, that—unless students are crystal clear on their career track, much like Adelina—I encourage students to avoid liberal arts majors altogether.

Mistake #3: Indecision is a Decision

Many a false step was made by standing still.
—FORTUNE COOKIE

In addition to seeking to become the perfect candidate (Ultra Specific Majors) and "keeping my options open" (Liberal Arts Majors), exists an equally poor decision: choosing *nothing*. That's exactly what I did.

I began my undergraduate career in the College of Education at Penn State. But, during the course of my freshman year, I slowly began to realize that pursuing a major in secondary education was not a good fit for me.

Although I sensed a void, the costs of being confined to an unfit major were rather minimal—at least, during my *freshman* year. After all, my classmates were taking the same general education classes as me. Then came sophomore year, when I realized my friends were becoming increasingly involved in their particular major. My engineering friends were taking engineering courses. My business friends were taking business courses. I, however, was still taking education courses despite knowing that I would eventually switch majors.

One night during my sophomore year, I had a revelation that shook me to the bones, one I quickly shared with my dad. In *We Learn Nothing*, author Tim Kreider perfectly described my experience:

> [W]e only get one chance at [life] with no do-overs. Life is an unrepeatable experiment…For whatever we do, even whatever we do not do, prevents us from doing its opposite. Acts demolish their alternatives. That is the paradox.

I realized that, if I chose a major, by definition, I restricted myself from choosing other majors. But importantly, if I chose to refrain from picking a major (what I was doing), I restricted myself even further, because I was choosing to pass on career-advancing opportunities. I suddenly realized that I could no longer afford to do nothing. *I had to choose something.* Through this experience, I learned that "indecision is a decision."

Many students are like my sophomore self: unsure of what to choose. To get a better idea, many students turn to the classroom, believing that exposure to different subjects will provide a better sense of what to do. While this may be true for many (e.g. Johnfrank Dieguez, experimenting in community college), it wasn't true for Ari Rose (Emory '09, Liberal Arts):

> I took the common idea of "go to college and you'll figure it out later." After two years in college, however, I was in the same place as I was freshman year. If anything, my exposure to more subjects only increased my interests and therefore complicated my decision in choosing a major. It became more difficult to choose, rather than less.

Ultimately, students like me, who decide to *not* choose a major, are in fact choosing a major: the very one they are in, including the common catch-all major, "Undecided." To excel in college, however, students must stop playing defense. Fortunately, the following section identifies the three categories of high-value majors, and provides a roadmap for how students can get off the sideline and into the game.

The Happy Medium: "Skills Ready" Majors

Majors…[are] the only strong signal to employers that you're prepared for the workplace.
—JEFF SELINGO, EDITOR OF THE CHRONICLE OF HIGHER EDUCATION

Between Ultra Specific majors and Liberal Arts majors lies a happy medium, a sweet spot that, if found, can catapult students into extraordinary success. These majors are more technical in nature and develop the practical skills employers want, enabling students to make an impact immediately after graduation. I call these majors "Skills Ready" majors, and they are the key to HACKing the major selection process.

Skills Ready majors fall under one of the following three categories:

1. Science, Technology Engineering, and Math (STEM);
2. Business; and
3. "Career-Related" Majors.

Let's take a closer look at each.

Skills Ready Major #1: STEM

Matt Brocker (Taylor '10, Engineering; Johns Hopkins '13, Informatics) is already a cyber security guru, and he only recently finished his formal education. Today, Matt works for a leading cyber security startup company located in Virginia, successfully leveraging both of his STEM degrees to land at the epicenter of the growing cyber security industry.

How did he get there?

In high school, Matt loved math. "Our high school held 'Physics Olympics,'" explained Matt, "where we built cool projects, such as mousetrap racecars." Matt loved tinkering with things so much he set out to explore college majors relating to science and math.

Once enrolled in college, Matt decided to major in Computer Engineering. "I knew that companies were increasingly outsourcing work to India, including white collar work," Matt said. "But I think that U.S. companies will always want their cyber security work to stay local."

While in college, Matt plunged himself headfirst into his studies. "I worked really hard," said Matt. "I did social things but less than the average student." Matt explains why his STEM workload was so demanding:

> My major was math heavy. Students got a math minor just by taking classes required for a Computer Engineering degree. Every semester seemed like the hardest, until the next semester came. The reason was that every new math class built upon my previous math classes. Every new science class built upon my previous science classes.

The rigor of Matt's STEM track has made him extraordinarily valuable to employers. But not simply because the STEM track was academically demanding, but more importantly, as Matt explains, it was utterly practical:

> STEM is really about the practical. For example, students spent lots of time in labs or learning to program. The academic side simply provides depth to understand the practical.

This magical blend of theoretical mixed with practical is what employers love. Most telling, even non-STEM employers are falling in love with STEM majors. "Previously, STEM work had been concentrated among an elite few workers," found a Georgetown study. "Today...STEM competencies are needed in a broader reach of occupations, and their use is growing outside of STEM."

For these reasons, STEM graduates are expected to receive the highest starting salaries among all college graduates. And the difference is huge. Consider that engineering graduates will earn double that of Education graduates. What's more, the average salary for a STEM graduate has continued to climb for years and is projected to have the largest wage growth over the course of a career.

Ultimately, for those seeking a STEM degree, students can expect a rigorous course load of math and science. As a reward for such intense studying, STEM graduates continue to find themselves as one of the most in-demand majors among employers. To see the states with the most STEM job opportunities, visit bit.ly/stemjobmap.

THE ADDED ADVANTAGE OF GOING STEM: COLLEGE SELECTION

Remember Stewart Butterfield, the multi-millionaire and graduate with two liberal arts degrees from two Elite Colleges? Unlike Butterfield, when students enter the STEM world, they don't need to attend Elite Colleges to achieve extraordinary success. In fact, the college a STEM student attends doesn't matter that much, period.

"Prestigious schools boost future earnings only in certain fields," reports the *Wall Street Journal* concerning a study that analyzed thousands of graduates. "[F]or fields like [STEM], it largely doesn't matter whether students go to a prestigious, expensive school, or a low-priced one—expected earnings turn out the same."

Most notably, this STEM advantage does not apply to other majors, including other Skills Ready majors. "Outside of STEM, it matters tremendously where a student receives a degree," concluded the *Wall Street Journal.*

Do you understand the significance? Now STEM majors can bargain shop during the college selection process, because a STEM degree from a General College can pack the same punch as a STEM degree from an Elite College. The only difference is the price tag. Just one more reason to major in STEM.

Skills Ready Major #2: Business

Nathan Davy (Florida '07, Business Management; Army '07 – '13) sports an extraordinary resume. But Nathan didn't hit the corporate world right after college to do it. Instead, shortly after graduation, Nathan became an infantry officer in the Army. While in the Army, Nathan went to Ranger school, served a deployment in Iraq, and received a Bronze Star for his services. After leaving active duty, Nathan quickly scored a job, where he is now responsible for over $5 million in revenue a year.

How did Nathan make an impact so quickly?

"In high school, I knew that I wanted to study Business in college," explained Nathan. "Both of my grandfathers were business guys, so I grew up knowing that business was the engine of job growth."

Although Nathan knew he wanted to pursue Business, after beginning college, Nathan wasn't sure which specific Business major to choose. "Based on high school, I knew I enjoyed economics," said Nathan. "But I hated advanced math."

To get a better feel, Nathan took the required entry-level Business courses. That's when Nathan began to narrow down his options. "I didn't really enjoy my finance class," explained Nathan. "Plus, it was pretty hard."

Around the same time, Nathan accepted a scholarship offered by Army ROTC, a program that prepares young adults to become officers in the U.S. military. Knowing his future with the Army, combined with the lessons learned from his introductory Business classes, Nathan decided to major in business management. "Business management made sense, because I knew that I would be managing people in the Army," said Nathan.

Although Army ROTC was rigorous, Nathan still found time to succeed academically. Nathan explains how the moderate demands of a Business major created room for ROTC:

> In terms of academic demands, Business majors are middle-of-the-road. Writing incredibly well is not required, but you do have to be competent. Doing advanced math is not required, but you do have to take calculus.

Unlike STEM, Business majors do not face the same intensity regarding academic pressures. Studies show that STEM majors study 50 percent more than business majors. That's why, in college, my Engineering friends poked fun at us Business majors, saying we "had it easy."

So does less academic rigor translate into fewer job prospects? Not at all. In fact, Business majors are the *most* in-demand major out of any other major, even topping STEM majors.

This demand translates into higher salaries. Today, Business majors are one of two non-STEM majors included inside the top-five highest paying majors. (The other is healthcare, which we'll cover next). In fact, Business majors are projected to have the second-highest wage growth over the course of a career, next to STEM majors, and not surprisingly, are the most common majors in college.

Ultimately, for those seeking a Business degree, students can expect a less rigorous course load relative to STEM majors, but receive similarly promising job prospects.

THE DOUBLE EDGED SWORD OF BUSINESS MAJORS

While it's true that Business majors have great job prospects, salaries for Business majors—more than any other major—maintain the most variability. Consider that the average annual salary of many Business majors early in their careers can be as low as $43,000 or as high as $100,000+. That's a big difference. It also explains how I, as a business student, had difficultly landing a job, while my fraternity brother, also a business student, landed on Wall Street after graduation.

So how can students enjoy the fruits of a Business major, while avoiding the soft spots? By picking a Business major that resembles a STEM major.

The world is increasingly moving toward a technical, numbers-driven marketplace. Some Business majors, but not all, deliver a curriculum geared toward number crunching. To maximize employment prospects, students should select a more technical Business major. Below is a list of the more technical Business majors (and thus more marketable) and less technical Business majors (and thus less marketable):

- Highly Marketable Business Majors: Economics, Management Information Systems (MIS), Finance, Supply Chain/Logistics, and Accounting

- Least Marketable Business Majors: Marketing, Business Management, International Business, Human Resources, and Hospitality Management

Skills Ready Major #3: Career-Related Majors

Zack Vincent (Florida State '14, Exercise Science; University of Central Florida Med School '19) started his college career as an aspiring chef. "I took culinary classes during high school," Zack said. "So I decided to enroll as a Food Science major at Clemson."

But Food Science left Zack unfulfilled. "My culinary arts classes just didn't challenge me," Zack explained. "They weren't stimulating."

So Zack made a radical change. Before beginning sophomore year, Zack transferred to Florida State and targeted a career in healthcare. "During my freshman year, I took Biology and Chemistry, which I loved," stated Zack. "I've been hooked on learning about the human body since then."

Exercise Science—a major Zack chose with the intention of leading to a career in medicine—represents a category of majors to which I refer as "Career-Related" majors: majors chosen with a specific, technical career in mind. Career-Related majors include Education, Social Work, and Healthcare.

Many Career-Related majors, healthcare in particular, are filled with high academic expectations. Zack explains how the pre-med track is among the most challenging:

I found myself sacrificing a lot, mainly my social life, just to pull the grades I needed. Most medical schools require close to a 3.70 GPA. Plus, the medical track requires difficult classes, such as bio chemistry and organic chemistry.

Nevertheless, Zack describes how hard work in a Career-Related major, and healthcare in particular, brings serious rewards:

There's a ton of demand at almost all levels of healthcare. Plus, the healthcare industry has something to offer everyone with every kind of interest. The challenge is just getting into the academic program. Once you do, the job outlook is awesome. I would do this track again in a heartbeat.

Reports reflect exactly what Zack describes. Healthcare majors have some of the lowest unemployment rates, including nearly 50 percent less than the average Liberal Arts graduate, and even lower than students with *graduate* degrees in nearly every field. That's amazing!

While healthcare majors are among the premier, there are other desirable Career-Related majors. For example, similar to healthcare, Education and Social Work majors sport low unemployment rates and lead to some of the most predictable, stable salaries, even if those salaries are lower than other Skills Ready Majors.

Ultimately, Career-Related majors provide students with some of the best career prospects inside the entire college arena.

PRACTICALITY OVER ACADEMICS: A TEACHER'S PERSPECTIVE

Ryan Heintzelman (Bloomsburg '10, History; Bloomsburg '11, Education) started out his college career knowing he wanted to become a teacher. He just wasn't sure how to best go about it. Today, he knows.

Ryan explains what aspiring teachers should expect in college:

Practical experience is even more important than academics. For academics, you're looking to maintain a 3.0 GPA. For experience, you must be able to enter a classroom and communicate your lesson by graduation. The ability to communicate clearly is what makes for the most employable teachers, not the best grades.

Ryan's experience reflects something at the heart of Career-Related majors: practicality. That's why employers inside Career-Related majors often mention practical experience as one of the most important line items on a resume. If you are inside a Career-Related major, you must enjoy working in the trenches of your particular industry, not just the academics of it.

The 3 Reasons to Pursue "Skills Ready" Majors

If a window of opportunity appears, don't pull down the shade.
—Tom Peters, business management guru

Some students object to pursuing a Skills Ready major on the basis that such a major is not in line with the industry or job they want to pursue. For example, "I love philosophy and want to work inside a job where I can think critically about the big issues on life," some might say. "Pursuing a Skills Ready major doesn't at all relate to what I want to do."

I completely disagree. Even for students with seemingly different interests, selecting a Skills Ready major still makes absolute sense. Let me give you three reasons why.

Reason #1—Flexibility: Focus on the First Job, Expand from There

A college major is not destiny. College is only the ante in the lifelong learning game.
—Anthony Carnevale, educational and workforce expert

If the purpose of college is to get a job, then the purpose of your major is to get your *first* job. This is difficult for students to initially grasp. They have been taught that selecting a major means choosing "what you want to do for the rest of your life."

But that couldn't be further from the truth. Studies show that the first job of 47 percent of college graduates is unrelated to their college major. In other words, nearly half of all students won't use their major immediately after graduation. What's more, 27 percent of college graduates have *never* worked in a field related to their major. In essence, just because you major in something, doesn't mean you'll actually do it after graduation—let alone the rest of your life.

Not only are students no longer marrying themselves to a particular job, they couldn't do it even if they wanted. Today, job *instability* is the new normal. In 1937, the average lifespan of an S&P 500 company (think the biggest and most popular companies in the world) was 75 years. Studies show, however, thanks to increasing rate of change, ten years from now, more than 40 percent of today's top companies will no longer exist.

In response, workers have pulled back their allegiance to one particular company. Today, on average, a person will have held over six jobs by the age of 26 and will have held 15 to 20 jobs before their career is over. Millennials change jobs every four years and half of them are considering leaving their employer within the next two years.

The rapid rise and fall of companies, coupled with workers job-hopping, means that career *flexibility* has never been more valuable, and a climb-the-ladder approach has never been more dangerous. College students need the ability to move from job to job, and even industry to industry, more than ever before. As a result, students should not pick a major with the mindset that

"I'll be doing this the rest of my life," but rather with an eye toward creating "career pathways," college tracks that open up multiple job opportunities across multiple industries. What are these majors? You guessed it: Skills Ready majors.

The story of Woody Bernardo (George Mason '06, Information Technology) shows just why. Immediately after college graduation, Woody began working at a technology company as a help desk technician—essentially grunt work in the IT industry.

In six short months, however, one of the premier consulting firms in Washington, DC, hired Woody. Think about that: many graduates today can't land a job with two or three years of experience, and Woody landed a great job within just six months. That's when Woody's career took off. "As part of my consulting job," explained Woody, "I worked on a project through the National Institutes of Health, a project aimed to cure certain childhood diseases—an awesome mission."

Despite the great job at the consulting firm, Woody has moved onto an even more exciting opportunity. Today, Woody works at Echo360, a multi-million dollar education technology company revolutionizing classroom learning.

Although Echo360 recruits workers with technical expertise, Woody's current role blends together a sales position and his technical background. Woody's core responsibility is to bring customers on board and continue to satisfy their needs—a non-technical role. Although Woody's technical background comes in handy—such as answering clients' questions—his technical training is required only a fraction of the time.

So why is Woody's technical experience important for a non-technical job? Because Woody can perform both technical and non-technical roles. "A technical background definitely gives me options, because I can do a sales job, or many other jobs that involve customer interaction," explained Woody. In other words, if a technical issue arises, Woody can complete it. If a non-technical issue arises, Woody can complete that, too.

Importantly, the opposite is *not* true. Graduates with a non-technical background cannot address technical issues. They are one-dimensional. For example, you wouldn't expect a History major to troubleshoot a computer program, would you?

Counter to our instincts, Skills Ready Majors, traditionally focused on a very narrow subject, actually offer *more* flexibility than non-Skills Ready Majors, focused more broadly.

TO PURSUE ART OR ENGINEERING?
THAT IS THE QUESTION

In college, Rhyan Johnson (Washington University in St. Louis '10, Engineering) was a unicorn of sorts, a rare college student who excelled in both math *and* art. Rhyan's dual talent, however, made for a complicated college life early on:

> I started college as a mechanical engineering major, because I thought it would balance math and design in an interesting way. My best grades were in multi-variable calculus and fashion design. My art professor told me that he never had taught an engineer before. He said that I had an identity crisis; and I felt that way, too. I remember frequently calling my parents trying to figure out my college life.

At one point, because of this identity crisis, Rhyan transferred out of the College of Engineering and into the College of Art. Her stay inside the College of Art, however, didn't last long, and she soon switched back into Engineering. Rhyan explains why:

> I decided to return to Engineering, mainly because I wanted a career. I knew that I could always teach myself art—at least the sort of art I wanted to do. It made more sense to me that I put my scholarship toward an engineering degree and continue taking art elective courses.

Rhyan's artistic abilities (and passion) begs the question: was Rhyan's move back into Engineering a smart one? The proof is in the pudding.

Today, Rhyan has a wildly successful career as an engineer, working at Amazon and developing the Alexa personality, a cutting edge artificial intelligence technology. Nevertheless, Rhyan is still an artist at heart. Shortly after college graduation, Rhyan co-founded Freely Collective (bit.ly/freelycollective), a nonprofit producing original, hand-crafted home and paper goods, whose proceeds go toward fighting human trafficking. Just a few years after college graduation, Rhyan is flourishing both as an engineer and as an artist.

Most importantly, Rhyan believes that majoring in Engineering allowed her the financial flexibility to co-found Freely Collective. "My career as an engineer allows me to pursue art," Rhyan said. "Although it's possible to support yourself as an artist, it can be a challenge. The engineering field, however, is continuing to grow and provide more jobs. I enjoy knowing I have options."

Again, pursuing Engineering (a Skills Ready major) allowed Rhyan more, not less, opportunity to pursue Art (a non-Skills Ready major).

Reason #2—The Timing Element: You Need to Provide Value. Now.

What employers want from college graduates now is the same thing they want from applicants who have been out of school for years, and that is job skills and the ability to contribute now. That change is fundamental, and it is the reason that getting a good job out of college is now such a challenge.
—PETER CAPPELLI, PROFESSOR

Remember the days when employees were hired, *then* trained, *then* expected to perform? Your parents do. Your professors do. You, of course, don't. In 1979, young workers received an average of 2.5 weeks of training per year. Back then, workers could learn "on the job." Today, however, only 21 percent of employees received *any* training in the previous *five years.* "On-the-job" training is dead.

When I was hired at a law firm, for example, I had less than one hour from stepping foot in my office to when I began working on a multi-million dollar deal. This is how my first day went:

9:00am: Arrived at law firm for first time as employee

9:10am: Completed crash course of the computer system

10:00am: Toured the office and met my coworkers (what I call the "dog and pony" show)

After the dog and pony show, I returned to my office, a short hour after first setting foot in it. There, one of the law firm partners awaited me, with a file the size of five telephone books in his hand. "Kyle, I want you to learn everything in here and explain it to me later today," he said. "Get back to me once you're finished."

Less than 30 seconds after returning to my office, I already had a serious assignment. "I don't even know if I have pens in my desk," I thought to myself. But that's the point. There's no time to waste. Employers want results. Now.

In light of these high expectations, companies are creating entire recruiting programs designed to hire only the top talent, while passing over everyone else. Who are these students? Those with Skills Ready majors. But the exact reason may surprise you.

Studies have shown that graduates with a Skills Ready major—more than any other major—score significantly higher on critical thinking and problem-solving abilities. It's these raw abilities—critical thinking and problem solving—that employers most want, not necessarily the subject information a student learned in his or her major.

That's why companies bend over backwards to hire Skills Ready majors. It's also why companies don't hire English majors, not because companies don't value communication skills, but because English majors often lack the critical thinking and problem solving skills companies most want. Ultimately, Skills Ready Majors provide one of the best ways for students to signal to employers that they possess the valuable skills of critical thinking and problem solving.

Reason #3—Better Jobs and Employment Prospects

Analyst: My thesis was a study in the way that friction ratios affect steering outcomes in aeronautical use under reduced gravity loads.

[Long silence]

Wall Street Executive: So you are a rocket scientist?

Analyst: I was. Yes.

Wall Street Executive: How did you end up here?

Analyst: Well it's all just numbers really. You're just changing what you're adding up. And if I may speak freely, the money is considerably more attractive here.

—Margin Call, 2011

Most students know that not all degrees are created equal, but few students know just how deep the difference runs. Studies have found that the difference between the highest and lowest-paying college majors equals *$3.4 million* over the course of a lifetime. To put these numbers into perspective, that's *four times* the amount a typical high school graduate earns in a lifetime.

Unfortunately, the opposite is also true. Because of the extremely low salaries for the lowest-paying college majors, the value of attending college is frequently *negative*. That means students are actually *worse off* by having gone to college. Alarmingly, one study found that nearly 25 percent—*one in four students*—is made worse off by college. Yikes.

The majors with the lowest salaries are those that emphasize creativity, interpersonal skills, holistic thinking, and other soft skills—that is, non-Skills Ready majors. To find out the amount you can expect to earn with your major, use these tools:

1. **Hamilton Project** (bit.ly/hamiltonmajor): calculates lifetime earnings for over 80 different majors for every phase of a career.
2. **NACE First-Destination Survey** (bit.ly/nacemajor): provides employment rates and average starting salary for recent college graduates by using info from nearly 250,000 graduates.
3. **PayScale** (bit.ly/payscalemajor): ranks highest to lowest-paying majors based on more than 40 million salary profiles.

THE MAGIC OF DOUBLE MAJORS: HOW TO BECOME A MATH-LOVING PEOPLE PERSON

At many colleges, as much as forty percent of students graduate with a double major. Daniel Davy (Florida State '13 Economics, History) was one of them.

Daniel graduated with an Economics degree (a Skills Ready major) and a History degree (a non-Skills Ready major), making him a math-loving, people person: someone who combines the quantitative skills of a Skills Ready major and the qualitative skills of a non-Skills Ready major. Although these two degrees are radically different, fusing both together has equipped Daniel with a massively marketable skill set. Daniel explains:

> The Economics degree honed my quantitative and critical thinking skills. The History degree sharpened my writing and communication skills. I never would have gotten the opportunities I did without both skill sets.

Just what are those opportunities? For starters, immediately prior to graduation, Daniel was awarded the highly prestigious Fulbright Scholarship, a merit-based grant for international educational exchange.

Daniel's Fulbright Scholarship, however, wouldn't begin until a year and a half after graduation. In the meantime, largely thanks to his double major, Daniel landed a position at the Florida State Capitol, working with the Economic Affairs Committee and helping draft legislation...as a 22-year old! Then, because of his experiences, a government think-tank snatched up Daniel, even though the think-tank knew Daniel was scheduled to leave the country soon thereafter.

Today, math lovers with interpersonal skills earn salaries that are much higher than just technical experts alone. In fact, studies show that by adding a technical skill, Liberal Arts graduates can nearly double their job prospects. For the super ambitious, double majoring in a way that demonstrates you are a math-loving, people person can supercharge performance—just like Daniel did.

Transferring Majors

Similar to the College Selection HACK, many students will have read the Major Selection HACK *after* they selected a specific major—and regret the major they chose.

For the reasons in this section, I encourage all non-Skills Ready Majors to transfer into a Skills Ready Major. If that's not possible, (e.g. university policy states it's too late), non-Skills Ready Majors can *still* expose themselves to the benefits of a Skills Ready Major by taking elective courses inside Skills Ready Majors. This way, students can still tell employers about their highly marketable Skills Ready Major coursework, even if that particular major doesn't appear on their transcripts.

HACKing Takeaways

- There is a danger in picking majors that are too narrow (Ultra Specific majors), majors that are too general (Liberal Arts majors), or not choosing a major at all (indecision is a decision).
- To supercharge college success, students should choose Skills Ready Majors, majors that develop technical and practical skills, and allows them to provide employers with immediate value upon graduation.
- Even though some Skills Ready majors may appear unrelated to the career a student wants to ultimately pursue, selecting a Skills Ready major is still the way to go.

Action Hack #4
Grades

Follow the "3.0 GPA Rule"

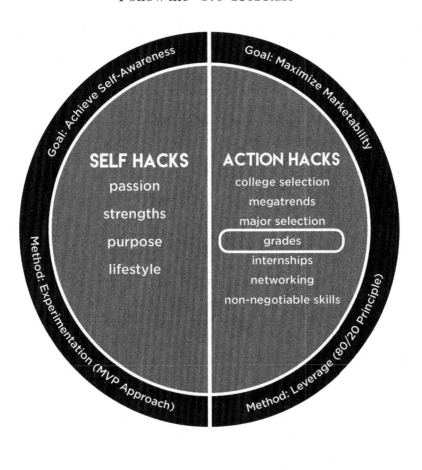

Goal: Achieve Self-Awareness

Goal: Maximize Marketability

SELF HACKS
passion
strengths
purpose
lifestyle

ACTION HACKS
college selection
megatrends
major selection
grades
internships
networking
non-negotiable skills

Method: Experimentation (MVP Approach)

Method: Leverage (80/20 Principle)

Our greatest fear in life should not be of failure, but of succeeding at things that don't really matter.
—Francis Chan, American preacher

It was after midnight...again. "The library will be closing in 10 minutes," a voice over the loudspeaker squawked. "Please gather your belongings and proceed to the exit." I rubbed my eyes, sensing that my 10:00pm cup of coffee had lost its effect an hour too early. I closed my calculus book and exited through the library doors, knowing that I would be back first thing in the morning. At least the cool Pennsylvania air on a night like this was refreshing.

Late nights at the library were common for me. After a few weeks, I'd tire of my secret study area secluded in the library book stacks. Then I would venture to the modern and airy atrium of the business building. After a few weeks at the business building, I would again tire and return to the library. My study locations varied. My study hours did not.

Perhaps those late nights were worth it. After all, I wore a yellow cord around my neck during my college graduation ceremony, signifying that I graduated with honors. I, along with the other top business students, stood and were recognized by the dean and those in attendance during the graduation ceremony.

"Those late nights were worth it, right?" someone once asked me. "You graduated with excellent grades."

No, those late nights were not worth it. I established my entire college approach on the belief that employers hire only the smartest graduates, and that the smartest graduates have the highest GPAs. I was so wrong. If I could redo college, those late study nights would be ground zero for things I would change.

The Grades HACK will outline why grades don't matter as much as you think, how to use battle-tested, non-studying tricks to boost your GPA, and how to optimize learning during the brief moments you actually study.

The Purpose of Grades

Whatever gets measured gets managed.
—Peter Drucker,
FOUNDER OF MODERN BUSINESS MANAGEMENT

Your GPA is basically a distilled snapshot of your college performance. If someone wants to quickly know how you performed at school, they can simply look at your GPA and draw all sorts of inferences. Here are some common inferences people *think* are true:

> **High GPAs (3.5-4.0):** you worked hard, attended all of your classes, and have Einstein-like intelligence.

Mid GPAs (3.0 - 3.49): you worked pretty hard, attended most of your classes, and are above average in intelligence.

Low GPAs (below 3.0): you partied more than you studied, barely attended classes, and are average to below average in intelligence.

Obviously, no one wants to be associated with the inferences made in the low GPA category. That's why everyone fights to get to the top. It may surprise you, however, that those who matter—the employers—actually don't draw inferences along these lines.

Thoughts On Grades From Those Who Matter Most: Employers

Never hire a human being who had a 4.0 in college. If they had a perfect GPA, it means they bought the act and never screwed around. Now a 2.0 is probably not so good. But the ones who had 3.0, yeah! Those are the freaks you want!
—Tom Peters, business management guru

All too often, students strive for perfect grades for no other reason than believing a successful college career demands perfect grades.

But let me ask you this: are your professors going to hire you after college? Didn't think so. Grades only matter to the extent employers care about them. Remember, the purpose of college is to get a job. That makes *employers* the most important group of people within your college career.

What may surprise you is that employers don't require 4.0 GPAs. In fact, many employers don't care about grades at all. Take it from Dave Nossavage (Misericordia '10, Math; Villanova '14, Statistics):

> College is so focused on grades, studying hard, getting A's. All this stuff looks great on paper, but no one actually cares. In applying to my company where I work, candidates prepare their resume, including GPA, courses completed, and topics of interest. The thing is my company never looks at that stuff. All they care about is what kind of individual are you? Are you a hard worker? Do you have experience? Do you have a track record of success outside of the classroom?

So what GPA do employers expect? According to studies, the minimum GPA most employers expect to see is a 3.0. After that point, higher grades have less and less impact. I call this the "3.0 GPA Rule."

Dave's classmate, Justin Muthler (Misericordia '10, Education), talks about his success in using the 3.0 GPA Rule:

> In college, I didn't work extremely hard, especially inside the classroom. Getting a 3.2 GPA was just as good as a 4.0 GPA. Ultimately, I graduated with a 3.5 GPA. Not once has anyone balked at hiring me because I graduated with a 3.5 and not something higher. In fact, they rarely ask for my transcripts.

Justin targeted a GPA slightly above a 3.0 and got it (actually, he even did better). As Justin demonstrates, you don't need perfect grades. Good enough grades are just that: good enough.

Ultimately, unless an exception applies (discussed next), most students merely need to achieve a 3.0 GPA. Stop stressing about your next exam and start realizing that you're stressing over something that isn't as important as you think.

Exceptions to the 3.0 GPA Rule

Nature provides exceptions to every rule.
—MARGARET FULLER, WOMEN'S RIGHTS ADVOCATE

The 3.0 GPA Rule does not apply to every student. Indeed, some students need a GPA higher than 3.0.

An exception to the 3.0 GPA Rule first applies to students who, with slightly more effort, can break into a prestigious opportunity with a higher GPA requirement. For example, to intern at JP Morgan—an excellent way to hone a personal brand in finance—students need a 3.2 GPA. That's why it's necessary to research the GPA requirements of the job opportunities you're interested in pursuing.

Also, every year, about 3 million students enroll in a post-college program, such as a masters or doctorate program. Graduate admissions offices typically evaluate a candidate on three equal bases: grades, experiences, and the relevant test (e.g. GRE, LSAT). That means for purposes of applying to graduate school, a student's grades can be one-third of importance. For some natural sciences and top med schools, the value can be more like one-half grades and one-half relevant test. Some of the elite graduate schools, such as Harvard, like to see a 3.5 GPA or better. If you are thinking of pursuing graduate school, the 3.0 GPA Rule does not apply to you.

Other than these few exceptions, the 3.0 GPA Rule applies to every student on campus—mainly those looking to land a job immediately after graduation.

Reasons to Avoid Competing on Grades

I have come to see grades as schools' drug of choice, and we are all addicted.
—SIR KEN ROBINSON, BRITISH AUTHOR AND PUBLIC SPEAKER

Not only do grades offer limited paybacks, but competing on the basis of GPA is very risky. Here's seven reasons why:

Reason #1: GPAs Don't Correlate to More Success

Employers are beginning to realize that success in college does not necessarily translate to success in the workplace. For example, the U.K. office of Ernst & Young recently announced that it scrapped its previous practice of requiring new employees to have at least a 3.0 GPA, opting instead to use a more holistic approach. Why? The company found little evidence that academic success correlated with how new hires performed on the job. Many other companies are following suit.

With the perception of grades shifting among employers, by going all-in on GPAs, students are investing in something with decreasing importance. When perception changes—like it is now—students who wager a college career on grades are betting on a falling market.

Reason #2: No One Cares About Grades After Your First Job

First, grades are important for grad school and, to a limited extent, for your first job. After that, nobody gives a damn.
—RAMIT SETHI, ENTREPRENEUR

By investing in GPAs, students are investing in something with a short shelf life. How short? According to, Laszlo Bock, senior vice president of people operations at Google, GPAs are almost meaningless as soon as students land their first job:

> Google famously used to ask everyone for a transcript and GPAs and test scores, but we don't anymore, unless you're just a few years out of school. We found that they don't predict anything.

Think of grades like this: grades help you land your first job, but your performance at your first job—not your grades—determines where you go from there. That's why investing in grades provides very little payoff throughout your life.

Reason #3: Everyone Already Competes on Grades

By competing on grades, students are in direct competition against the smartest people in the class, not to mention the smartest people from other schools applying for the same job. "You have to compete against everyone else who will be trying to get jobs using the same criteria: grades," said entrepreneur Ramit Sethi.

The greatest achievements, however, come from zigging when everyone else is zagging. Think about it. Henry Ford made car ownership possible by standardizing the assembly process, while every car manufacturer used varying procedures. "Any customer can have a car painted any color that he wants so long as it is black," said Ford.

Use students' GPA obsession to your advantage. Choose a different battle to fight and compete where it's less crowded, providing more room for success.

Reason #4: Diminishing Returns

It takes a lot of energy to go from a B to an A—much more so than going from a C to a B. Trying to compete at the top of the GPA spectrum means each fraction of a GPA point requires more and more energy. It can be exhausting trying to reach the top.

Then, if a student reaches the top, now he or she is forced to expend a massive amount of energy just trying to stay there. After all, receiving a B in a class can sink a 4.0 GPA faster than a B factored into a 3.0 GPA. Laborious work demands more laborious work. That's not how students should invest their college years.

Reason #5: Everyone Already Has A's

In classrooms today, the average GPA is close to a 3.5, and 45 percent of all grades administered are A's, the most common grade awarded. "At elite schools, at this point, if an upperclassman does the work, it is almost impossible to give them less than a B-plus, and even, increasingly, an A-minus," said William Deresiewicz, a Yale professor. Today, nearly every student is scoring A's.

Since so many students have A's, to separate from the pack, students need a nearly unblemished GPA—a 4.0 or darn close. And, as we discussed, maintaining GPA perfection is often utterly exhausting.

Reason #6: No Room for Interpretation

Everyone knows that a 3.7 GPA is higher than a 3.6, but is a student with a 3.6 GPA and internship experience at an elite company more valuable than a student with a 3.7 GPA and no internship experience? That's a good question. The student with a 3.6 GPA can argue that it is. And she should. And because she can use her experiences, for example, to make a case for her value, all of a sudden she becomes a viable candidate for any position against the 3.7 GPA student. But if students chalk a college career up to one number, they eliminate themselves from being competitive against every student with a better GPA.

This reason explains why students with mediocre grades can outcompete students with the best grades. A job candidate's profile is always more complex than merely a GPA. Don't create a college career where you pin your career prospects to one number.

Reason #7: No Room for Exploration

Obsessing over GPAs can limit experimentation that is so critical to a successful college career—basically everything we covered in the Self-HACKs. Take it from Rhyan Johnson (Washington University in St. Louis '10, Engineering):

> Before high school, I was used to getting straight A's. Later, I qualified for, and was accepted into, a magnet high school, where I started getting B's and C's. I was disappointed at first, but this in many ways prepared me for college. I learned how to work hard, balance a busy schedule, and give myself grace regarding grades.

> During college, I witnessed many successful high school students enroll only in majors in which they were almost guaranteed A's in their classes. They would rather settle for a career track they disliked than receive a B. If that's your mindset, you will likely study something that's not your passion.

By solely fixating on grades, students eliminate their ability to explore inside the relative safety of college. It's no surprise then that many 4.0 GPA students are completely miserable after college.

If you learn anything from this book, know that failure is good. But if you allow GPAs to be a measure of your success, you will never conduct the experimentation necessary for living a fulfilling life. And that is the ultimate failure.

In the end, great grades only show that you're a great test taker. "I would always hire a B-student who can show me she understands technology and is passionate about what she does, over someone who shows me he spent four years in the library and has no tolerance for risk or real skills (except test-taking)," said technology entrepreneur Ramit Sethi.

How to Score Higher Grades With Ease

It is vain to do with more what can be done with less.
—WILLIAM OF OCCAM, ORIGINATOR OF OCCAM'S RAZOR

Even though students should avoid competing exclusively on grades, it's still important to satisfy the 3.0 GPA Rule. Here are five methods to scoring higher grades without an ounce of studying.

Method #1: Professor Selection

A professor can mean the difference between a crushing amount of homework and a doable workload. Use these two tricks to ensure you're selecting the best professor possible.

RateMyProfessors (bit.ly/rateprofs)

With over 17 million ratings for 1.6 million professors across 7,000 schools, students can use this site to target professors known for doling out an easy A. Rocky Bernardo (George Mason '05, Economics) talks about the magic of RateMyProfessors:

> I was getting D's in my classes. But then I used RateMyProfessors to find easier professors. Eventually, I only took classes with professors with high scores. Soon I started knocking down much better grades.

Using RateMyProfessors takes a mere five minutes and will save students huge headaches and boatloads of time every semester.

The "Signup-and-Drop" Method

Many colleges allow students to "drop" a class within the first few weeks of the semester with no penalty. Use this policy, in conjunction with "Syllabus Week," to your advantage.

Syllabus Week is the first week of college classes where professors provide an overview of the semester, including course load, projects, and general expectations. This overview allows students to survey the course difficulty, assess the professor quality, and decide whether a better alternative exists elsewhere.

In college, my schedule forced me to take a History course with one of two professors, both of whom received mediocre reviews on RateMyProfessors. Instead of blindly choosing, I signed up and attended *both* History classes during Syllabus Week.

During the first class I learned that one professor would be much more demanding than the other. I wasn't looking for Ph.D. rigor in a History class. As a result, I dropped the harder professor's class and stayed enrolled in the easier professor's class. Simply by attending one class, I saved myself a lot of unnecessary stress. Ultimately, choosing the right professor is one of the easiest ways to score higher grades with less effort.

Method #2: Strategic Reading

Frequently, reading assignments consume an unnecessarily large chunk of time. Thanks to strategic reading, however, students can cut down on the workload by (1) identifying what to read, (2) reading efficiently and effectively. Let's address each in turn.

Identifying What to Read

Here's the big idea: *don't do all of your reading,* as most of it is irrelevant. To identify what *not* to read, ask yourself the following questions:

- Will there be a test or quiz on the material?
- Is the reading something that I will need in order to be able to do the homework?
- Will I need to discuss this out loud in class?

If the answer to all of these questions is *no,* then don't do the reading. For technical courses (e.g. STEM), it's often sufficient to largely skip reading altogether, and put time into doing homework problems. To compensate for not reading, simply fill in the gaps during class with great notes.

Reading Efficiently and Effectively

After filtering out unnecessary reading, use these three techniques to read, digest, and comprehend the remaining reading assignments faster than ever:

- **Focus on Keywords.** "Keywords" signal a main idea is coming, including "thus," "therefore," and "as a result." Punctuation and formatting can provide a similar function, including colons ":" and words that are italicized and bolded. Finally, just like blog posts, focus on headings to quickly takeaway the big idea. Upon reaching any of these items, slow down and focus on the main point. After digesting the main point, continue zipping through to the next keyword.
- **Paragraph Location.** Most literature is structured as follows: (1) beginning: frames the issue, (2) middle: provides evidence in support, and (3) conclusion: provides key takeaway. Paragraphs inside the *beginning* and *concluding* sections are the most important, because they frame and answer the critical concept. The middle merely provides the underlying reasons for the critical concept, many of which

are either obvious or so abstract that professors don't expect you to master them.

- **Eye Speed.** Research shows that when people read, their eyes jump around, thereby slowing down the reading process. Focus on keeping your eyes moving at a consistent speed across every sentence, which has been shown to *triple* reading speed.

In summary, students can trim away hundreds of hours of study time by simply knowing what to read and reading it effectively and efficiently.

Method #3: Class Attendance

Many students skip class. In fact, studies show that classes, on average, are a little less than 50 percent full, and nearly 25 percent of students miss a year's worth of classes.

Here's some advice that may surprise you: *don't skip class.* Not only can class skipping become addictive, it actually provides a low payoff. Why? In class, many professors teach—and often explicitly state—*exactly* what's on the exam, cutting hours off of your study time. Plus, there is often an attendance requirement, boosting your GPA just by showing up.

Occasionally, however, there are good reasons to skip class (e.g. networking events, last-minute exam prep). If you must skip, do so in a class that meets one of the following:

- **Attendance Not Required.** Skip classes that don't penalize your GPA, not the ones that do.
- **Large Classes.** Skip classes held inside large classrooms, such as lecture halls, where absences are difficult to notice.
- **Boring Classes.** Skip classes with boring, droning professors.
- **Grades Determined Outside of Class.** Skip classes that base grades on readings, not lectures, or take-home papers, not in-class exams.

In general, students should make every effort to attend class and only use these class-skipping tricks when absolutely necessary.

Method #4: Note Taking

Drafting your own notes is fine, as it forces students to digest information in real time. Nevertheless, it's still a good idea to cross-reference them with the notes of stellar students. As a result, no matter if you take your own notes, or are just looking for someone who does, use these two tricks to score some of the highest quality notes on campus.

Buy Class Notes from A-Quality Students

When I attended Penn State, an off-campus company bought the notes taken by A-quality students in every class. Many colleges, particularly bigger ones (another advantage of big schools), have similar off-campus companies. If, for whatever reason, you skipped plenty of classes throughout the semester, or you simply don't like organizing your own, buy these notes.

Befriend Students Who Have Previously Taken Your Class

In law school, everyone made "outlines," a summary of the professor's lectures from the semester. Although I began law school making my own, I soon realized that doing so consumed an absurd amount of time. Plus, I realized that dozens of crisp, polished outlines were available from other students who previously took the class. By gaining access to these outlines, I saved myself hundreds of study hours.

Often times, groups or organizations will have a cache of notes, too. That's exactly what Cari Lutkins (Alabama '16, Political Science) used:

> My sorority had this catalogue called "Easy A's and Stay-Aways." Every semester students submitted a list of easy teachers—the "Easy A's"—along with the hard teachers—the "Stay-Aways." All the responses were stored in a Google Doc and shared with everyone. Obviously, I took the "Easy A's" teachers.

Ultimately, students should focus on obtaining stellar notes from other students and supplement their own notes as needed.

Method #5: Test Taking Strategies

Frequently knowing *how* to approach exams provides more value than knowing the content on the exams. Importantly, the exam format determines the optimal test taking strategy. Let's look at the most common exam formats: multiple choice and essay exams.

Multiple Choice Exams

Multiple choice exams are perhaps the easiest exam format to master, as they simply require memorizing and regurgitating facts. To streamline this process, do the following:

- **Identify Core Concepts.** From the reading, select bolded terms, definitions, and other specific details the professor highlights. Be sure to include concepts on which the professor lectured at length.
- **Memorize.** Enough said.

In this process, the biggest time drain is identifying core concepts. Fortunately, others have already done that for you. Simply use StudyBlue (bit.ly/studyblueflashcards), an online platform that crowdsources flashcards for nearly every college subject possible. I used StudyBlue to study for my Bar exam, saving me hundreds of hours from having to wade through 35 legal subjects.

Essay Exams

Essay exams test the *main idea* of concepts, and consequently, require more preparation than multiple choice exams. In the next section, I'll show you how to *learn* main concepts with warp speed. This section, however, will show students how to *deliver* the main concept on an exam. Rocky Bernardo (George Mason '05, Economics) explains what's at the heart of this delivery:

The thing about my economics exams is that I had to support my points. I had to read the book and make arguments. But some teachers preferred arguments that others did not. I befriended students who had previously taken the class and used their notes to assert the arguments I knew that the teacher would find persuasive.

In other words, Rocky approached essay exams with the intention of giving the audience exactly what they wanted. That audience is the professor. As a result, students must figure out what the professor wants and give it to them.

Learning Still Matters: The Optimal Way to Study

When you first start to study a field, it seems like you have to memorize a zillion things. You don't. What you need is to identify the core principles...that govern the field.
—JOHN REED, AUTHOR

Even though the Grades HACK teaches students how to score easy A's, *learning* is still important at college. Otherwise, once hired, if the student can't perform basic job functions, he or she won't stay employed for long.

There are two ways to approach learning: the efficient way and the inefficient way. Unfortunately, 80 percent of students engage in the inefficient way, which includes reading and rereading textbooks to memorize content. This approach doesn't work for three reasons: (1) it's time consuming; (2) it doesn't result in long-term retention; and (3) it's deceiving, as a growing familiarity with the text feels like mastery of the content when it's not.

Fortunately, the learning process can be boiled down to the follow four-steps, which allows students to learn faster, spend less time in the library, and position themselves to succeed once hired.

Step #1: Deconstruct the Skill

Knowing *what* to study is much more important than knowing *how* to study. To determine what to study, it's necessary to first deconstruct—or break down into the simple pieces—whatever you're trying to learn.

Surprisingly, making things simple requires serious thought, as it forces reducing complexity, eliminating redundancy, and scrapping irrelevancy. To provide an idea of how much simplicity is required, in law school, professors frequently spent an hour covering *one* legal case. In my deconstruction process, I condensed each case into one or two *sentences,* a challenging exercise. You must be equally persistent in simplifying lectures, notes, and assignments.

After sifting through the concepts and simplifying their parts, hone in on the highest value pieces—most likely, those that constitute the basic concepts as well as those that the professor spent significant time covering.

Ultimately, deconstruction involves (1) breaking down concepts into simple bits, and (2) focusing most of your attention on the bits that matter most.

Step #2: Learn to Self-Correct

The goal here is to study just enough—but no more—than what it takes to reach a critical point in learning. What point is that? The point at which a student learns significantly less from one additional hour of studying than what he learned the previous hour.

To reach this point in rapid fashion, students must learn enough to "self-correct"—that is, know enough content to identify mistakes and recognize how to correct them along the way. For example, many students read everything before beginning to study. That's a mistake. Instead, they should read just enough to have a basic understanding of the subject and then *test* themselves. As soon as possible, students want to engage in *active learning*: applying knowledge in an effort to understand how the concepts relate to one another and stand on their own. Students who memorize every concept before engaging in active learning actually retain less.

Step #3: Remove Practice Barriers

There are two important barriers to remove in the learning process. The first barrier is general distraction. Studies show that the average person pulls out their phone 85 times a day and Internet searches consume 60 percent of people's working hours. That's a huge time-suck and can't happen. When studying, I turn my phone completely off to make sure not only am I not interrupted, but I don't even *anticipate* being interrupted. Studies show that the mere *presence* of a phone limits productivity.

Second, a less obvious barrier, are logistical activities, such as sending an email to set up a group study. Scheduling time to study is not the same thing as actually studying. Don't fall into a black hole of thinking so.

To further minimize distractions, I use:

- **White/Ambient Noise:** SimplyNoise (www.simplynoise.com), a free white noise app, Coffitivity (www.coffitivity.com), coffee shop ambient noise, or RainyMood (www.rainymood.com), a rain ambient noise.
- **Technology Tricks:** RescueTime (www.rescuetime.com), analyzes how productively I use time on my computer, and StayFocused (bit.ly/stayfocusedforchrome), a Google Chrome extension that restricts time spent on time-wasting sites (e.g. Facebook).

Step #4: Study for 20 Hours

By following these principles, studies show that twenty hours of study time (that's it!) is all that is required to learn a subject.

To learn something in twenty hours, however, students must optimally structure this study time. To start, use "batching," that is blocking out uninterrupted time periods spanning several hours. I prefer three to four hour chunks. Studies show that out of these batching periods, learning occurs best in 45 to 50 minute learning intervals, followed by a 10-minute break. Continue to repeat this process for all twenty hours.

To take learning to the next level, in the middle of the 45 to 50 minute learning interval, carve out a 5-minute window and introduce a *different* concept from the one you're studying. Switching gears, even briefly, helps the brain retain the different concept more permanently than it otherwise would.

HOW OPTIMIZED LEARNING ALLOWED ME IN LAW SCHOOL TO LEARN IN TWO DAYS WHAT PREVIOUSLY TOOK A SEMESTER

In law school, professors assigned students an absurd amount of reading, ranging up to 200 pages of dense legal cases, *everyday*. Being a high achiever–but mainly not knowing any better–I attempted, at least initially, to keep pace.

The problem, I later discovered, was that I had no idea how to apply this four-part, optimized learning process to reading. But when you're reading 200 pages of legalese every day, optimized learning is not only efficient, it's necessary.

Eventually, I began to implement optimized learning so effectively that I could learn in *two afternoons* what previously took the entire semester. How? Thanks to the polished notes of previous students, I knew exactly what to expect on the exam (Step #1). Next, I tested my understanding of each concept through practice problems (Step #2), while locking myself away all day in the library (Step #3), which allowed me to batch study (Step #4).

I am not an exception. Millions of students have done the same. For example, in preparation to pass the "Bar," the exam authorizing legal practice, law school graduates, relying on optimized learning, learn upwards of 35 legal subjects in two to three *months*, what otherwise took three *years* to study in law school. In other words, with optimized learning, millions of law school graduates have learned at ten times the rate compared to when they were students.

By only using twenty hours to study—thereby freeing up extraordinary amounts of time—students can reinvest this excess time into higher value activities, such as internships (Action HACK #5), networking (Action HACK #6), non-negotiable skills (Action HACK #7), or by revisiting any of the Self-HACKs. Learning efficiently, and only spending the time necessary to satisfy the 3.0 GPA Rule, is perhaps the best way inside the entire college landscape to recover time, double down on high value activities, and supercharge a college career.

Working Around Sub-3.0 GPAs

Expect problems and eat them for breakfast.
—Alfred Montapert, author

Inevitably, there will be some students—many students—who score or graduate with less than a 3.0 GPA. When I interviewed graduates for this book, I was surprised by how many of them struggled at some point in college with a low GPA. Several were even on academic probation. In other words, if you fall below a 3.0 GPA, you're not alone. Fortunately, however, low GPAs don't have to limit success.

SUB 3.0 GPAs DON'T GUARANTEE LIMITED SUCCESS

- **Cory Briggs (Harvard '14, Sociology):** "During my freshman year, I struggled with grades, which landed me on academic probation. I was in danger of getting kicked out of Harvard."

  However, despite his low grades, during college, Cory worked for the Cleveland Browns, an NFL football team. Currently, Cory works at a premier real estate company in DC and is on track to eventually run the company. Cory is living proof that a student's worst fear–failing out of school–can't limit success.

- **Alex Rekas (NoVA '07, Mathematics; James Madison '10, Studio Art):** "During my first semester, I scored a 2.5 GPA. I even had two F's on my transcript."

  However, recently, Alex launched his own startup company (bit.ly/alexrekas), using his unique background in art and math, to develop websites for clients.

Even though a sub 3.0 GPA won't prevent you from landing a great job, you still want to minimize its negative effects. To do so, use these three tricks:

Trick #1: Leave GPA Off Resume

If you have a sub 3.0 GPA, don't list it on your resume. If employers want to know what your GPA is, make them specifically ask you.

Here's the reality: most employers won't ask. Take it from Zach Winterer (Sam Houston '15, Accounting), someone who graduated with a sub-3.0 GPA:

> During college, I interviewed for seven jobs. To my surprise, only one asked me about my grades and the other six never asked at all. The one company that did ask, waited until the second round, but then seemed to care very little about my low

GPA. Instead, they were more concerned that I was personable, sociable, and had previous work experience. The next day they offered me a job. The company was ranked #2 for my industry in the Houston area.

Six of Zach's seven employers didn't ask him about his grades, demonstrating that students are frequently not required to disclose their GPA in the first place.

Trick #2: Have an Explanation

If an employer asks for your GPA, it's not the end of the world. Just make sure you have a good story that explains why you didn't score higher. Maybe you worked throughout the semester and didn't have enough time to study. (That's actually a great reason because it shows you have practical experience). Maybe you were sick and couldn't focus. Or maybe it was your freshman year and it took time to figure things out. No matter your story, it's important to tell the truth.

Trick #3: Embrace Interestingness

In 2014, I had checked every box expected of me: good grades, college graduation, practicing attorney. As a result, I looked at my future and asked, "What is the next box I must check?" I, however, didn't see an obvious answer, except to work 40 years until one day I could (hopefully) retire. After all, that's exactly what everyone else was doing.

But I didn't want to be like everyone else, so I did something radical: left my job and rode my bicycle coast-to-coast for a 58-day, 3,167-mile adventure across southern America (highlight video at bit.ly/wineycycling).

The decision to leave my job wasn't an easy one, particularly working for a panel of esteemed judges inside one of America's fastest growing jurisdictions. Ideally, I wanted to keep my job but realized leaving came with no guarantees. Thankfully, the judges graciously allowed me to leave, holding my job for my return.

The benefits of my cross-country ride have been more than expected. Not only does it serve as a lifetime memory, it has equipped me with a significant advantage: *interestingness*. I now have a talking point distinct from everyone else, separating me from the crowd.

Every college student, including those with low grades, can gain an edge by embracing interestingness. Being interesting has nothing to do with grades—at least not directly—but can pack just as big of a punch. Take it from legendary investor Chris Sacca:

> As I look around, who I've hired, who I like to work with, who I back, they are interesting. They are people you want to be around, you want to spend time with, you want to hear their answers....And if I can give advice to someone who...[isn't] sure

how they want to get ahead or distinguish themselves, I think pursuing a course of life that embraces interestingness.

Sacca understands that many people who he has hired are not the ones with the most glittering GPA. He wants people who are *different,* who are interesting. By being interesting, students no longer blend in with the crowd, distinguishing them from other students, even those with 4.0 GPAs.

BEING INTERESTING: HOW AN IVY-LEAGUER SUCCESSFULLY CHOSE INTERESTINGNESS OVER GRADES

India Perdue (Dartmouth '19, Government and Sociology) is the only student who, when I interviewed her, had yet to graduate from college. At the time of the interview, she had just completed her freshman year. But I did this for good reason: India is currently living out advice that seems so contrary to our instincts. India not only does not stress about grades—she doesn't even know what her grades are! "After my first semester, I have no idea what my GPA is," said India. "I have intentionally not looked at them."

India is an *Ivy League* student. She's supposed to be smart, right? Isn't this a reckless move? Not at all. Listen to India explain the success she has already experienced outside of the classroom just in her freshman year alone:

> I helped re-launch a blog for an on-campus organization. Quickly after our re-launch, we had 3,000 visitors in two months across 50 different countries. It's still a baby project, but I'm leading it. Our blog is an extension of our journal, which thirty other schools have modeled. I get to play a key part.

> In addition, I sit on an executive board that governs the renovation of a house which will soon accommodate 30 people. As an executive board member, I am involved in helping shape the future of this organization, its house, and its tenants, for years to come.

What's the method to India's madness? She invests her time heavily in relationships. "I spend lots of time getting meals with people, developing relationships, getting mentored," India said. "I want to put great minds around me. It's a priority for me. I build studying into the spaces in between."

Unbelievable to most, India puts grades second and relationships first. *And she does this intentionally.* Give me India's resume, even if it comes with a mediocre GPA, over any boring 4.0 GPA student's resume. India possesses interestingness.

Ultimately, by using the Grades HACK, student can allocate the optimal amount of study time, develop more efficient study habits, and invest their saved time into higher college activities.

HACKING TAKEAWAYS

- Students should maintain a GPA of a 3.0 or above. After that, it's best to allocate time that would otherwise be spent studying to higher value activities.
- Betting college success on grades is not only exhausting, more importantly, it's risky and foolish.
- For students who score below a 3.0 GPA, there are still ways to impress employers.

ACTION HACK #5
Internships

Get inside the internship funnel

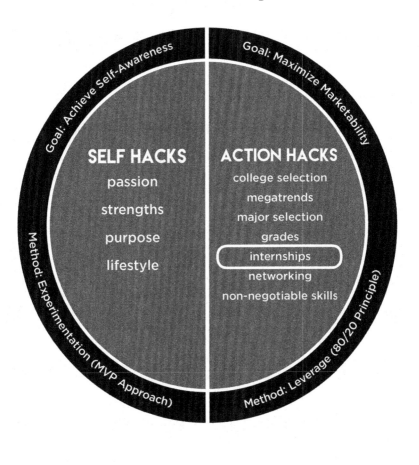

There are two ways to beat the cruelty of the environment: you can become stronger or you can become smarter. We chose the latter.
—John Medina, molecular biologist

"Big Law" is the dream of many law school students. It was mine. Big Law is the name for large, prestigious law firms located in the heart of cities. Big Law is where 25-year-old new law school graduates go to make $160,000 and work 80+ hour weeks. In law school, that's what I wanted.

The entry point into Big Law, however, is very clear: *internships*. And not just any internship, a summer internship at a Big Law firm occurring between the student's first and second year of law school.

To illustrate the consequences of missing the Big Law train, for everyone else outside of the Big Law world, there is a huge drop-off in salary, where many law school graduates make as little as $40,000 per year.

The path to a career leading to a $160,000 salary or a $40,000 salary turned on *one* internship. That's the power of internships for all students.

The Internship HACK explains why internships are extraordinarily valuable, the step-by-step process for landing one, and the three things students need to make an internship a wild success.

The 3 Reasons Why Internships are a Gold Mine

It's not enough to do things right, you must also do the right things. Smart people fail everyday because they execute flawlessly on the wrong goals.
—Chico Mendes, three-time Brazilian jiu jitsu medalist

Internships contain extraordinary value—perhaps more so than any other single activity inside the college landscape. Below are the top three reasons why.

Reason #1: Best Onramp to a Job

Internships are much more than just an activity to check off your college to-do list. They aren't just the price of admission into the job market. Studies show that no matter the industry and no matter the company size, all employers unanimously agreed on the same thing: internships are the *single most important credential* during the hiring process, beating out GPA, college reputation, major, and even volunteer experience and extracurricular activities. As a result, a *portfolio of amazing internship experiences can propel you past a 4.0 student, even one from the likes of Harvard.*

Matt Mullenweg is the founder of WordPress and was named one of Business Week's Most Influential People on the Web. This guy clearly knows a thing or two about running a business. Here's what Mullenweg says about who he hires and why:

I think because I dropped out of college, I was very entranced with people with Masters or Ph.Ds. Turns out that has no correlation with how effective that person was in our organization. So what we started to do is look back to the first couple people and say, "How can we sort of set up a hiring system where you actually do the work that you do on the job?" And that's all you're judging them by. You don't care about anything else.

According to Mullenweg, his company only hires people who can best complete the assignments that they will face during their actual job—the essence of an internship. Not surprisingly, employers widely acknowledge that the primary focus of internships is to convert students into full-time, entry-level employees. Amazingly, in 2015, over half of all internships converted into full-time hires. Just by interning, students have a 50 percent chance of landing a job.

Reason #2: Experimentation Haven

It is better to see once than to hear a hundred times.
—MIKHAIL GORBACHEV, SOVIET STATESMAN

Not only are internships a great way for employers to test you, they are a great way for students to test employers. Indeed, internships are the poster child of a Steering Wheel Feedback Loop:

Cheap: internships cost nothing (or count as college credits you otherwise would take), and employers often pay students;

Reliable: internships mirror students' potential future working conditions, providing the most accurate feedback possible; and

Quick: internships require only one summer or semester (basically eight to ten weeks); while this may appear like a big investment, a few weeks out of an entire college career is merely a fraction of total time spent at college.

To best use internships in the experimentation process, use these three questions as a guide:

1. Do you enjoy the customers (e.g. general public, specific clients)?
2. Do you enjoy the working environment (e.g. high-stress, high demand or low-stress, low demand)?
3. Do you enjoy your colleagues (e.g. gossipers or empowerers)?

Answering these questions is invaluable for determining whether a student should pursue converting an internship into full-employment, transition to a different company within that industry, or leave the industry altogether.

Reason #3: Love and Money

Students simply love internships. Over 75 percent of graduating students with internship experience reported they were either "very satisfied" or "extremely satisfied" with their internship experience, while only six percent reported to be either "not very satisfied" or "not at all satisfied."

Not to mention, students are often generously paid for interning (unpaid internships discussed later). For example, in 2015, the average hourly wage for a bachelor's degree-level intern equaled $17.20, a six-year high. Some of the highest-paying internships paid closer to $20.00 per hour. If your part-time job cannot compete with those wages, you're selling yourself short.

How to Land an Internship

Simplicity is the ultimate sophistication.
—Leonardo da Vinci

There are many ways to score an internship. However, as The 80/20 Principle predicts, only a few of the methods are the most effective. The following represents the three best ways for students to obtain an internship in record time.

Method #1: Gaining "Relevant Work Experience"

Studies show that 93 percent of employers—basically all of them—said that "relevant work experience" is the most important qualification to landing an internship.

This is where underclassmen students get antsy. "How can I gain 'relevant work experience' without the opportunity to gain experience in the first place?" Great question. Here's how.

According to employers, "relevant work experience" does not necessarily mean that students must already have an internship or prior work experience in that field. Instead, "relevant work experience" means simply demonstrating passion and interest in the field. "You don't necessarily need to have a lot of internships," explained the dean at Brandeis University. "You just need any kind of experience that shows you're passionate."

Here are some great ways to demonstrate "relevant work experience," even if you began college with no experience at all.

1. **Volunteering:** Typically, there is only one reason people do something for free: they genuinely like it. Demonstrating that you like something so much that you don't need paid shows an employer how seriously you take what you do.

2. **Part-Time Jobs:** Four out of five students work part-time during college. Working part-time, even if it's not directly related to your career path, is a terrific opportunity to develop professional skills like teamwork, time management, and customer service—qualities employers want.

3. **Student Organizations:** Joining a student organization, and *actively* (that's the key) participating allows you to gain practical skills inside a particular industry.

4. **Professor Understudy:** Work closely with a professor to research, write, and generally advance the project he or she is tackling. Not

only will you gain hands-on experience, you'll establish a relationship and secure a job reference you'll definitely need in the near future.

5. **Do Your Own Thing:** Start freelancing—the process of writing, designing, and otherwise selling services—by using Upwork (www.upwork.com) or Freelancer (www.freelancer.com). You'll gain practical skills and begin to build a portfolio, which you can later show to employers.

Method #2: Tackling the Logistics

There are two logistical items that are important for scoring internships: (1) getting face-to-face, and (2) early planning. Let's take a look at each.

Getting Face-to-Face

Studies show that employers prefer to hire interns from on-campus recruiting activities, because they want to meet interns in person. As a result, students must get face-to-face with employers, too, whether that's at a career-fair, on-campus interviews, or coffee breaks.

Early Planning

On average, employers begin planning for internship recruitment seven months before the position is scheduled to start. That means for a summer internship, students must start applying during the fall semester.

Regardless of how freshman and sophomore year go, research shows that students must intern by *junior* year, as employers strongly rely upon junior summer internships in the hiring process following graduation.

Most importantly, each internship builds upon itself for the next. That means if students obtain a *good* internship freshman or sophomore year, they set themselves up for a *great* internship junior and senior years. And by locking down a great internship junior or senior year, students position themselves to land an *extraordinary* job upon graduation. That's why you must start interning as early as possible.

Method #3: Using Internship Tools

Use these three tools to cut through the noise and find an internship that's right for you.

1. **Your school's job listing site and alumni network:** Gain access to your school's database, if there is one.
2. **LinkedIn (www.linkedin.com):** To search for internship listings, go to the jobs tab at the top of the page and type "internship" in the search box. You can refine your search by filling in the boxes on the right side of the page. The most valuable aspect of LinkedIn is instantly seeing which of your contacts works at a company or knows people who work there. Use your parents' profile to search their LinkedIn networks for contacts, too.

3. **Glassdoor (www.glassdoor.com):** Glassdoor's main attraction is that it offers an instant way to search for salaries, company reviews, and descriptions of job interviews.

The 3 Things Needed from Every Internship

The mechanic that would perfect his work must first sharpen his tools.
—CONFUCIUS, ANCIENT CHINESE PHILOSOPHER

Once a student scores an internship, to maximize the internship's personal brand effect, he or she must walk away with the following three things:

1. A brand name company
2. A captivating 3-5 minute story
3. A great recommendation

Let's look at each one in turn.

Internship Item #1: Brand Name Company

Consider the following students' profile. Which is a more attractive candidate?

Student #1

- College: HACKiversity
- Year: Junior
- GPA: 3.5
- Internship: ABC Company, the leading company in the industry
- Internship Description: answered telephone calls, made copies, and served coffee at the conference espresso bar

Student #2

- College: HACKiversity
- Year: Junior
- GPA: 3.5
- Internship: XYZ Enterprise, a company few people know
- Internship Description; (i) analyzed the most important issues facing the industry, saving supervisor 100 hours, (ii) independently resolved structural problems in company, saving company $100,000, and (iii) completed projects directly responsible for generating $50,000 in additional revenue

With the exception of internships, Student #1 and Student #2 are identical. Student #1 has the internship brand name, but failed to gain relevant experience, while Student #2 failed to secure the internship brand name but gained lots of relevant work experience. Who do the employers prefer?

Most would say Student #2. After all, relevant work experience is the key to gaining an internship in the first place, so why wouldn't relevant work experience be the key to a successful internship? But it's not. Once students are inside the internship world, the game shifts from gaining relevant work experience to interning at a brand name company. Student #1 wins. Why? As long as a student can sell his or her internship experiences to employers (covered in Internship Item #2), the internship game is all about maximizing the two to three lines on a student's resume. That's exactly what brand name companies do.

Andrea Lucas (South Carolina '10, Public Relations, English) explains how interning at Disney, one of the premier media companies in the world, single-handedly opened many opportunities following graduation:

> The Disney brand name on my resume led to multiple job offers right out of college. Interviewers always asked about that internship, and I was even considered further along in my college program because of the weight that the Disney name carried.

As Andrea stated, what she did at Disney did not matter for purposes of landing a job after graduation. All that mattered was that she interned there in the first place.

Similarly, Matt Syme (Texas Christian University '10, Journalism) interned at ESPN, also one of the premier media companies in the world. Matt explains how a previous prestigious internship landed him at ESPN, and then how ESPN created a new world of possibility after graduation:

> I landed at ESPN because I previously interned at Fox Sports Southwest, a really great company. That was my edge to landing at ESPN. After I finished in Bristol [headquarters], suddenly ESPN became the heavy hitter on my resume. In fact, the ESPN name pulled more weight than TCU, my college. Interning at ESPN gave me a chance to stand out that TCU didn't.

Matt's story shows how internships can even overshadow college reputation. Today, Matt has used his internships to begin working at Cvent, a cutting edge technology company recently purchased by an investment firm for $1.65 billion.

Matt and Andrea are not exceptions. Researchers have shown time and time again that students who work at high-status companies consistently land better jobs. As a result, interning at a great company can launch a successful career right out of the college gates.

Internship Item #2: Captivating 3-5 Minute Story

Interviewers are busy people. They can't afford to take an hour out of their day to interview a college kid. That's why interviews are typically short—no more than 35 to 40 minutes. Within that time, there's a lot of ground to cover. You meet the other person, share a little about yourself, discuss the position, and ask relevant questions. That doesn't leave the interviewer much time to dive deeply into every one of your internship experiences. As a result, on average, describing one internship experience should take no more than three to five minutes.

Such a narrow time window is perfect for you, because during a job interview, all you need is *one good story* relating to your previous internship. As long as you did at least one thing noteworthy, it doesn't matter if you spent the rest of the internship fetching your boss' coffee.

For example, during law school, I interned at Morgan Stanley, a premier Wall Street bank. While there, I spent most of my time designing a promotional PowerPoint presentation for my boss. But I never mention my Power-Point creation during an interview. Instead, I emphasize the analytical component of my internship, even though it was less than 15 percent of my overall experience. Why? Because that's what employers want to hear.

To kick my story up another notch, I add in some "buzzwords," industry jargon that gives the interviewer a sense that I know what I'm talking about. Here's a snippet from my three to five minute story that I typically share with interviewers, sprinkled with the right amount of buzzwords:

> Clients frequently complained about *market volatility*. For these folks, I focused on analyzing investments that minimized volatility while maximizing *return on investment*. To accomplish this, I used both *technical* and *fundamental analysis* coupled with a *macro* view of global economics in order to find the best *investment vehicle* to fit the client's *risk profile*. For example, if a client called and said he was *bullish* on the housing market, I tried to find him a *high-yielding* asset.

Seem impressive? Employers think so. That's why they ask me about it during every interview, even for non-finance positions. And there's not one mention of PowerPoint.

Ultimately, during most interviews, you only have time to hit the highlights. And since you were the one who interned, you can decide what those highlights are. This puts you in a huge advantageous position.

Internship Item #3: Great Recommendation

Interns: it's not what you're going to learn this summer…It's going to be who you meet.
—Gary Vaynerchuk, founder of www.winelibrary.com

The last thing you'll need to HACK internships is to walk away with a great recommendation. To accomplish this, you need to develop relationships.

But there is a special kind of relationship that matters more than anything else: the "Referrer," the person who will offer you a recommendation to future employers. The Referrer certifies that you existed, showed up to work, and performed well. Typically, the Referrer will be your supervising boss.

How do you identify the best Referrer at your internship? Use these three easy methods:

Method #1 – Ask Previous Interns: if you know students who previously interned at the company, ask who wrote them a letter of recommendation.

Method #2 – Ask People Around the Office: once working at your internship, ask your coworkers to identify people at the office who are outgoing, selfless, and helpful. Take someone out to lunch and pick their brain. They'll share.

Method #3 – Use Your Instincts: after a while, you'll figure out who is nice enough to offer you a recommendation. Make sure, however, that the Referrer is nice *and* dependable. You don't want to count on an overly busy executive to refer you, no matter how nice he or she is.

Obviously, you must give the Referrer a reason to refer you. One of the best pieces of advice I've received for establishing early wins at the office is to act like you're 35 years old. Yes, I know you're likely much younger. But what I mean is that when you enter the internship, don't act like a novice, even though you are. If you are smart and competent, step up and do whatever you are capable of doing in a mature way. You'll develop a great reputation early on.

Finally, on your last day, be sure to provide a hand-written thank you note to at least your supervisor and the Referrer, if they are different people.

One of the biggest mistakes students make with internships is failing to stay in contact. They soon realize their mistake when they are applying to a job and need a recommendation, but realize they haven't spoken to the Referrer in two or three years. Don't let that happen to you.

THE "ONE MORE THING" HACK: USING WRITTEN LETTERS OF RECOMMENDATION

When I worked on Wall Street, my boss was so impressed with my work he said, "Kyle, if you ever need a recommendation, tell them to call me. I'll give you a great recommendation." True to his word, my boss gave me a great recommendation...twice. Obviously, this type of phone conversation is great. But you can do even better by adopting the tactics of Apple co-founder, Steve Jobs.

Jobs was a master showman. He spent virtually every second of his presentations dazzling the audience with the latest iPod and iPhone technologies. And just when everyone thought they had seen everything, Jobs was famous for saying, "But there's one more thing." That's when Jobs showcased something even more spectacular about the product.

Use this same tactic when applying for your next internship or first full-time job. But in order to do so, you'll need a *written* recommendation letter from the Referrer. That's why written recommendations *in your possession* are the best.

Here's how I used the "One More Thing" HACK. After law school, I clerked for one of the most respected judges in Virginia. Prior to leaving my clerkship, I asked him to write me a letter of recommendation. Graciously, he did. He then emailed me a copy. Bingo.

When I later applied for an attorney position at a law firm, I put the judge's job recommendation letter to good use. Following my in-person interview, I reached out to the attorneys and thanked them for their time—something everyone does (or should do). But to separate myself from the pack, I attached the judge's written letter of recommendation to the same email. I got the job.

Unpaid Internships: Opportunity or Exploitation?

The point of working now isn't to make $15 / hour when you're a Sophomore washing dishes at the dining commons. The point is to make $100K when you graduate as a Senior because you had the relevant skills and experience.
—LEO THOM, FORMER LINKEDIN WEB DEVELOPER

Unpaid internships are occurring with increased frequency. Today, nearly half of all internships are unpaid, and that trend is expected to continue into the future. This flood of unpaid internships has been unleashed due to nearly every college student—92 percent to be exact—having interned at least once prior to graduation.

With so many students from which to choose, companies have opted to simply not pay them, which has led some to call such practices "modern day exploitation" and "deeply unfair." Nevertheless, despite the absence of pay, college students keep applying.

So the question is: if an unpaid internship is your only internship opportunity, should you take it? Katharine Lucas (Savannah College of Art and Design '14, Writing) explains why the answer is clearly yes:

> During my junior year, I completed an unpaid internship working for my college's PR team. It was high-stakes and high-pressure—and I wasn't paid. But I used the lessons learned during my unpaid internship to land a paid job immediately after my unpaid internship. At that point, I was still a junior.
>
> My new job was located in Virginia, but I was still going to school in Georgia. The fact that my boss allowed me to work remotely as a college student tells you how much she valued my skill set—something I mainly built during my unpaid internship. I worked at that company during my junior and senior year and continued to work there after I graduated.

Although she wasn't paid, and was a lot of work, Katharine used her unpaid internship to build a skillset that someone was willing to pay for, while she was still a *junior*. Clearly, even unpaid internships have power.

Katharine's experiences reflect what studies have found: nearly 80 percent of all employers agree that even an unpaid internship has a positive impact in the hiring process, higher than students who volunteer, enroll in graduate school, and work in an unrelated career path during college.

I realize, however, that some of you simply may not be able to afford an unpaid internship, no matter how great the benefit. If you're one of these people, I wish I had an easy answer. But I don't. *You need to find a way to intern.* Maybe that means working a part-time job during the semester so that you can afford to complete an unpaid internship in the summer. Or maybe that means eating out less during the school year or reducing your Starbucks trips. Whatever the solution, you need to make one. It may not be fair, but HACKing college is not about fair. It's about results. And internships—even unpaid internships—produce spectacular results.

Ultimately, maximizing internship prospects is like throttling up a bulldozer while your classmates tackle the same task with a shovel. Masters of the internship game maintain a substantial advantage over their classmates. This means you must organize your college career around interning. Get out of the library and do what employers really care about.

HACKing Takeaways

- Internships are the *best* way to land a fulltime job after graduation.
- In order to land an internship, students need "relevant work experience," which can be anything from a previous internship to involvement in a related club or organization.
- To maximize an internship's marketability, a student must leave with (i) a brand name company, (ii) a captivating 3-5 minute story, and (iii) a great recommendation.

ACTION HACK #6
Networking

Connect with the "Connector"

*Relationships are all there is. Everything in the universe
only exists because it is in relationship to everything else.
Nothing exists in isolation. We have to stop pretending we
are individuals that can go it alone.*
—MARGARET WHEATLEY, WRITER

With a bourbon and coke in hand, he sunk into the chair beside me at our law firm's weekly Friday afternoon happy hour. "So, Kyle, how do you like working here so far?" asked the law firm's president. At that point, I had been working at the firm for only a month. "It's great!" I said. "Everyone is very friendly and I enjoy the subject matter."

Five minutes into the conversation, the law firm president asked me a question that almost made my jaw bounce off the floor. "When you were in law school, did you…wait…*where did you go to law school again?*" This guy just hired me *a month ago* and couldn't remember my law school. Shouldn't my law school have been the primary consideration in him having hired me? I thought employers obsess over that stuff. But if the law school from which I graduated was so important, how could he forget so quickly? This is a sharp guy, after all.

Moments later, he explained why. "Before I hired you, I called your former boss at the courthouse," continued the law firm president. "He spoke very highly of you. I think very highly of him, which means I think very highly of you. He's really a bright guy. He said the same about you."

I couldn't believe it. I didn't get the job because of my school's reputation, my GPA, or my extracurriculars. *I got the job because of my network.*

This is a lesson I should have learned years earlier. In fact, research shows that referred individuals are *ten times more likely* to be hired than non-referred applicants. This is a huge imbalance, and it means that students must invest their time making connections. Students must stop thinking of networking as something *additional* they must cram into their schedule. Networking must be something as regular as going to class.

The Networking HACK shows students how to optimize the power of networking around key people, how to connect with these key people, and how to make networking feel more natural, even for those who typically hate networking.

Who You Want in Your Orbit: Connectors

*Sometimes the most ordinary things could be made extraordinary
simply by doing them with the right people.*
—NICHOLAS SPARKS, AUTHOR

Five months before I had my conversation with the law firm president, I was having a much different conversation with three judges at the courthouse, the place where I worked before the law firm and immediately following graduation. "Kyle, we like you, and we like your work," one judge told me, as the other three nodded in agreement. "We'd like to hire you permanently," he said, knowing my one-year contact was ending. Humbling to hear from a panel of esteemed judges. A week later I received a full time, permanent job offer.

Despite the compliments, I knew it was time for me to move on with my career and my life. As a result, I submitted my resignation letter. In doing so, I guaranteed that I was headed for unemployment as I quit my job with no Plan B.

Over the course of the next five months, I applied to job after job. Day after day, month after month, I received rejections. On the rare occasion I was asked to interview, I was—you guessed it—rejected. In total, I was rejected nearly 100 times in five months (is that a record?).

But, as they say, you only need one. And that break occurred at a warehouse brewery (surprised me, too), where my law school was hosting an alumni event. I went for the beer and to see old friends—not realizing what was about to happen.

I was at a table, talking with my friends, when a former classmate sat down. I recognized her from school, but had never really talked with her before. Frankly, I had forgotten her name. In short order, I introduced myself and she the same.

"Where are you practicing?" she asked me.

"Actually, I'm not," I responded. "I turned down a job offer a few months ago and have been looking for work since. Specifically, I've been looking for work as a transactional attorney—you know, contract stuff."

"We are looking to hire a transactional attorney!" she exclaimed. "Forward me your resume on Monday, and I'll make sure it gets to the right person."

So I did. Two weeks later I had a full time job.

Little did I know, my law school classmate was no ordinary classmate. She regularly goes out to happy hours with local lawyers, rubs elbows with judges, and generally has a pulse on the local legal market. Plus, because of her outgoing personality, she regularly chats with everyone inside the law firm where she works, allowing her to become aware of events before they actually occur. That's how my classmate knew the law firm was looking to hire another attorney, even though no formal email had been sent and no job posting had occurred. There's a special name for people like my classmate. They are called "Connectors", and they are the key to HACKing networking.

The Value of the Connector

If you want to go fast, go alone. If you want to go far, go together.
—African Proverb

In networking, the ultimate goal is to reach the Decision Maker, the person who determines whether you're hired. In my case, the Decision Maker was the law firm president. In the world of networking, there are two pathways to the Decision Maker: knowing the Decision Maker directly or knowing the Decision Maker through someone else who knows the Decision Maker.

Most of the time knowing the Decision Maker directly isn't possible, because he or she is often too busy, protected by a secretary, or generally uninterested in taking calls from complete strangers. So that means students often need to access the Decision Maker through someone else.

What's the best way, then, to indirectly reach the Decision Maker? The 80/20 Principle states that not all relationships are of equal value. While the majority of people don't know many Decision Makers, a few people know a significant number of Decision Makers. These highly-connected people are the Connectors, just like my former law school classmate who introduced me to the law firm president.

Most importantly, the biggest advantage to knowing a Connector is not just the access he or she provides to *one* Decision Maker, but the access provided to *multiple* Decision Makers. Consider that Connectors, by their very nature, have many relationships, and many relationships translates into a higher probability of connecting with more Decision Makers. As a result, targeting relationships with Connectors produces more networking opportunities than students could ever achieve by simply trying to reach the Decision Maker alone.

The rest of this section will show students the step-by-step methods to find, attract, and seize opportunities to meet Connectors, thereby exposing students to exponentially more opportunities than otherwise possible.

How to Connect with the Connectors

Ask and it will be given to you.
—Matthew 7:7

Before diving into specific tactics, it's important to first understand the reception students will likely receive in the process of finding Connectors. Unfortunately, many students believe that the reception will likely be cold at best and rejection at worst. But did you know that people are more willing to help than you think? In fact, Stanford conducted a study which found that people dramatically underestimate how likely others are to help.

To illustrate people's helping inclination—and the incredible paybacks from a simple ask—remember the following story about my law school classmate. George Mason held an open house for accepted students in an attempt to convince those on the fence to enroll. At the open house, one of my soon-to-be classmates approached the dean, and asked if the dean could do anything to offset the cost of attendance. With virtually no pushback, the dean instructed my friend to complete certain paperwork, thereby qualifying him for a $15,000 per year scholarship. He made $45,000 ($15,000 x 3 years) just by asking! That's how inclined people are to help. Use this to boost your confidence as you reach out to the Connectors.

Here are seven of the best methods I and other students use to connect with the Connectors.

Method #1: Start With What's In Common

Cari Lutkins (University of Alabama '16, Political Science) is a networking superstar. But she wasn't always. "In college, I was looking for an internship," Cari said. "Once I sent out 35 emails without knowing the person on the other end, hoping to land a position, but I only got two replies."

So Cari decided to start networking close to home, where she already knew a lot of people. Cari eventually stumbled across a less obvious choice. "One day I went through my LinkedIn network and found that one of my old high school teachers had retired and now worked at this cool company as a second career," said Cari. "I messaged him and got the job."

Cari began her networking efforts by focusing on something *everyone* has in common with someone else: a shared place of growing up. Similar to Cari, begin networking by looking for commonalities close to home, such as in your community (friends, family, neighbors), high school (classmates, teachers), or former job (boss, coworkers). By starting close to home, students take advantage of a natural commonality.

Most importantly, the threshold for establishing a commonality capable of leading to opportunities is remarkably low. As Cari explains, basically any commonality will do:

> I always look people up on LinkedIn and see if we have anything or anyone in common. I frequently use the Alabama connection. Since Alabama is a big football school, it's an easy conversation starter, particularly with guys. If that doesn't work, I expand as far as using an SEC school to establish a commonality. Really, anything remotely close will work.

Lastly, once you meet someone, it's important to remember commonalities for the sake of future conversations. For example, Cari's networking savvy landed her a prestigious internship at the U.S. Capitol, where she made a deliberate effort to remember people's names and story—something which, Cari explains, has paid serious dividends:

> Everyone I met during my internship on the Hill I kept in a spreadsheet, including their name, address, and a paragraph about them. That way, the next time I reach out to them I can follow up on something we previously talked about. Now that I'm job searching, I've seen this strategy work miracles. If I just email these people, they remember me just because I mentioned something memorable from our previous conversation.

In only a few months of working in DC, Cari repeated this process more than a dozen times. As a result, from this strategy, Cari landed a job deep within the 2016 presidential campaign, where she worked with some of the top influencers in her political party. Today, less than a year removed from graduation, Cari works closely with high-level politicians inside the White House.

Method #2: Ask for an "Informational Interview"

The fastest way to change yourself is to hang out with people who are already the way you want to be.
—Reid Hoffman, co-founder of LinkedIn

Before the law firm hired me, my friend, who is a Connector, introduced me to Kelsey, an attorney and former law clerk to Justice Ruth Bader Ginsburg, a U.S. Supreme Court Justice, a position capable of opening any door inside the legal world. When I met Kelsey at her office, she tapped her deep understanding of the legal market to explain how I could best pursue my then-current job search.

To get me in the door, my Connector friend arranged something known as an "informational interview," a meeting in which a potential job seeker (that was me) seeks advice on their career (from someone like Kelsey).

Informational interviews are not traditional interviews, but rather are *natural conversations* between two people, accelerating their effectiveness. Similar to a traditional interview, however, informational interviews allow students to tell their story—thereby marketing themselves—but without the awkward pressures of a traditional interview. Furthermore, an informational interview presents the person giving career advice (such as Kelsey) with an opportunity to introduce students to various Decision Makers at his or her company and throughout the industry.

To take full advantage of an informational interview, spend 90 percent of the time asking for advice using open-ended, easy-to-answer question, such as:

- What is the culture in your industry?
- Why did you choose to pursue your career path?
- Are you happy you chose this profession? Would you do it again?

Do not ask questions that can be found through a quick online search (e.g. where the person attended college). Show them that you did your homework.

Use the last 10 percent of the time to ask open-ended questions, but this time, ones direct enough to explore job opportunities:

- If you were in my shoes, what would you do?
- Is there a person in particular you recommend I speak with?
- What resources do you think I should use moving forward?

Aim to finish the interview in 20 minutes. *Do not exceed 30 minutes.* Many overly nice people—particularly those generous enough to conduct an informational interview—will not interrupt the conversation at the 30-minute mark. But they will regret having gone over 30 minutes, as they are likely swamped with work. That's why it's your job to end the interview yourself.

If you don't have a Connector friend like I did, you can also ask someone directly for an informational interview. I prefer email.

Visit bit.ly/kylewineyemailtemplates for a word-for-word template I've used to contact people directly for informational interviews.

BOOST YOUR EMAIL EFFECTIVENESS BY 900 PERCENT IN LESS THAN 10 SECONDS

Over 2.6 billion people use email. On average, people send or receive 122 business emails per day. That means if you want to be an effective networker, you better be an effective email writer.

The most valuable real estate on an email is the subject line. Studies show that the best email subject lines are overly straightforward (e.g. "Following up on Sales Position") and have up to a 900 percent open rate compared to tacky, ambiguous ones ("Want a Gift Idea? We have the Answer!"). Take ten seconds to write a subject line *telling* what's inside, not *selling* what's inside.

Here are three other easy-to-use and highly effective email tricks:

- **Use Old Email Threads.** If you've previously contacted a person—and they responded—but some time later you want to rekindle the conversation, use the *old email thread.* That way your email won't appear "cold," as if coming from a stranger, but rather "warm," as an extension of an existing conversation.

- **Forward a Stale Email Back to Recipient.** The best way to gently remind someone who has failed to respond to an email (typically within 48 hours; if they're important, within four or five days) is by forwarding them the same email to which they didn't respond. In the forwarding email, include a one to two sentence reminder, such as "Hi John, I haven't heard from you since I sent this. I wanted to make sure you received it. Thanks."

- **Guilt Them into Answering.** When a Connector recommends connecting with a particular person, use the following highly effective subject line: "[Name of Mutual Friend] Recommended We Connect." The recipient will be intrigued by why your mutual friend wants you two to connect, and feels pressured to respond out of fear that silence might get back to the mutual friend.

Method #3: Go Where the Connectors Are

One of the best ways to meet Connectors is to attend events, especially ones on campus. To determine if the people attending the event are Connectors, use Klout (bit.ly/KloutConnectors), a service that measures a person's influence. You can also find groups of Connectors using Meetup (bit.ly/meetup-connectors), the world's largest network for local groups.

Once you meet face-to-face with a Connector, focus on the following:

- **Tell Your Story.** Share your "elevator pitch," a 90-second memorable story that captures the Connector's attention, so that the next time you two meet, the Connector says, "Oh, you were the guy/girl, who…"
- **Obtain Contact Information.** You want a convenient way to contact the Connector. One of the most effective (and least awkward) ways is to hand them your business card—something I regret not making in college—and ask for theirs in return. To obtain business cards for as little as $0.02 per card, visit VistaPrint (bit.ly/vistaprintbusinesscards), or design more elegant cards for free using Canva (bit.ly/canva50themes).

Method #4: Bring the Connectors to You

During *HACKiversity's* promotional process, I spoke at a conference, attended by hundreds of students from across eleven different universities. Many of the students were Connectors at their colleges. Speaking at the conference forced Connectors to come to me.

You can do the same by scheduling a time to present an engaging topic with an organization or club at your college, one that will likely attract the type of Connectors you want. Leaders of organizations are always looking for engaging content. Make their lives easy by giving them a reason to allow you to speak. If speaking doesn't interest you, help organize, or better yet—*be* the organizer—of the event. Then, watch a gathering of like-minded people come to you.

Method #5: Provide Value

Networking is fundamentally about helping someone else,
before you go back and ask for anything.
—RAMIT SETHI, ENTREPRENEUR

Regrettably, many students approach networking as if the sole purpose is to receive something. Of course, when people are treated as a commodity, something to be used and disposed of, the relationship never goes anywhere.

At its core, networking is not about receiving, but rather about creating relationships. One of the best ways to begin creating relationships is by providing value to someone's life. By providing value, you become "top of mind," the first person considered when an opportunity arises.

One of the best ways to provide value is through volunteering—something I did by mentoring an inner city kid as part of Little Lights Urban Ministries (www.littlelights.org). Through my mentorship, I've had the opportunity to meet local politicians, community figureheads, and business leaders. I didn't start mentoring because I wanted to meet these folks. It just happened as a byproduct of my service. But that's how volunteering works. To get involved as a mentor, check out Big Brothers Big Sisters (www.bbbs.org), United Way (www.unitedway.org), and MENTOR (www.mentoring.org).

If mentoring kids isn't your thing, find something else, even if it's something you don't think you'll inherently enjoy. For example, I recently helped one of my friends successfully run his re-election campaign for a local public office. Although I don't inherently enjoy politics, I very much value our relationship. The campaign trail set before us a common goal, which allowed us to regularly interact. To explore dozens of causes and volunteer opportunities in your local area, visit VolunteerMatch (www.volunteermatch.org).

Often times, opportunity will come directly to you. In those cases, do what billionaire and founder of Virgin Records, Richard Branson, recommends: "say yes," even if you have to learn along the way. "Saying yes" can add so much value that one expert networker developed the "five-minute" favor: a rule whereby you agree to do something for *anybody* that will take you five minutes or less.

Ultimately, just find a way to make someone's life better, and people, including Connectors, will remember you the next time an opportunity arises.

Method #6: The Hail Mary

Imagine that you have a Connector in mind, but you have no way to access them. No common connection exists. You don't have their email address. What are you supposed to do?

There's a solution. Download Rapportive (bit.ly/downloadrapportive), a Google Chrome extension. Rapportive works inside your Gmail interface and shows the LinkedIn profile of your intended recipient. This sets the stage for the magic.

Suppose, for example, you want to connect with Nick Hungerford, CEO of Nutmeg, a London-based finance company. Actually, I did. Using Rapportive and educated guesses, I found Nick's email address by watching his LinkedIn bio appear upon entering his correct email address. Here are several common email formats upon which I relied to find the correct email address:

- nick@nutmeg.com
- nhungerford@nutmeg.com
- nick.hungerford@nutmeg.com
- nickh@nutmeg.com
- nickhungerford@nutmeg.com
- n.hungerford@nutmeg.com

Sure enough, on my second try, Nick's LinkedIn profile popped up inside my Gmail screen, meaning that I had found his correct email address. By using this trick, in less than 30 seconds, I scored a CEO's email address. I'll let you experiment to see which email address is Nick's. (If Nick didn't know about *HACKiversity* before, he will now).

HOW TO LAND A DREAM JOB WITHOUT KNOWING THE CONNECTOR

Mark Bowles (University of North Carolina '10, Business Administration) recently landed a great job at Cisco, one of the world's premier tech companies. Mark explains how, despite not being initially able to identify the right Connector, his efforts eventually afforded him access to the Decision Maker:

> To get my job, I asked 15 people connected to Cisco for help. I just emailed and asked. Only five people responded. Three of those conversations were with people in the department where I ultimately got my job. Eventually, these three people put me in touch with the Decision Maker. When I interviewed with the Decision Maker, I was able to speak intelligently about the position, department, and company simply because the three people had already explained everything to me.

Out of Mark's 15 emails, only three of them found a Connector—someone with access to the Decision Maker—a rate of 20 percent. Unlike exams, however, 20 percent is a great score, as it only takes one, maybe two, connections to grab the Decision Maker's attention. If finding the Connector is not obvious, keep looking and cast a wide net. "You want to target people in the department you want to work or people high up the chain—ideally both," Mark said. The payoff, as Mark's story illustrates, is worth it.

Method #7: Once You're In, Expand

One of the biggest missed opportunities students make in networking is *not* asking for the person to connect them again. Students are so shocked that someone actually took ten minutes to speak to them that they simply go home, wrap up the phone call, or stop emailing because they don't want to be a pest.

But networking all-stars pursue more Connectors. "After I reach out, I ask the person to connect me with one to two other people," said Cari Lutkins (University of Alabama '16, Political Science). "Assuming the conversation went well, here's exactly what I say:"

> [Person's Name]
>
> Thank you so much for your advice. As I mentioned, I'm trying to enter the field of [industrial engineering]. Do you have anyone in mind that could help me with [finding a summer internship]? I haven't yet met anyone doing [process engineering work]. Could you connect me with anyone you think would be helpful?
>
> Thanks!

This is the exact approach I've taken with gathering dozens of testimonials for this book. I started by asking my friends to share their story. Soon I ran out of friends with good stories. But my friends have friends, and their friends have friends, too. So after every conversation, I always asked the person if he or she had any other people in mind who were potentially willing to chat with me. They usually did. That's why collecting so many testimonials was easy. Use this same approach to connect with additional Connectors.

A CONNECTOR YOU'LL NEED: ONE PROFESSOR

In college, I rarely attended office hours, time professors make available to meet with students. When I applied to law school, however, my application requested three letters of recommendation, including one from a professor. Whether students apply to graduate school or a job immediately after graduation, they will almost always need a professor's recommendation. Fortunately (and accidently), all because of *one* meeting, I had a professor lined up. Here's how.

My favorite professor was my dry-humored, entertaining, and approachable business law professor. With intriguing stories about a subject I found interesting, I wanted to learn more about pursuing law as a career.

One week I emailed the professor and scheduled a meeting, which lasted about 45 minutes. While I don't remember our entire discussion, I remember one thing in particular: we didn't discuss much relating to law school. In the end, I left his office without a better understanding of law school than when I entered.

Fast forward to a year and an half later, during my law school application process, when I needed a professor's letter of recommendation. Since I had rarely gone to office hours throughout college, my business law professor was the best relationship I had, even though it was a weak one. I wasn't sure he remembered me.

Nevertheless, I scheduled another appointment, intending to ask for a letter of recommendation. Soon after arriving, I popped the question. "Kyle, I'd be happy to!" the professor exclaimed in response. "I remember having great conversations with you in my office!" he explained.

I remember thinking, "Conversations? Plural? We only chatted once!"

My professor's willingness demonstrates the low bar existing for students looking to develop necessary and (extremely) beneficial professor relationships. Remember that most professors simply want their students to succeed.

To maximize the chances of securing a great letter of recommendation, focus on these three things:

- **Be Memorable.** Ensure the professor knows your name. To best accomplish this (i) attend office hours three times throughout the semester (no need to spend more than ten minutes per appearance), and (ii) actively engage the professor by asking questions relating to upcoming exams, assignments, or anything else noteworthy. For added effect, in class, sit within the "reverse T," the professor's field of vision that includes the front row and the center of the room.

- **Target Professors in Whose Class You Excel.** In the letter of recommendation, you want the professor to describe you as intelligent. Scoring great grades in the professor's class is perhaps the best reason for the professor to talk you up. For added bonus, target professors who are likely talented writers, such as those with Liberal Arts backgrounds.

- **Ask in Person.** Don't ask for a letter of recommendation over email. Appearing in-person and asking for a recommendation face-to-face demonstrates professionalism and enhances the likelihood of the professor remembering who you are.

Ultimately, connecting with a professor doesn't take much effort, but the rewards are huge. Whether you're applying to graduate school or a job immediately after graduation, you'll likely need a letter of recommendation.

How to Ruin Your Network

There are two common mistakes students commonly make, which quickly, and unnecessarily, destroy their network.

Mistake #1: "I Won't See These People Again"

It's a small world after all.
—IT'S A SMALL WORLD (AFTER ALL), 1962

I saw it all the time. Obnoxious fraternity guys trying to pick up girls. Or drunken girls face planting on the concrete floor from one too many Jell-o shots. I even saw one girl publicly urinate on a street corner after a late night of binge drinking. The rationale was always the same: "I don't care. It's not like I'll see these people again, anyway."

But you know what? You do. You always do. Or you see the friend of these people, who happens to be your lab partner. Or these people see you on Facebook, Twitter, or Snapchat. Even at Penn State, a college with one of the largest student populations in the world, I routinely saw students on campus from the prior weekend.

The popular theory known as "six degrees of separation" explains how these repeated interactions are possible within a sea of strangers. The theory states that anyone can reach anyone else in the world through a short chain of acquaintances, at most six hops removed from the start of the chain. In other words, we live in a small world.

The idea of a small world means that it's important to establish great relationships with your classmates early. But the opposite is also true. Because you'll inevitably encounter many of your classmates—both during and after college—it's important to leave a good impression. Today, your reputation can spread faster than ever before. Make sure people are spreading a good one.

Mistake #2: Waiting to Network Until You Need Your Network

You build your network before you need it. When someone comes to me for advice on how to build a network because they need a job now, I tell them it's useless. People can tell the difference between desperation and an earnest attempt to create a relationship.
—KEITH FERRAZZI, "THE MICHAEL JORDAN OF NETWORKING"

At its core, networking is about relationships. That's why you must begin networking as early as possible in your college career. When you ask a Connector to introduce you to a Decision Maker, your existing relationship with the Connector makes the introduction much more likely to occur, because the Connector doesn't feel like you are using him or her. Instead, the Connector feels like they are helping out a friend, or even an acquaintance, a game-changing difference. Ultimately, to make networking successful, you don't have to know the Connector all that well, but having a preexisting relationship—at least to some extent—is vital to winning over the Connector.

Close the Deal: Ask for an Introduction to the Decision Maker

Starting strong is good. Finishing strong is epic.
—ROBIN SHARMA, MOTIVATIONAL SPEAKER

Once you have established a relationship with the Connector, it's time to close the deal. Remember, you ultimately want to reach the Decision Maker. The Connector is simply the best way to do it.

Mark Bowles (University of North Carolina '10, Business Administration) provides a word-for-word exchange between him, the Connector, and the Decision Maker, which ultimately helped land him a job at a fast-growing startup company immediately after college. Use Mark's exchanges as a guide for your own networking:

Mark's Email to the Connector

Hi [Connector],

Hope you're doing well, even after Brazil's embarrassing result last summer. I don't know if I've yet recovered from it! [Immediately, Mark uses soccer to establish a commonality].

Anyway, I was wondering how well you know [Decision Maker]. He's VP of Sales at a company I'd like to work for as an Inside Sales Rep. Do you know him well enough to introduce me? [Mark gets right down to asking].

Thanks,
Mark

Connector's Response to Mark

Hey man!

Yeah, I still have nightmares about that game.

I do know [Decision Maker], and I can definitely connect you!

Connector Introduces Mark to the Decision Maker

Hi [Decision Maker],

Hope you're doing well! Wanted to introduce you to my former classmate and co-worker, Mark Bowles. Mark and I worked together at [XYZ Company] at UNC Chapel Hill.

Mark is very interested in joining your company's team, so I thought it would be a great idea to connect you. He is a phenomenal teammate and hard worker. I know any organization would greatly benefit from having him. I highly recommend him!

I will let you two take it from here.

Thanks,
[Connector]

Mark's Email to the Decision Maker

Hi [Decision Maker],

[Company ABC] grabbed my interest on LinkedIn earlier this week when I discovered the company and the open Inside Sales position. I'd love to talk with you about this position and how my startup experience will add value to your sales team. [Mark tells Decision Maker what's in it for him.]

If you're interested, I can email you my resume and we can go from there. [Mark keeps it short and sweet.]

Thank you,
Mark

Decision Maker's Reply to Mark

Mark,

[The Connector's] recommendation goes a long way with me. Email me at decisionmaker@companyabc.com or just call me at 555.555.5555. It would be great to connect tomorrow before I head out of town for a few weeks.

[Decision Maker]

If you have already spoken with a Connector, and want a word-for-word email template I use to ask Connectors to introduce me to Decision Makers, visit http://bit.ly/kylewineyemailtemplates.

In the end, optimized networking comes down to Connectors, those highly networked individuals who can introduce you to multiple Decision Makers. Investing your networking efforts into a few, strategic relationships can open dozens of opportunities all without laboring to open each yourself.

HACKing Takeaways

- Students must embrace networking as something "I must do to succeed at college," not as "something extra I will do if I have time."
- To network most effectively and efficiently, find a Connector.
- Use your relationship with the Connector to gain access to the Decision Maker, the person responsible for deciding whether or not to hire you.

Non-Negotiable Skills

Demonstrate the 3 C's

A satisfied customer is the best business strategy of all.
—MICHAEL LEBOEUF, AUTHOR

Inside all of the internships and jobs I've worked throughout my life, I routinely heard employers fire off the same complaints regarding college students: "Students don't have the skills we need," they say, or "students can't provide what I'm looking for, so I don't bother hiring them at all." These complaints refer to the "skills gap," the difference between the skills employers want and the ones that students actually have.

The skills gap is a problem bigger than many believe. For example, studies show that over 80 percent of hiring managers said it was "difficult" to hire a candidate with the right skills. What's more, over 63 percent of CEOs admit they are "extremely concerned" about the availability of skills they need *right now* to run their business, and only 11 percent of business leaders think colleges are preparing graduates to be successful in the workplace.

Colleges know it, too. "Colleges and universities…accomplish far less for their students than they should," said Derek Bok, former Harvard president.

Alarmingly, the skills gap exists despite all-time highs in college graduation rates. That means no longer is a typical college career enough to develop the skills employers want. Unless you HACK college, that is. The Non-Negotiable Skills HACK shows students the skills employers actually want, how students can rapidly acquire them, and how doing so separates students from the crowd.

How to Solve the Skills Gap: "Non-Negotiable Skills"

I have come to understand that there is a core set of survival skills for today's workplace…skills that are neither taught nor tested, even in our best school systems.
—TONY WAGNER, AUTHOR

As The 80/20 Principle predicts, only a few skills matter most. It's these skills that all graduates who want to outperform must possess. These skills are so important that a national survey found that over 93 percent of business leaders indicated that they are *more important* than a candidate's undergraduate major.

I call these skills "Non-Negotiable Skills" due to the high regard in which employers hold them. These are skills that all employers—regardless of industry or major—want in their employees. The Non-Negotiable Skills can be easily remembered as the "3 C's": communication, collaboration, and creative problem solving.

Before learning how to develop the 3 C's, however it's first important to understand the added—and perhaps biggest—advantage to developing the 3 C's: protection from automation.

Automation: The Bigger Reason for Developing the 3 C's

I've learned that people will forget what you said, people will forget what you did, but people will never forget how you made them feel.
—MAYA ANGELOU, AMERICAN POET AND CIVIL RIGHTS ACTIVIST

Imagine going through college, diligently learning the tricks of a trade in a new industry, only to find that, upon graduation, supercomputers have replaced Excel spreadsheets, 140 characters have replaced print journalism, or solar energy has replaced fossil fuels. This is precisely what is happening today to thousands of college graduates thanks to automation.

The world is now engaged in what some have called a "Race Against the Machine." Not only can computers perform like a human, they are beginning to look like a human, too. Recently, Rodney Brooks, a serial robotics entrepreneur, presented a TED Talk showcasing a robotic initiative which he had spearheaded: Baxter. Baxter is built like a human, including two "arms" and a "head," but looks like a friendly cartoon avatar, as the monitor that represents Baxter's face projects two blinking eyes that move and focus on activities.

It is robots like Baxter, and the artificial intelligence within, that led Oxford University to release a study that found 47 percent of all U.S. jobs are in danger of being replaced by computers. *That's nearly one-half of the entire labor force!* Indeed, Baxter represents a coming heyday for robotics, whereby virtually any sort of work, including white-collar, will be disrupted, or extinguished. To see how vulnerable your future job is to computerization, visit bit.ly/automatingcollegejobs.

Many think that the upcoming automation wave is a science fiction fantasy. But you can already see signs. Consider that lawyers—once thought untouchable by automation—are currently using automated text-mining techniques to read through thousands of documents. Financiers—traditionally perceived as indispensible—are increasingly automating paperwork. Even corporate executives are automating as much as 20 percent of their work.

While automation will inevitably destroy many jobs, computers don't necessarily have to put you out of work. It's not all doom and gloom. By embracing the 3 C's, students can insulate themselves from the rise of the machines. "Computers are still very poor at simulating human interaction," explained a Harvard researcher.

The remaining sections explore how students can learn the 3 C's in record time and how doing so can transform a college career.

C #1: Communication

Today, computers are performing technical work (e.g. complex math) previously done by employees. Now it's up to workers to interpret and present conclusions generated by computer calculations, rather than do the calculations themselves. That's why the value of communication skills is at an all-time high. In fact, employers have said that communication is the most important out of the 3 C's. To HACK communication, students must master two particular skills: speaking and writing.

Speaking

There are two types of speakers: those that are nervous and those that are liars.
—MARK TWAIN, WRITER

Most college students are required to take a public speaking course, which they rely upon to demonstrate their communication abilities. The problem with doing the same is that you won't stand out. Plus, employers complain that communication is one of the 3 C's that graduates lack most. Clearly, in-class public speaking won't excite an employer.

Here are several easy ways to catch employers' eyes, while developing speaking skills:

- **Public Speaking Competitions.** Often colleges host on-campus speaking competitions. Enter to compete and, no matter the outcome, include your entry on your resume. For maximum impact, film your presentation and post it on LinkedIn.
- **Create Your Own Speaking Event.** During law school, I spoke at the George Washington's Tech Collective club, where I pitched my idea for a financial services start-up company. Setting up my presentation was incredibly easy. Within a few email exchanges to the club's contact person, I quickly arranged a time to talk at the group's next meeting.
- **Leadership Positions.** These roles frequently require students to speak to a group. Combining leadership with public speaking equals a double win.
- **Toastmasters** (www.toastmasters.org). With over 345,000 members across 142 countries, this organization is the world leader in communication and leadership development.

Use these resources to demonstrate that you possess professional communication skills above your classmates.

Writing

It's publish or perish.
—DANIEL BERNSTEIN, PROFESSOR

Today, nearly 40 percent of students enter college requiring courses in remedial writing. By graduation, things don't get much better. Nearly 36 percent of graduates failed to show any improvement in their writing skills since freshman year.

HACKing college is all about creating the right perception and the right perception requires demonstration. But before students can demonstrate superior writing abilities, they must actually be a good writer. As a result, students should avoid using AP credits to waive out of writing classes. Instead, enroll in writing classes, even advanced writing classes, and receive feedback on papers. Let me be clear: *you need this skill for the rest of your life.* Learn how to write well now.

Once students develop great writing skills, it's time to demonstrate. Similar to speaking, relying on your classroom assignments is not enough. Every student does that, and employers aren't impressed. You can be different.

Here are several ways for students to demonstrate superior writing skills:

- **Start a Blog.** In a short afternoon, I used WordPress.org (www.wordpress. org), which powers over 24 percent of the web, to build the website for HACKiversity (www.kylewiney.com), including its blog. If you are willing to forgo a customized domain name, use WordPress.com (www.wordpress. com) and receive a free blog (e.g. www.kylewiney.wordpress.com).
- **Publish Newspaper Articles.** Submit articles or op-eds to the editor of your college newspaper. Once published, post the article on LinkedIn.
- **Enter Writing Competitions.** Colleges often host writing competitions, which students can join and, if chosen, can win significant recognition.

Whatever you do, make sure your writing projects are visible. Even if employers never read what you've published (and they probably won't), the simple fact that it's published is enough to impress.

HOW REPRESENTING 10,000+ STUDENTS PAYS A CAREER WORTH OF DIVIDENDS

Senior year of college Avery Peechatka (Penn State '09, Economics; George Mason Law '13) scored a highly competitive position: representing a college class of more than 10,000 students as the communications chairperson of Penn State's senior class gift program. "I planned our communication strategy and drafted press releases," said Avery, "to raise hundreds of thousands dollars. Plus, I pitched our campaign to countless executives, administrators, and students."

Avery admits that he completely underestimated the extent to which employers would ask about this experience. "At first, I thought this experience would merely serve as a line item on my resume, but is has proved so much more valuable," Avery explained. "During nearly every job interview since, employers go straight to this experience, even though it happened nearly a decade ago. That's how badly employers want proof of effective communication skills."

Fortunately for Avery, leading a communications campaign on behalf of 10,000+ students gave employers exactly what they wanted. "My interviewers always seemed impressed, regardless the type of position I was interviewing for," explained Avery. "On multiple occasions, interviewers *pitched me* ideas on how I could replicate this past experience to benefit their company."

C #2: Collaboration

The ability to deal with people is as purchasable a commodity as sugar or coffee. And I will pay for that ability more than any other under the sun.
—John D. Rockefeller, 20th Century businessman

Previously, companies had rigid hierarchies with clear positions of authority and tightly defined responsibilities. Workers stayed within these parameters, and if they performed well and didn't misbehave, they eventually received a promotion. Orders were barked out by the higher-ups and flowed down from the top.

Today, that has all changed. Karen Bruett, a business developer for Dell, explains the reality of the modern office structure:

> The way work is organized now is lots of networks of cross-functional teams that work together on specific projects. Work is no longer defined by your specialty; it's defined by the task or problem you and your team are trying to solve or the end goal you want to accomplish. Teams have to figure out the best way to get there.

As a result, employers want to see teamwork, or your ability to "collaborate," which includes the ability to communicate verbally and non-verbally, to listen, and to ask great questions.

To demonstrate collaboration, many students join clubs, sports, or organizations. Today, however, it is no longer good enough to merely be an organization member. Instead, more than 80 percent of employers look for *leaders* of organizations. To maximize marketability, students must become the head of something, anything—a group project, a club, the student government—or found their own organization.

I know this may sound daunting, but it's really not. The threshold for a "leadership" position is actually quite low. For example, during my junior year at Penn State, I took a business management class that simulated running a company. The students in the class were broken into five-person groups. Within those groups, the teams made managerial decisions using whatever system they devised.

Within our group, I quickly emerged as the leader, which meant I made our final decisions. No one voted me in. We didn't have a formal election system. It just happened. Given the casual nature of it, I didn't consider myself as the group's "leader," just someone who directed our decisions in running a fictitious company.

During the middle of the same semester, I talked with Zach, one of my friends from business school, who was taking the same course. "I had an on-campus interview with a company yesterday," Zach told me. "They wanted to know if I held any leadership positions."

"What did you tell them?" I asked.

"Well, since I never held an official leadership position," responded Zach, "I just told them about how I led our five-person team in our business management class."

"Were they impressed?" I asked surprised, knowing how informal my leadership position was within the same class.

"They were!" exclaimed Zach. "They liked that I presented my ideas to the team in such a way that I convinced them to follow my suggestions. I think I got the job!"

I couldn't believe this. Zach had demonstrated leadership abilities to an employer using a simple classroom project. It was the same "position"—if you can even call it that—which I held but never considered a leadership role.

But that's the point. You don't have to become the student body president. You just need something—anything—to show that you've led other people, even if that something is as small as a group project that everyone is required to do.

USING FANCY JOB TITLES TO DAZZLE EMPLOYERS: A PERSONAL STORY

In college, I ran to become my fraternity's president, a group of more than 200 people. I lost by *one* (controversial) vote. Despite losing the presidency, my fraternity brothers elected me into another position: "First Executive Counselor." Sounds fancy, right? It wasn't. In reality, I was the maintenance guy, the "Mr. Fix It" of our fraternity house. I sanded and waxed floors for our winter formal, fixed (many) broken windows, and changed plenty of light bulbs. For most of the college crowd, blue-collar, handyman work is not sexy. And it was certainly not as sexy as serving as the fraternity's president.

During interviews, however, when employers asked me about the position, I never claimed to be "Mr. Fix It." Instead, I discussed how the position "tasked me with the responsibility for overseeing the operations of a multi-million dollar fraternity house filled with over 40 (unruly) brothers." (Forty of the 200 brothers lived in the house). No matter what the job actually entails, to supercharge your perception as a great leader, find a position with a fancy title. Then it's all about finding *one* good story to share with employers.

Ultimately, being the First Executive Counselor was not glamorous. But the name was: *First* Executive Counselor. The name gave me a resume line item, a conversation piece, and most importantly, evidence that I not only belonged to a group, but *led* a group.

C #3: Creative Problem Solving

*The best way to put distance between you and the crowd is to do
an outstanding job with information.*
—BILL GATES, FOUNDER OF MICROSOFT

Colleges have traditionally produced "knowledge workers," graduates who specialize in handling or using information, such as computer programmers, lawyers, and business folks.

But the days of the knowledge worker are crumbling. Compared to previous decades when information was buried inside books, which were buried inside libraries, information is now readily available to anyone, anywhere, anytime. For example, Wikipedia, a free encyclopedia, contains so much information that printing it out in its entirety would require more than four football fields of shelving. There is so much free information that business expert Peter Diamandis is fond of saying that Google affords today's student access to more information than Bill Clinton had during his presidency.

Importantly, the rise of free, abundant information is driving two major forces:

1. **Devaluation of "Knowing" Information.** The value for the ability to recall facts and figures is plummeting through the floor, even as many colleges base their entire curriculum on teaching students this way. One study even found that, thanks to the increasing speed of technology, four-year degrees are becoming outdated by a student's junior year; and
2. **Soaring Value for "Applying" Information.** The ability to apply information in a way that arrives at new solutions is a skill that is in short supply and high demand. That skill is called "creative problem solving."

In essence, in today's economy, it's no longer about *what* you know but rather *what you can do* with what you know. There's a special name for the kind of person who excels at creative problem solving: "Smart Creatives," a term coined by Google.

A Smart Creative is someone with technical depth, business savvy and creative flair. They are willing to work hard, question the status quo, and attack things differently. At the heart of a Smart Creative is a hands-on approach to getting things done. It's about producing results.

As a result, ground zero for becoming a Smart Creative is to have an understanding of your field. At Google, for example, Eric Schmidt, Google's former CEO, said this means that a Smart Creative is a computer scientist, or at least understands the structure of the systems behind the magic we see on our screens everyday.

One of the best ways to becoming a Smart Creative, and branding yourself as one, is to build a prototype. Remember: Smart Creatives are masters at *doing*. Paul Graham, co-founder of Y Combinator, the first startup incubator, explains the importance of doing in today's economy:

> I asked managers at Yahoo, Google, Amazon, Cisco and
> Microsoft how they'd feel about two candidates, both 24, with

equal ability, one who'd tried to start a startup that tanked, and another who'd spent the two years since college working as a developer at a big company. Every one responded that they'd prefer the guy who'd tried to start his own company.

In other words, students today must be practitioners, not just bookworms, even if they produced a product that failed. That's how desperate employers are for students capable of doing.

If you're in college right now, one of the best ways to establish yourself as a Smart Creative is to start something outside of class. Anything. It can be a business, a non-profit, an organization, or a service. *Just start doing.*

Ultimately, Non-Negotiable Skills, as represented by the "3 C's," are must-have supplemental skills that employers want to see. As an added bonus, developing the 3 C's insulates students from the ever-growing automation wave, which will significantly disrupt how work is done, and consequently, the value of a college degree.

HACKING TAKEAWAYS

- All employers want to see certain skills. Because of their importance, I call these skills "Non-Negotiable Skills."
- The Non-Negotiable Skills are: communication, collaboration, and creative problem solving.
- In addition to their marketability, Non-Negotiable Skills provide even more value by protecting students from the ever-growing automation wave.

BRINGING IT TO A CLOSE

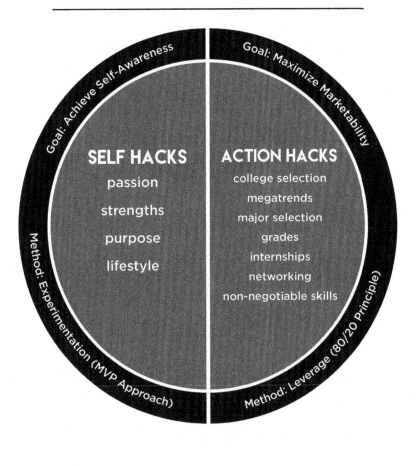

Goal: Achieve Self-Awareness

Goal: Maximize Marketability

SELF HACKS

passion

strengths

purpose

lifestyle

ACTION HACKS

college selection

megatrends

major selection

grades

internships

networking

non-negotiable skills

Method: Experimentation (MVP Approach)

Method: Leverage (80/20 Principle)

HACKING COLLEGE: A RECAP

Tell the audience what you are going to tell them, tell them, and then tell them what you have told them. —ARISTOTLE

Congratulations! You now know how to achieve more by doing less in college. To recap, here was everything we covered:

The Self-Awareness Cornerstone. This is everything left of the centerline. The Self-Awareness Cornerstone provided the principles for helping students determine *what* to do at college. Each of the four Self-HACKs contained in the Self-Awareness cornerstone represent the step-by-step action items for helping students develop self-awareness—that is, understanding the things that make them tick—and is the fastest way to get there. Here are the highlights:

<u>The two big picture concepts:</u>

Goal:	Achieve self-awareness
Method:	Experimentation (MVP approach)

<u>The individual HACKs:</u>

Self HACK #1:	*Passion* – never follow your passion, but never be without it, either
Self HACK #2:	*Strengths* – go all-in on your strengths, go all-out on your weaknesses
Self HACK #3:	*Purpose* – find your *Why?*
Self HACK #4:	*Lifestyle* – lifestyle design first, college planning second

The Execution Cornerstone. This is everything to the right of the center-line. The Execution Cornerstone provided the *"how"* principles for helping students maximize their marketability. Each of the seven Action HACKs contained in the Execution Cornerstone represent the step-by-step action items designed to maximize a student's marketability, which are distilled into the purest forms thanks to the use of leverage. Here are the highlights:

The two big picture concepts:

Goal:	Maximize marketability
Method:	Leverage (The 80/20 Principle)

The individual HACKs:

Action HACK #1: *College Selection* – go elite, but if not elite, seek value
Action HACK #2: *Megatrends* – ride the waves of the next megatrends
Action HACK #3: *Major Selection* – select "Skills Ready" majors
Action HACK #4: *Grades* – follow the 3.0 GPA Rule
Action HACK #5: *Internships* – get inside the internship funnel
Action HACK #6: *Networking* – connect with the "Connector"
Action HACK #7: *Non-Negotiable Skills* – Demonstrate the 3 C's

Before wrapping up, I want to signoff with a heartfelt message to students, parents, administrators, and more.

A MESSAGE TO STUDENTS

Twenty years from now you will be more disappointed by the things that you didn't do than by the ones you did do. So throw off the bowlines. Sail away from the safe harbor. Catch the trade winds in your sails. Explore. Dream. Discover.
—MOTHER OF H. JACKSON BROWN, AUTHOR

In 2006, I stepped onto college campus with virtually no idea what I was doing. In writing this book, I kept my naïve 18 year-old self in mind. "What do I wish I would have known back then?" served as my guiding question.

When telling people I was writing a book about "everything I wish I would have known before freshman year," many said that college students wouldn't care and will continue to approach college the way they always have. But if you've read this far, it's clear that you—much like I do—take your hopes and dreams seriously. It's my belief that there are thousands—if not millions—of these students. In truth, I wrote this book for you.

While many disagree with certain educational policies, nearly everyone agrees that college represents a remarkable time in a student's life—a time to spread wings, experience the world, and become exposed to different people and ideas. There's something truly beautiful about that.

Regrettably, students often allow the pressures of college performance to obscure this beauty. While I'm not dismissing the importance of college performance (indeed, I wrote an entire book about it), that's not the end goal of college. "Wait," you say, "I thought the purpose of college is to get a job?" Well, it is…sort of. But let me ask you a deeper question: "What's the purpose of getting a job?"

During my law school application process, I attempted to answer this question inside my personal statement, which explored what it meant to be a "success." I proposed three possible ways to define success. First, I proposed that success is illusory, that it's this hocus-pocus, fluffy concept that doesn't really exist. I rejected this proposition. Second, I proposed that success is "making a name for oneself," focused on accumulating treasure and protecting oneself from life's uncertainties. I rejected this idea, too.

I then proposed that success is best represented by a quote from Ralph Waldo Emerson:

> To leave the world a bit better, whether by a healthy child, a garden patch or a redeemed social condition…to know even one life has breathed easier because you have lived—this is to have succeeded.

It is ultimately this definition, that at the age of 22, I embraced as my definition of success. My hope is that this book helps you breathe a little easier at college, to live a little more, and to find your own version of success in life.

A Message to Teachers, Administrators, and Parents

The significant problems we face cannot be solved at the same level of thinking we were at when we created them.
—Albert Einstein

At the beginning of my college career, I majored in education. Why? Because I care about students. Like you, I want the best for the next generation. But the world has shown that everything has changed. Education itself must change with it.

New realities face college students today. Equipping students to succeed in this new era is going to require a new approach. But most importantly, a new approach means nothing if there aren't people willing to implement it. Those people can be—in fact, *must* be—you.

In order for students to succeed, teachers, administrators, and parents must embrace this reality. In short, students need you. I hope this book encourages you to think about the way in which you approach education. The next generation does, too. In fact, they are counting on you.

A MESSAGE TO POLICY MAKERS

*A good hockey player plays where the puck is. A great
hockey player plays where the puck is going to be.*
—WAYNE GRETZKY, FOUR-TIME STANLEY CUP CHAMPION

We are currently in an economy like never before. Overseas workers are performing jobs previously held by college graduates. Computers are automating white-collar jobs. Recent college graduates can't find work. All of these things are true. But what's also true is that learning has never been cheaper and more accessible. Experiences have never been more available. Opportunities have never been more valuable. We are now living in a world of extremes. For those who reap, they reap in abundance. For those who flounder, they flounder longer.

Within this book, I've laid out how college students can thrive in the midst of the current economic realities. But here, I want to use my research, conversations, and experiences to offer predictions where I think education is going:

Prediction #1 – The Flight To Quality Will Continue to Grow. Despite some speculation that every college is poised to undergo major disruptions, that won't happen. As more people, both domestic and abroad, demand a college education, they will increasingly flock to Elite Colleges.

Prediction #2 – The Flight to Value Will Skyrocket. Students applying to General Colleges will become increasingly price sensitive to tuition rates, resulting in two major consequences: (a) exploding demand for community colleges, and (b) soaring demand for flagship public universities (e.g. Arizona State). Flagship public universities will offset cuts in public funding by finding ways to scale.

Prediction #3 – The Death of the Middle Will Strike. Outside of the Elite Colleges and the highest-value General Colleges are the over-priced General Colleges, which largely include $50,000+ a year liberal arts schools and basement-dwelling state schools. Without extensive government funding, these schools will struggle to survive, and many will fail.

Prediction #4 – "Disruptive" College Platforms Will Struggle. Currently, many startup companies are trying to replace the entire college curriculum. They won't. Degrees from traditional four-year colleges, particularly Elite Colleges and valuable General Colleges, will retain significant value. The reason is that employers will hesitate to equate the value of a degree awarded by an unknown startup company to a degree awarded by Harvard, for example.

Prediction #5 – Personalized Education Will Explode. Cookie-cutter responses to career and educational questions will grow in their ineffectiveness. In its place will emerge personalized career tracks, which will no longer recommend college as the one-size-fits-all solution.

Prediction #6 – Inequalities in Job Prospects Will Widen. The sheer magnitude of new economic forces will continue to polarize the success (or lack thereof) that college students experience immediately upon graduation. Students who play by the old rules will incur more damage than ever before. Students who embrace these new realities will position themselves for more success than ever before.

Ultimately, I encourage you all to put down this book. Take action and be fearless. Create a college career—and help others create a college career—that fosters success. The world is waiting.

MORE SECRETS TO ACHIEVING MORE BY DOING LESS

Ways to Keep in Touch

- Subscribe to the *HACKiversity* podcast on iTunes!
- Questions, success stories, or feedback to share? I would love to hear from you! Email me at kyle@kylewiney.com.
- Share your *HACKiversity* story with the hashtag #HACKiversity on social media.
- For ongoing blog posts on achieving more by doing less visit kylewiney.com/blog and subscribe to the *HACKiversity* newsletter.

Want to Help Spread the Word?

If you enjoyed *HACKiversity* and think others could benefit, share the love using the following ways:

- Write a review on the retailer's site where you purchased the book.
- Write a review on Goodreads to help others decide whether to purchase a copy.
- Gift a copy to a friend, classmate, family member, teacher, or administrator. The potential HACKer audience is big!
- Share your *HACKiversity* story on social media with the hashtag #HACKiversity.

THOSE WANTING MORE: THE FEW BOOKS THAT MATTER MOST

The books mentioned below are among those that interviewees and I mentioned when asked, "What is the one book that changed your life the most?" In true 80/20 form, this list represents books hand selected from the most common responses, which I paired with its corresponding college HACK. Finally, by using the reading tricks listed under the Strategic Reading section, which is located in the Grades HACK, students can read approximately 100 pages in forty minutes (2.5 pages per minute), allowing them to digest the books below in only a few hours.

College Basic #1: What Is the Purpose of College?

Academically Adrift: Limited Learning on College Campuses (144 pages)
By Richard Arum and Josipa Roksa

This book showcases the startling findings produced from a study conducted by the authors: nearly half of all college students fail to demonstrate any improvement in learning during the first two years of college, and the results aren't much better for all four years. This book single handedly casts a blow to anyone who believes the purpose of college is for students to learn.

College Basic #2: Why Your Current College Approach Will Fail

College (Un)Bound: The Future of Higher Education and What It Means for Students (215 pages)
By Jeffrey Selingo

Selingo is the editor at large for the *Chronicle of Higher Education* and has one of the best pulses for the higher education market. This book demonstrates the utter failure of conventional college approaches by one of the world's leading experts.

Excellent Sheep: The Miseducation of the American Elite and the Way to a Meaningful Life (242 pages)
By William Deresiewicz

Deresiewicz is a former Yale professor and saw firsthand how a conventional college approach produced a large number of very smart but completely confused graduates—the ultimate failure.

Self-Awareness Cornerstone

The Lean Startup: How Today's Entrepreneurs Use Continuous Innovation to Create Radically Successful Businesses (290 pages)
By Eric Ries

In addition to forming the backbone of the Self-Awareness Cornerstone, this book is cited by nearly every entrepreneur and high-performing individual around. By introducing a revolutionary approach, this book demonstrates how people and businesses can efficiently and effectively succeed in the new economy.

Passion HACK

Drive: The Surprising Truth About What Motivates Us (230 pages)
By Daniel Pink

Typical external motivators (e.g. money, prestige) were effective in the industrial era because work was mechanical and uncreative in nature. Today, however, the same motivators are ineffective, as the nature of work has changed. What we need is to find work that unleashes our intrinsic motivators. This book makes a compelling case for why and how this can be done.

Strengths HACK

Now, Discover Your Strengths (258 pages)
By Marcus Buckingham and Donald O. Clifton

Clifton is considered the "Father of Strengths-Based Psychology." This book upends the notion that "good is the opposite of bad" by demonstrating that, in order to excel, individuals must understand their strengths.

Purpose HACK

The Reason for God: Belief in an Age of Skepticism (240 pages)
By Timothy Keller

This book represents one of the top three most influential books in my life. In it, Keller makes a compelling case for the existence of God, and therefore, instills a sense of deep and profound purpose in what we do. The way in which this book has revolutionized my worldview cannot be overstated.

The Purpose Driven Life: What On Earth am I Here for? (338 pages)
By Rick Warren

My gateway into Keller's *The Reason for God,* Warren masterfully illustrates how God has a purpose for everyone's life. Armed with this knowledge, stress plummets, simplicity soars, and satisfaction endures.

Start With Why: How Great Leaders Inspire Everyone to Take Action (228 pages)
By Simon Sinek

Many people know *what* they do, but few people know *why* they do it. This book demonstrates that those who are fueled by their *why*—their purpose, cause, or belief—are happier and outperform those who aren't.

Lifestyle HACK

The 4-Hour Workweek: Escape 9-5, Live Anywhere, and Join the New Rich (376 pages)
By Tim Ferriss

Another one of the top three most influential books in my life, Ferriss demonstrates how bucking conventional wisdom can lead to more freedom, success, and happiness than playing by the same old rules as everyone else. In essence, Ferriss provides the best step-by-step approach in lifestyle design.

Execution Cornerstone

The 80/20 Principle: The Secret to Achieving More with Less (255 pages)
By Richard Koch

One of the first books that illuminated how my grind-it-out college approach was not only ineffective but also unnecessary. This book convinced me that only a few things in college truly mattered (same in life), and that by focusing all my effort on those few things, I would be better off. Not surprisingly, the Execution Cornerstone is built upon the principles in this book.

The 22 Immutable Laws of Marketing: Violate Them at Your Own Risk (132 pages)
By Al Ries and Jack Trout

This book explains how my fraternity brother, despite doing everything "wrong," created a better personal brand than me, someone who did everything "right." This book contains the principles students must follow in order to create an effective personal brand.

The 7 Habits of Highly Effective People: Powerful Lessons in Personal Change (342 pages)

By Stephen R. Covey
One of the landmark books of personal productivity, Covey identifies the seven principles that empower people to do more with less. Not surprisingly, this book has largely inspired *HACKiversity*.

College Selection HACK

Will College Pay Off? A Guide to The Most Important Financial Decision You'll Ever Make (188 pages)
By Peter Cappelli

Unlike conventional wisdom, which says that everyone must pay $100,000+ for a college education, this book provides a personalized response to the question contained in the book's title.

Megatrends HACK

Bold: How to Go Big, Create Wealth, and Impact the World (279 pages)
By Peter H. Diamandis and Steven Kotler

This book convincingly asserts that the world's biggest problems are now the world's biggest business opportunities by pinpointing where these business opportunities are and how to unlock them.

The Industries of the Future (249 pages)
By Alec Ross

This book identifies the location, size, and impact of the world's next megatrends along with the skills necessary to benefit from these opportunities.

Major Selection HACK

There is Life After College: What Parents and Students Should Know About Navigating School to Prepare for the Jobs of Tomorrow (255 pages)
By Jeffrey Selingo

Another great book by Selingo, which demonstrates the wide disparities that exist among the different majors. This book explains how some majors lead to great opportunities while many don't.

Grades HACK

The 4-Hour Chef: The Simple Path to Cooking Like a Pro, Learning Anything, and Living the Good Life (639 pages)
By Tim Ferriss

Although appearing as a cookbook (and it is), this book is fundamentally a toolkit for optimized learning. The subject just happens to be food. With the right approach, Ferriss demonstrates how it's possible to become fluent in Japanese in one year, Mandarin Chinese in six months, German in three months, and Spanish in eight weeks. Now that's optimized learning!

Internships HACK

The First 90 Days: Proven Strategies for Getting Up to Speed Faster and Smarter (257 pages)
By Michael Watkins

The goal for every intern is to reach as quickly as possible the "break-even point:" the point at which the intern contributes as much value as he or she consumes. Watkins provides a step-by-step approach for students to reach the break-even point before 90 days, the typical length of an internship.

Networking HACK

Never Eat Alone: And Other Secrets to Success, One Relationship at a Time (367 pages)
By Keith Ferrazzi and Tahl Raz

This book demonstrates the value of networking and how students can make the most of each networking opportunity no matter the setting in which they find themselves.

Superconnect: Harnessing the Power of Networks and the Strength of Weak Links (261 pages)
By Richard Koch and Greg Lockwood

Once again, Koch masterfully applies the concepts of leverage, but this time, to networking. Koch demonstrates why connectors are so powerful and how individuals can take advantage.

Non-Negotiable Skills HACK

The Global Achievement Gap: Why Even Our Best Schools Don't Teach the New Survival Skills Our Children Need – and What We Can Do About It (305 pages)
By Tony Wagner

Dismissing conventional wisdom, Wagner beautifully outlines the skills and abilities students need to thrive inside the new economy. He also illustrates what happens when students fail to develop these skills...and it's not good.

How Google Works (260 pages)
By Eric Schmidt and Jonathan Rosenberg

This book provides a window into how one of the most innovative and disruptive businesses hires employees. Google has made a habit of hiring "Smart Creatives," those people with technical depth, business savvy, and creative flair, who are also the future of the modern workforce.

GRATITUDE AND ACKNOWLEDGMENTS

If I have seen farther, it is by standing on the shoulders of giants.
—SIR ISAAC NEWTON

If you found this book valuable in any way, it's no doubt due to the stories shared by the 40+ students and college graduates I interviewed. Most of the conversations lasted hours, and some were held with people I never met. Each was incredibly giving of their time. I am incredibly grateful for how their story has reshaped—for the better—the way in which students approach college.

HACKiversity started as a jumbled idea, and frankly, a Plan B to another entrepreneurial project to which I took too big of a bite in trying to launch. During a random phone call, I floated the idea of a "college playbook" past my good friend, Avery Peechatka. Avery encouraged me to write the book in an effort to fill the shortage of quality advice out there. Without Avery's encouragement, I never would have begun writing. Thanks, Avery, for being such an ally throughout my entrepreneurial pursuits and, more importantly, for being a great friend.

In addition, what you're holding wouldn't be possible without the stellar work of my copy editor, Angie Peechatka. Angie's dedication to the book never faded and belief in the message never waned. Angie's extraordinary attention to detail, listening skills, and raw talent were indispensible in shaping *HACKiversity* into what it is today. Without her, this book would be a hotbox of jumbled thoughts. (I know, because I tried other copyeditors.) Angie, you were a true blessing throughout this whole process. A true Big Win!

Without marketing efforts, *HACKiversity* would have reached no one. A heartfelt thank you to Andrea Lucas for her eye for photography and graphic design wizardry. Andrea's hard work and exceptional abilities created visuals that made my rookie web development skills appear more than they are. Andrea breathed her creative insights into launching *HACKiversity*, and without it, this book would be unread by those who need it most.

There is another gang of selfless creatives who gave their time and effort into making *HACKiversity* better. Thanks to Woody Bernardo, who offered many essential critiques to my website and all things marketing. Thanks to Alex Rekas for developing parts of my website and for finding the tools to make *HACKiversity's* upcoming promotional contest possible. Thank you to Glorianna Picini for taking on a new challenge and bringing to life the stellar book trailer that exists today. Finally, thank you to Jonathan Lynch for sharing his professional acting insight into what makes a great video.

A special thanks to Gret Glyer for his generosity in connecting me to a wide-array of promotional opportunities, which have undoubtedly helped spread the word about *HACKiversity*. More importantly, Gret has made possible a remarkable upcoming trip to Africa for one lucky college student as part of *HACKiversity's* promotional process. Thanks, Gret!

The finished product in your hands is thanks to the priceless insights I received from those who offered their time to read and re-read my drafts. This includes Elise Domouchelle, Tyler Brodie, Mackayla Brodie, Justin Muthler, Beth deButts, Grafton deButts, Avery Peechatka, Gret Glyer, Jim Kreighbaum, Jackie Winey, Doug Winey, Andrea Lucas, Danielle Nadler, Becky Semidey, Gus Cavanaugh, David Perdue, Melody von Kahle, Matt Bowles, Bethany Malskis, Jessica Martinson, Erin Jansen, Anita Kamwendo, Brynn Biddle, Monica Gingerich, Sarah Hawk, Ian Batt, Mary Biddle, and Adelina Longoria.

I am deeply grateful for a wonderful and supporting family. Those people certainly include my Aunt Annie and Uncle Dave. Their support, including financial support of both my bicycle and mission trip, allowed me to have many of the experiences I've shared with students throughout *HACKiversity*. Without them, this book wouldn't be what it is.

I am also deeply grateful to both my grandparents, Lerch and Grandma Jean. Without their continued, unwavering support, I would not have been able to enjoy life to the extent I have. Together, we share many memories, including my days working at the office, our family vacations and holidays, and many more. Those memories are treasures I'll forever cherish.

I am also deeply grateful to my both my parents, Jackie and Doug, or just Mom and Dad. Their generosity in paying for my college tuition allowed me to gain the experiences and see the need for writing *HACKiversity* in the first place. But more importantly, their nearly three-decade commitment to one another through marriage is a precious gift to our family, and one I've grown more and more to appreciate. It's because of this foundation that I have any success at all.

Outside of my family, I am the beneficiary of extraordinary influences and mentors. These people include David Perdue, Rob Lemos, Jonathan Little, and Judge Thomas Horne. These individuals have both taught and demonstrated the value of living a life of significance, and what making a difference in people's lives looks during the day-to-day.

Most of all, I am grateful for the love and grace I experience daily from God through Jesus Christ, for bringing me this far in my journey, and for the promise of hope, peace, and rest, in this life and the next.

NOTES

My Story and Why You Need This Book

1. *Sir Ken Robinson quote:* "How to escape education's death valley | Sir Ken Robinson." YouTube. May 10, 2013. Accessed February 06, 2017. http://www.youtube.com/watch?v=wX78iKhInsc.

What Is The Purpose of College?

2. *Lloyd Blankfein quote:* Abkowitz, Alyssa. "Goldman's Blankfein on Skipping School Work, Wishing to be Chinese." The Wall Street Journal. June 10, 2015. Accessed January 24, 2017. http://blogs.wsj.com/chinarealtime/2015/06/10/goldmans-blankfein-on-skipping-school-work-wishing-to-be-chinese/.

3. *today, anyone can take a semester's worth of online courses—for free—in MIT's top-ranked Supply Chain Management master's program:* Lapal, Rachel. "MIT Pilot program reimagines admissions process, introduces "MicroMaster's."." EdX Blog. October 07, 2015. Accessed February 06, 2017. http://blog.edx.org/edx-courses-time-on-campus-a-new-path-to-an-mit-masters-degree.

4. *36 percent failed to show any improvement:* Selingo, Jeffrey J. *College (un)bound: The Future of Higher Education and What It Means for Students.* (Boston: Houghton Mifflin Harcourt, 2013), 25.

5. *Kevin Spacey quote:* How To Become Successful - Best Motivational Videos Compilation for 2017. November 15, 2016. Accessed January 24, 2017. https://www.youtube.com/watch?v=zlluSzNDDUM.

Why Your Current College Approach Will Fail

6. *Paula Poundstone quote:* I Love That Quote. Accessed January 24, 2017. http://www.ilovethatquote.com/adults-are-always-asking-kids-what-they-want-to-be-when-they-grow-up-because-theyre-looking-for-ideas/.

7. *The Big Short:* The Big Short. Directed by Adam McKay. By Charles Randolph, Adam McKay, and Michael Lewis. Performed by Christian Bale, Steve Carell, Ryan Gosling. United States: Paramount Pictures, 2015. Film.

8. *In 2008, more than 35 percent of recent college graduates were underemployed:* Bowyer, Chris. "Overqualified and Underemployed: The Job Market Waiting for Graduates." *Forbes*, August 15, 2014. http://www.forbes.com/sites/thecollegebubble/2014/08/15/overqualified-and-underemployed-the-job-market-waiting-for-graduates/.

9. *By 2015, that number jumped to 50 percent:* Parcells, Nathan. "What 50,000 Students Have to Say About College Recruiting." *Looksharp* (web log), July 1, 2015. https://www.looksharp.com/blog/what-50000-students-have-to-say-about-college-recruiting.

10. *A major source of worry and concern for Millennials is debt:* 2014 Wells Fargo Millennial Study. PDF. Wells Fargo, 2014. https://www.myirionline.org/docs/default-source/research/click-here.pdf?sfvrsn=0.

11. *over 40 million people carry more than $1.3 trillion in student loan debt:* Ellis, Blake. "40 million Americans now have student loan debt." *CNN Money*, September 10, 2014. http://money.cnn.com/2014/09/10/pf/college/student-loans/.

12. *student loan debt grows by $2,700 every second:* Munk, Jonathan. "Universities can't solve our skills gap problem, because they caused it." *Crunch Network*, May 8, 2016. https://techcrunch.com/2016/05/08/universities-cant-solve-our-skills-gap-problem-because-they-caused-it/.

13. *"What you thought you were going to get in quality of life by going to that college, you've just undermined with the amount of debt you're taking on.":* Jacobs, Peter. "MARK CUBAN: This is just the start of the college implosion." *Business Insider*, March 5, 2015. http://www.businessinsider.com/mark-cuban-sweet-briar-college-college-debt-bubble-crisis-2015-3.

14. *That number is an eye-popping 27.8 million students:* Ginder, S.A., Kelly-Reid, J.E., and Mann, F.B. (2015). Postsecondary Institutions and Cost of Attendance in 2014-15; Degrees and Other Awards Conferred, 2013-14; and 12-Month Enrollment, 2013-14: First Look (Preliminary Data) (NCES 2015-097). U.S. Department of Education. Washington, DC: National Center for Education Statistics.

15. *there are over 150.6 million college graduates or students:* Itbach, Philip G., Liz Reisberg, and Laura E. Rumbley. *Trends in Global Higher Education: Tracking an Academic Revolution.* 2009. World Conference on Higher Education, United Nations Educational, Scientific and Cultural Organization. Conf 402. Paris, France: UNESCO, 2009. vi.

16. *more people will hold a college degree than since the beginning of human history:* Robinson, Sir Ken. "Do schools kill creativity?" Speech, TED Talks. February 2006. Accessed December 5, 2016. http://www.ted.com/talks/ken_robinson_says_schools_kill_creativity.

17. *Ken Robinson quote:* Ken Robinson and Lou Aronica, *Creative Schools: The Grassroots Revolution That's Transforming Education* (New York: Viking 2015), 15.

18. *Thomas Friedman interviews CEO of Indian tech company:* Friedman, Thomas L. *The world is flat: a brief history of the twenty-first century.* New York: Farrar, Straus and Giroux, 2005, 6-7.

19. *the cost of your degree averages about $120,000 for a 4-year public university and $250,000 for a 4-year private university; two million adults over the age of 60 are still paying off their student loans:* Wagner, Tony, and Ted Dintersmith. *Most likely to succeed: preparing our kids for the innovation era.* New York, NY: Scribner, 2015, 150 & 152.

20. *Seth Godin quote:* "Seth Godin for teens on being different, college, and loving failure." Interview. *Teenage Professional Network* (audio blog), August 14, 2014. https://www.youtube.com/watch?v=dPsR3S1DK8c.

21. *the stock market doubled over a four-year period in the '80s and more than tripled over a four-year period in the '90s:* "Compound Annual Growth Rate (Annualized Return)." Moneychimp. Accessed December 18, 2016. http://www.moneychimp.com/features/market_cagr.htm.

22. *The 90's stock market boom, for example, had a probability of about 0.4 percent of occurring:* Moneychimp. Accessed December 18, 2016. http://www.moneychimp.com/features/market_cagr.htm.

23. *employees who stay in companies longer than two years earn less than 50 percent of what routine job switchers make over the course of a lifetime:* Keng, Cameron. "Employees Who Stay In Companies Longer Than Two Years Get Paid 50% Less." Forbes, June 22, 2014. http://www.forbes.com/sites/cameronkeng/2014/06/22/employees-that-stay-in-companies-longer-than-2-years-get-paid-50-less/.

24. *"They figure that kids can straighten the emotional stuff out in his/her 20's, but no one can go back and get the Yale undergrad degree.":* Lythcott-Haims, Julie. "Kids of Helicopter Parents Are Sputtering Out." *Slate*, July 5, 2015. http://www.slate.com/articles/double_x/doublex/2015/07/helicopter_parenting_is_increasingly_correlated_with_college_age_depression.html.

Self-Awareness Cornerstone

25. *Dan Roam quote:* Kaufman, Josh. *The personal MBA: master the art of business.* New York, NY: Portfolio/Penguin, 2012.

26. *Charlotte Gilman quote:* A-Z Quotes. Accessed January 13, 2017. http://www.azquotes.com/quote/786753.

27. *Self-awareness is so powerful that studies have found it served as the strongest predictor of overall success:* Lipman, Victor. "All Successful Leaders Need This Quality: Self-Awareness." Forbes. November 18, 2013. Accessed January 13, 2017. http://www.forbes.com/sites/victorlipman/2013/11/18/all-successful-leaders-need-this-quality-self-awareness/#6f9debd457b4.

28. *Peter Guber quote:* "Self-Awareness is the Most Important Skill for Career Success." LinkedIn. May 7, 2015. Accessed January 13, 2017. https://www.linkedin.com/pulse/i-were-22-self-awareness-most-important-skill-career-success-guber.

29. *Despite self-awareness leading to huge upside, today, less than 30 percent of people are self-aware:* Diedorff, Erich C., and Robert S. Rubin. "Research: We're Not Very Self-Aware, Especially at Work." Harvard Business Review. March 12, 2015. Accessed January 13, 2017. https://hbr.org/2015/03/research-were-not-very-self-aware-especially-at-work.

30. *For example, 70 percent of high school seniors believe they have "above average" leadership skills:* Grant, Adam M. *Originals: how non-conformists move the world.* NY, NY: Viking, an imprint of Penguin Random House LLC, 2016, p. 33.

31. *Reid Hoffman quote:* Hoffman, Reid, and Ben Casnocha. *The Start-up of You: Adapt to the Future, Invest in Yourself, and Transform Your Career.* New York, NY: Crown, 2012, p. 7.

32. *Under this system, you might excel, or you might struggle. You would never ride a bike:* Wagner, Tony, and Ted Dintersmith. *Most Likely To Succeed: Preparing Our Kids For The Innovation Era.* New York, NY: Scribner, 2015, p. 28.

33. *Entrepreneurs call this the "Minimum Viable Product" (MVP) approach:* Holiday, Ryan. *The Obstacle Is The Way: The Timeless Art Of Turning Trials Into Triumph.* New York: Portfolio/Penguin, 2014, p. 82.

34. *In general, there are two ways to receive feedback from experimentation:* Ries, Eric. *The Lean Startup: How Today's Entrepreneurs Use Continuous Innovation To Create Radically Successful Businesses.* New York: Crown Business, 2011, p. 21.

35. *Xunzi quote:* Tutoring Services." Lemonade Accounting. November 05, 2016. Accessed January 13, 2017. https://lemonadeaccounting.wordpress.com/tutoring-services/.

36. *John Le Carree quote.* BrainyQuote. Accessed January 24, 2017. https://www.brainyquote.com/quotes/quotes/j/johnlecarr143875.html.

37. *Experiments are fact-finding missions that, over time, inch scientists toward greater understanding:* Catmull, Ed, and Amy Wallace. *Creativity, Inc. Overcoming the Unseen Forces That Stand in the Way of True Inspiration.* S.l.: Random House Publishing Group, 2014, p. 113

38. *For example, a career services director at the University of Texas says:* Robinson, Ken, and Lou Aronica. *Finding your element: how to discover your talents and passions and transform your life.* New York: Viking, 2013, p. 29.

39. *Research shows that only one in five young people have a clear vision of what they want to accomplish in life:* Damon, William. *The path to purpose: helping our children find their calling in life.* New York: Free Press, 2008, p. 5.

40. *Thomas Tusser quote:* The Quote Garden. December 08, 2016. Accessed January 13, 2017. http://www.quotegarden.com/debt.html.

41. *Not surprisingly, nearly 20 percent of college graduates with student loans eventually give up on their preferred line of work:* Bowyer, Chris. "Overqualified and Underemployed: The Job Market Waiting for Graduates." Forbes. August 15, 2014. Accessed January 13, 2017. http://www.forbes.com/sites/thecollegebubble/2014/08/15/overqualified-and-underemployed-the-job-market-waiting-for-graduates/.

42. *Michael Jordan quote:* BrainyQuote. Accessed January 24, 2017. http://www.brainyquote.com/quotes/authors/m/michael_jordan.html.

43. *Use these three steps to increase the likelihood of failing successfully:* Burnett, Bill, and Dave Evans. *Designing Your Life: How to Build a Well-Lived, Joyful Life.* New York, NY: Borzoi, 2016, p. 192.

44. *Ironically, the more you risk failure—and actually fail—the greater your chances of success:* Maxwell, John C. "Failing Forward Quotes." Goodreads. 2017. Accessed January 13, 2017. https://www.goodreads.com/work/quotes/614412-failing-forward-how-to-make-the-most-of-your-mistakes.

Passion HACK

45. *Austin Kleon quote:* "How will I pay the bills?" *Austin Kleon* (web log), February 19, 2015. Accessed January 13, 2017. http://austinkleon.com/2015/02/19/how-will-i-pay-the-bills/.

46. *Paul Graham quote:* "The Top Idea in Your Mind ." *Paul Graham* (web log), July 2010. Accessed January 13, 2017. http://www.paulgraham.com/top.html.

47. *That's because an "interest" is something you're excited or curious about:* Brown, Kerry. "Warrior Leadership – Passion Vs. Interest." LinkedIn. April 14, 2015. Accessed January 13, 2017. https://www.linkedin.com/pulse/warrior-leader-

ship-passion-vs-interest-kerry-brown.

48. *"Are you going to go to your sweetie and say, 'Marry me! You're interesting": Why You Will Fail To Have A Great Career.* Performed by Larry Smith. TED-Ed. August 15, 2013. Accessed January 13, 2017. https://www.youtube.com/watch?v=gDkJ-ry6aSk&list=FLTGRfJFM8zXE7_rluTTLF2Q&index=1, min. 6:00.

49. *Instead, passion is a deep, emotional conviction that drives us to achieve our vision of something meaningful:* Covey, Stephen R. *The 8th Habit: From Effectiveness To Greatness.* New York: Free Press, 2005, p. 66.

50. *When asked the question, "What is the most important thing for a sixteen-year-old to do this summer vacation?":* Ferriss, Tim. "Peter Diamandis on Disrupting the Education System, The Evolution of Healthcare, and Building a Billion-Dollar Business." *Four-Hour Work Week* (audio blog), July 17, 2015. Accessed January 13, 2017. http://fourhourworkweek. com/2015/07/17/peter-diamandis-on-the-education-system/, min. 22:00.

51. *Legendary basketball coach John Wooden explained:* Wooden, John, and Steve Jamison. *Wooden: A Lifetime of Observations and Reflections on and Off the Court.* New York: McGraw-Hill, 1997, pp. 175-77.

52. *Studies show that students who are driven by the internal satisfaction of the activity itself actually outperform students who are not:* Pink, Daniel H. *Drive: the surprising truth about what motivates us.* New York, NY: Riverhead Books, 2009, p. 75.

53. *Not to mention, these same students have higher self-esteem, better relationships, and greater general well-being:* Pink, Daniel H. *Drive: the surprising truth about what motivates us.* New York, NY: Riverhead Books, 2009, p. 78.

54. *Simon Sinek quote:* DeMers, Jayson. "Feeling Stressed? Relax With Aristotle, Churchill, and More." Inc.com. October 16, 2014. Accessed January 24, 2017. http://www.inc.com/jayson-demers/40-quotes-to-help-you-relieve-stress.html.

55. *In just a few decades, human performance has grown faster and farther than at any other point in history:* Kotler, Steven. *The rise of superman: decoding the science of ultimate human performance.* Boston: New Harvest, Houghton Mifflin Harcourt, 2014, p. ii.

56. *For example, in 1960, a surfer rode a 25-foot wave (two-in-a-half stories high), considered the biggest wave ever caught at the time:* Kotler, Steven. *The rise of superman: decoding the science of ultimate human performance.* Boston: New Harvest, Houghton Mifflin Harcourt, 2014, p. 24.

57. *Then, in 1996, a surfer caught a 35-foot wave (three-in-a-half stories high):* Kotler, Steven. *The rise of superman: decoding the science of ultimate human performance.* Boston: New Harvest, Houghton Mifflin Harcourt, 2014, p. 24.

58. *Fast forward to 2000. Laird Hamilton, an extreme surfer, found himself on the shores of Teahupoo:* Kotler, Steven. *The rise of superman: decoding the science of ultimate human performance.* Boston: New Harvest, Houghton Mifflin Harcourt, 2014, p. 25.

59. *In 2011, Garrett McNamara caught a spectacular 78-foot goliath:* "Guinness World Records can confirm that Garrett McNamara has entered the record books for surfing the largest ever wave." Guinness World Records. May 09, 2012. Accessed January 24, 2017. http://www.guinnessworldrecords.com/news/2012/5/video-78-foot-wave-surfed-by-garrett-mcnamara-confirmed-as-largest-ever-ridden-41598/.

60. *"Flow" is the state in which people are so involved in an activity that nothing else seems to matter:* Csikszentmihalyi, Mihaly. *Flow: The Psychology Of Optimal Experience.* New York: Harper & Row, 1990, p. 4.

61. *To identify flow activities, experts have developed the "flow test":* Flow, The Secret to Happiness. Performed by Mihaly Csikszentmihalyi. TED. October 24, 2008. Accessed January 13, 2017. https://www.youtube.com/watch?v=fX-IeFJCqsPs, min. 14:00.

62. *William Shakespeare quote:* "To Thine Own Self Be True - Meaning, Origin, and Usage." Literary Devices. May 29, 2015. Accessed January 13, 2017. http://literarydevices.net/to-thine-own-self-be-true/.

63. *It was 1976 and Steve Wozniak quit his 9-5 job:* "Steve Wozniak." Biography.com. April 14, 2015. Accessed January 13, 2017. http://www.biography.com/people/steve-wozniak-9537334#founding-apple-computer.

64. *Apple's success is no secret, going on to become the most valuable public company in the world:* Wieczner, Jen. "Apple Takes Back Title of World's Most Valuable Company." Fortune.com. February 03, 2016. Accessed January 13, 2017. http://fortune.com/2016/02/03/apple-facebook-amazon-google/.

65. *Steve Wozniak quote:* "50 Entrepreneurs share priceless advice." December 07, 2014. YouTube. Accessed January 13, 2017. https://www.youtube.com/watch?v=QoqohmccTSc, min. 4:00.

66. *Miguel de Cervantes quote:* A-Z Quotes. Accessed January 24, 2017. http://www.azquotes.com/quote/609617.

67. *Although Emotional Intelligence 2.0 comes as a book, it can be used for much more than reading:* Bradberry, Travis, and Jean Greaves. *Emotional Intelligence 2.0.* San Diego, CA: TalentSmart, 2009.

68. *Ev Williams self-test:* 50 Entrepreneurs share priceless advice. December 07, 2014. YouTube. Accessed January 13, 2017. https://www.youtube.com/watch?v=QoqohmccTSc, min. 7:00.

69. *Seth Godin self-test:* Godin, Seth. *Linchpin: are you indispensable?* New York: Portfolio, 2010, p. 98.

70. *Elon Musk self-test:* "11 Of The Best Success Lessons from Billionaires - Who Wants to Be a Billionaire?" YouTube. January 26, 2016. Accessed January 13, 2017. https://www.youtube.com/watch?v=nI2bQj_80pI, min. 6:40.

71. *The "Enjoyment" Exercise:* Robinson, Ken, and Lou Aronica. *Finding Your Element: How To Discover Your Talents And Passions And Transform Your Life.* New York: Viking, 2013, p. 79.

72. *Johann Wolfgang von Goethe quotes:* All the Best Quotes. March 04, 2016. Accessed January 13, 2017. https://chatna.com/johann-wolfgang-von-goethe-quotes/.

73. *To construct an absurdly cheap trip use the following tools:* Ferriss, Timothy. *The 4-Hour Work Week: Escape 9-5, Live Anywhere, And Join The New Rich.* Chatham: Vermilion, 2011, pp. 263-64.

74. *Today, there are more than 700 crowdfunding sites:* Diamandis, Peter H., and Steven Kotler. *Bold: how to go big, achieve success, and impact the world.* New York: Simon & Schuster, 2015.

75. *AmeriCorps facts:* "AmeriCorps." Corporation for National and Community Service. Accessed January 13, 2017.

http://www.nationalservice.gov/programs/americorps.

76. *Peace Corps facts:* "Peace Corps." *About.* Accessed January 13, 2017. https://www.peacecorps.gov/about/; see also *Fact Sheet.* PDF. Peace Corps, December 17, 2015. http://files.peacecorps.gov/multimedia/pdf/about/pc_facts.pdf.

77. *Service Year facts:* "Service Year Alliance." The Aspen Institute. Accessed January 13, 2017. https://www.aspeninstitute.org/programs/service-year-alliance/.

78. *Benjamin Franklin quotes:* BrainyQuote. Accessed January 24, 2017. https://www.brainyquote.com/quotes/quotes/b/benjaminfr132478.html.

79. *"The Law of Magnetism":* Maxwell, John C. *The 21 irrefutable laws of leadership: follow them and people will follow you.* Nashville, Tenn.: Thomas Nelson.

80. *Herbert Bayard Swope quotes:* BrainyQuote. Accessed January 13, 2017. https://www.brainyquote.com/quotes/quotes/h/herbertbay164646.html.

81. *Envy says, "I must be like you to be happy":* Warren, Richard. *The purpose-driven life: what on earth am I here for?* Grand Rapids, MI: Zondervan, 2002, p. 329.

82. *Yale student's email to professor quote:* Deresiewicz, William. *Excellent Sheep: The Miseducation of The American Elite and The Way to a Meaningful Life.* New York, NY: Free Press, 2014, p. 11.

83. *Professor and motivational expert Edward Deci found:* Deci, Edward L., and Richard Flaste. *Why we do what we do: understanding self-motivation.* New York: Penguins Books, 1996, pp. 26-29.

84. *Honore Gabriel Riqueti quote:* A-Z Quotes. Accessed January 13, 2017. http://www.azquotes.com/quote/587737.

85. *One of the most moving things I've ever heard on this point is from Steve Jobs:* "How to live before you die." Steve Jobs: How to live before you die | TED Talk | TED.com. Accessed January 13, 2017. https://www.ted.com/talks/steve_jobs_how_to_live_before_you_die, min. 8:00.

Strengths HACK

86. *Carl Jung quote:* Buckingham, Marcus, and Donald O. Clifton. *Now, Discover Your Strengths.* New York: Free Press, 2001, p. 124.

87. *In fact, according to a Gallup survey, 77 percent of individuals chose to focus on the F in algebra:* Marcus Buckingham and Donald O. Clifton, *Now, Discover Your Strengths* (New York: Free Press, 2001), 123.

88. *Gallup found that whether it asked Americans, British, French:* Marcus Buckingham and Donald O. Clifton, Now, Discover Your Strengths (New York: Free Press, 2001), 121.

89. *W. C. Fields quote:* BrainyQuote. Accessed January 24, 2017. https://www.brainyquote.com/quotes/quotes/w/wcfields108002.html.

90. *Simon, American Idol, quote:* "American Idol -10 Worst Auditions These Guys Suck." December 22, 2012. YouTube. Accessed January 16, 2017. https://www.youtube.com/watch?v=bwdHe1-Us90, min. 9:00.

91. *Gary Vaynerchuk quote:* "Gary Vaynerchuk's Top 10 Rules For Success." February 04, 2016. YouTube. Accessed January 16, 2017. https://www.youtube.com/watch?v=vqJrJ8cxEQ, min. 1:30.

92. *Steve Harvey quote:* "Steve Harvey - You Have to Jump." YouTube. January 13, 2016. Accessed January 16, 2017. https://www.youtube.com/watch?v=kILVFRlUtT8, min. 1:15.

93. *Usain Bolt set a world record in the 100-meter dash in 9.58 seconds:* Bethea, Charles. "How Fast Would Usain Bolt Run the Mile?" The New Yorker. August 01, 2016. Accessed January 16, 2017. http://www.newyorker.com/news/sporting-scene/how-fast-would-usain-bolt-run-the-mile.

94. *Bolt can sprint up to 23 miles per hour:* Zaldivar, Gabe. "Breaking Down Usain Bolt's Amazing Speed." Bleacher Report. August 3, 2012. Accessed January 16, 2017. http://bleacherreport.com/articles/1283999-usain-bolt-mph-breaking-down-amazing-speed-from-olympic-sprinter.

95. *Simms responded, "Usain has never run a mile.":* Bethea, Charles. "How Fast Would Usain Bolt Run the Mile?" The New Yorker. August 01, 2016. Accessed January 16, 2017. http://www.newyorker.com/news/sporting-scene/how-fast-would-usain-bolt-run-the-mile.

96. *Peter Drucker quote:* Burns, Daniel. "Managing Oneself -- A Classic Read from Peter Drucker." LinkedIn. July 14, 2014. Accessed January 16, 2017. https://www.linkedin.com/pulse/20140714022442-19165072-managing-oneself-a-classic-read-from-peter-drucker.

97. *Thomas Watson quote:* Upbin, Bruce. "Jay-Z, Buffett and Forbes on Success and Giving Back." Forbes. September 23, 2010. Accessed January 25, 2017. http://www.forbes.com/forbes/2010/1011/rich-list-10-omaha-warren-buffett-jay-z-steve-forbes-summit-interview.html.

98. *"It's not either-or," said Stanford psychologist Carol Dweck:* Dweck, Carol S. *Mindset: the new psychology of success.* New York: Random House, 2006, p. 5.

99. *Instead, modern research makes clear that our strengths are a function of our efforts and our natural abilities:* Buckingham, Marcus, and Donald O. Clifton. *Now, Discover Your Strengths.* New York: Free Press, 2001, p. 29.

100. *Our natural abilities affect our success more than the work we invest:* Buckingham, Marcus, and Donald O. Clifton. *Now, Discover Your Strengths.* New York: Free Press, 2001, p. 30.

101. *a DiSC assessment provides a personalized report into how you respond to conflict, what motivates you, what causes you stress, and how you solve problems:* "DiSC Profile - What is DiSC®? The DiSC personality test explained." DiSCProfile.com. Accessed January 16, 2017. https://www.discprofile.com/what-is-disc/overview/.

102. *The purpose of these resources is to determine your strengths, not to anoint you with one:* Buckingham, Marcus, and Donald O. Clifton. *Now, Discover Your Strengths.* New York: Free Press, 2001, p. 78.

103. *reoccurring patterns of thought, feeling, and behavior—known as "themes":* Marcus Buckingham and Donald O. Clifton, *Now, Discover Your Strengths* (New York: Free Press, 2001), pp. 78-79.

104. *Jack Welch quote:* Sherman, Erik. "Think You Know Your Competitive Advantage? Maybe Not." Inc.com. September 11, 2014. Accessed January 16, 2017. http://www.inc.com/erik-sherman/think-you-know-your-competitive-advantage-maybe-not.html.

105. *Blimey Cow statistics:* YouTube. Accessed January 16, 2017. https://www.youtube.com/blimeycow/about.

106. *Tom Rath quote:* Tom Rath (personal website). March 04, 2015. Accessed January 16, 2017. http://www.tomrath.org/can-anything-want-myth/.

107. *As a high school sophomore, Jordan failed to make the varsity team:* Gordon, Jeff. "A Biography of Michael Jordan as a High School Basketball Player." LIVESTRONG.COM. December 20, 2015. Accessed January 16, 2017. http://www.livestrong.com/article/450727-a-biography-of-michael-jordan-as-a-high-school-basketball-player/.

108. *Jordan would later recall, "It was embarrassing not making the team. They posted the roster and it was there for a long, long time without my name on it:* Gordon, Jeff. "A Biography of Michael Jordan as a High School Basketball Player." LIVESTRONG.COM. December 20, 2015. Accessed January 16, 2017. http://www.livestrong.com/article/450727-a-biography-of-michael-jordan-as-a-high-school-basketball-player/.

109. *Michael Jordan quote:* Gordon, Jeff. "A Biography of Michael Jordan as a High School Basketball Player." LIVESTRONG.COM. December 20, 2015. Accessed January 16, 2017. http://www.livestrong.com/article/450727-a-biography-of-michael-jordan-as-a-high-school-basketball-player/.

110. *during his sophomore year, Jordan played junior varsity and produced several 40-point games:* Gordon, Jeff. "A Biography of Michael Jordan as a High School Basketball Player." LIVESTRONG.COM. December 20, 2015. Accessed January 16, 2017. http://www.livestrong.com/article/450727-a-biography-of-michael-jordan-as-a-high-school-basketball-player/.

111. *Jordan scored 35 points during his first varsity game:* Gordon, Jeff. "A Biography of Michael Jordan as a High School Basketball Player." LIVESTRONG.COM. December 20, 2015. Accessed January 16, 2017. http://www.livestrong.com/article/450727-a-biography-of-michael-jordan-as-a-high-school-basketball-player/.

112. *Jordan was so good as a high school basketball player:* Gordon, Jeff. "A Biography of Michael Jordan as a High School Basketball Player." LIVESTRONG.COM. December 20, 2015. Accessed January 16, 2017. http://www.livestrong.com/article/450727-a-biography-of-michael-jordan-as-a-high-school-basketball-player/.

Purpose HACK

113. *Arno Penzias quote:* "30 Day Question Challenge – Day 29 – The Jugular Question." Archer's Paradox. April 16, 2014. Accessed January 16, 2017. https://wp.vcu.edu/enochhale/2014/04/16/30-day-question-challenge-day-29-the-jugular-question/.

114. *Whenever Toyota encountered a problem, Toyota workers asked "Why?" five times:* Ohno, Taiichi. "Ask 'Why' Five Times About Every Matter." Toyota Motor Corporation Global Website. March 2006. Accessed January 16, 2017. http://www.toyota-global.com/company/toyota_traditions/quality/mar_apr_2006.html.

115. *"Go directly to the source and keep asking, 'Why?' Taiichi Ohno, former Toyota vice president explained:* Ohno, Taiichi. "Ask 'Why' Five Times About Every Matter." Toyota Motor Corporation Global Website. March 2006. Accessed January 16, 2017. http://www.toyota-global.com/company/toyota_traditions/quality/mar_apr_2006.html.

116. *Consider this example from Toyota:* Ohno, Taiichi. "Ask 'Why' Five Times About Every Matter." Toyota Motor Corporation Global Website. March 2006. Accessed January 16, 2017. http://www.toyota-global.com/company/toyota_traditions/quality/mar_apr_2006.html.

117. *Robert F. Kennedy quote:* Goodreads. Accessed January 16, 2017. http://www.goodreads.com/quotes/145501-the-purpose-of-life-is-to-contribute-in-some-way.

118. *One of the best descriptions I've encountered is from leadership guru Tony Robbins:* Schnall, Marianne. "An In-depth Interview With Life Coach Tony Robbins." The Huffington Post. April 29, 2012. Accessed January 16, 2017. http://www.huffingtonpost.com/marianne-schnall/life-purpose_b_1461184.html.

119. *William Damon has highlighted two common characteristics of purpose:* Damon, William. *The path to purpose: how young people find their calling in life.* New York: Free Press, 2009, p. 33.

120. *In short, purpose is an "ultimate concern":* Damon, William. *The path to purpose: how young people find their calling in life.* New York: Free Press, 2009, p. 34.

121. *"The only way for us to have long-term happiness," explains Tony Robbins, "is to live by our highest ideals, to consistently act in accordance with what we believe our life is truly about":* Robbins, Anthony. *Awaken the giant within: how to take immediate control of your mental, emotional, physical & financial destiny.* New York, NY: Summit Books, 1991, p. 357.

122. *Mark Zuckerberg quote:* Goldman, David. "Mark Zuckerberg only works 50 to 60 hours a week." CNNMoney. April 15, 2015. Accessed January 16, 2017. http://money.cnn.com/2015/04/15/technology/mark-zuckerberg-hours/.

123. *Warren Buffett vowed to donate more than 99 percent of his wealth to philanthropy:* Buffett, Warren. "My philanthropic pledge." Warren Buffett pledge as part of the $600 billion challenge - Jun. 16, 2010. June 16, 2010. Accessed January 16, 2017. http://archive.fortune.com/2010/06/15/news/newsmakers/Warren_Buffett_Pledge_Letter.fortune/index.htm.

124. *Harvard professor Clayton Christenson explains why he encourages all of his students to put purpose before school:* Christensen, Clayton M., James Allworth, and Karen Dillon. *How Will You Measure Your Life?* New York, NY: Harper Business, 2012, p. 204.

125. *Mission Statements of Top Performers:* Vozza, Stephanie. "Personal Mission Statements Of 5 Famous CEOs (And Why You Should Write One Too)." Fast Company. February 25, 2014. Accessed January 16, 2017. https://www.fastcompany.com/3026791/dialed/personal-mission-statements-of-5-famous-ceos-and-why-you-should-write-one-too.

HACKiversity

126. *Ralph Waldo Emerson quote:* Goodreads. Accessed January 16, 2017. http://www.goodreads.com/quotes/144907-the-world-makes-way-for-the-man-who-knows-where.

127. *Daniel Pink explanation of rewards in Industrial Age:* Pink, Daniel H. *Drive: the surprising truth about what motivates us.* New York, NY: Riverhead Books, 2009, p. 42.

128. *Scientists found that when people use this Industrial model in the 21st century workplace:* Pink, Daniel H. *Drive: the surprising truth about what motivates us.* New York, NY: Riverhead Books, 2009, p. 37.

129. *today only 38 percent of workers believe that they are part of something meaningful:* A Purpose-Driven Work Force." Inc. com. July 07, 2016. http://www.inc.com/aflac/a-purpose-driven-workforce.html.

130. *As Pink describes, the solution is built on findings that scientists and researchers have time and time again made:* Pink, Daniel H. *Drive: the surprising truth about what motivates us.* New York, NY: Riverhead Books, 2009, p. 145.

131. *Researchers have found that people motivated by purpose have:* Pink, Daniel H. *Drive: the surprising truth about what motivates us.* New York, NY: Riverhead Books, 2009, p. 89.

132. *Alice in Wonderland quote:* Alice-in-Wonderland.net. Accessed January 16, 2017. http://www.alice-in-wonderland. net/resources/chapters-script/alice-in-wonderland-quotes/.

133. *only one in five people between the ages of twelve and twenty-six have a clear vision of where they want to go:* Damon, William. *The path to purpose: how young people find their calling in life.* New York: Free Press, 2009, p. 8.

134. *That's why researchers have called them "drifting dreamers":* Arum, Richard, and Josipa Roksa. *Academically Adrift: Limited Learning On College Campuses.* Chicago: University of Chicago Press, 2011, p. 3.

135. *Dan Hardy quote:* Hardy, Darren. *The Compound Effect: Multiplying Your Success, One Simple Step at a Time.* New York, NY: Vanguard Press, 2010, p. 62.

136. *Erin Brockovich description:* "Erin Brockovich." Erin Brockovich. IMDB. Accessed January 16, 2017. http://www. imdb.com/title/tt0195685/.

137. *purpose emerges largely from our unique experiences, opportunities, and challenges:* Christensen, Clayton M., James Allworth, and Karen Dillon. *How Will You Measure Your Life?* New York, NY: Harper Business, 2012, p. 197.

138. *Jim Collins quote:* "Good to Great Quotes by James C. Collins." GoodReads. Accessed January 16, 2017. https:// www.goodreads.com/work/quotes/1094028-good-to-great-why-some-companies-make-the-leap-and-others-don-t.

139. *research has indicated that students frequently found their Why? by asking, "What is something important in the world that can be corrected or improved?":* Damon, William. *The path to purpose: how young people find their calling in life.* New York: Free Press, 2009, p. 96.

140. *Johann Wolfgang von Goethe quote:* Goodreads. Accessed January 16, 2017. http://www.goodreads.com/ quotes/6774650-tell-me-with-whom-you-consort-and-i-will-tell.

141. *In one study, members of different groups felt like their spark originated with them:* Coyle, Daniel. *The Talent Code: Greatness Isn't Born: It's Grown, Here's How.* New York: Bantam Books, 2009, p. 108.

142. *But in reality, the study found that each group member had actually identified and formed a link with similar people before ever committing to becoming what they had become:* Coyle, Daniel. *The Talent Code: Greatness Isn't Born: It's Grown, Here's How.* New York: Bantam Books, 2009, p. 108.

143. *That's why our peers shape our ambitions more directly and with greater impact than any other source:* Arum, Richard, and Josipa Roksa. *Academically Adrift: Limited Learning On College Campuses.* Chicago: University of Chicago Press, 2011, p. 67.

144. *Stephen Covey quote:* "Books - 7 Habits of Highly Effective People." Stephen R. Covey. Accessed January 16, 2017. https://www.stephencovey.com/7habits/7habits-habit2.php.

145. *I got the idea from a Stanford commencement speech given by Steve Jobs:* "Steve Jobs' 2005 Stanford Commencement Address." YouTube. March 07, 2008. Accessed January 16, 2017. https://www.youtube.com/watch?v=UF8uR6Z-6KLc, min. 9:00.

Lifestyle HACK

146. *Tim Ferriss quote:* Ferriss, Tim. "Should You Start a 'Startup' or Build a Cash-Flow Business?" *Should You Start a 'Startup' or Build a Cash-Flow Business?* (audio blog), October 9, 2015. Accessed January 16, 2017. http://fourhourworkweek.com/2015/10/09/should-you-start-a-startup-or-build-a-cash-flow-business, min. 6:00.

147. *Barry Schwartz quote:* Schwartz, Barry. *The paradox of choice: why more is less.* New York: Ecco, 2004, p. 141.

148. *Henry Thoreau quote:* BrainyQuote. Accessed January 16, 2017. https://www.brainyquote.com/quotes/quotes/h/ henrydavid379350.html.

149. *But more than that, you also need to feel like you can provide for your basic needs in the future:* Rath, Tom, and James K. Harter. *Wellbeing: the five essential elements.* New York: Gallup Press, 2010, pp. 61-63.

150. *research shows that well being does not generally increase for household incomes in excess of $75,000:* Kahneman, Daniel. *Thinking, fast and slow.* New York: Farrar, Straus and Giroux, 2013, p. 397.

151. *research has found that the richest Americans, those earning more than $10 million annually:* Robinson, Ken, and Lou Aronica. *Finding Your Element: How To Discover Your Talents And Passions And Transform Your Life.* New York: Viking, 2013, p. 127.

152. *despite being the richest country in the world, the United States barely squeaks inside the top-20 happiest countries in the world:* Boyer, Lauren. "These Are the 20 Happiest Countries in the World." U.S. News. April 24, 2015. Accessed January 16, 2017. http://www.usnews.com/news/articles/2015/04/24/world-happiness-report-ranks-worlds-happiest-countries-of-2015.

153. *Ultimately, being poor makes people miserable, but being rich does not, on average, improve a person's well being:* Kahneman,

Daniel. *Thinking, fast and slow*. New York: Farrar, Straus and Giroux, 2013, p. 396.

154. *Potts explains why Charlie's belief is just plain wrong:* "How to Earn Your Freedom…And A Motorcycle Ride Across China?" Tim Ferriss (audio blog), April 10, 2015. Accessed January 16, 2017. http://fourhourworkweek. com/2015/04/10/how-to-earn-your-freedom, min. 8.

155. *Dead Poets Society quote:* IMDb. Accessed January 16, 2017. http://www.imdb.com/title/tt0097165/quotes.

156. *To help you in your own lifestyle design process, ask yourself these three questions:* Chamorro, Marcella. "Follow Your Ideal: 3 Steps to Creating Your Dream Life." Possibility of Change. December 31, 2016. Accessed January 16, 2017. http:// www.thechangeblog.com/dream-life/.

Execution Cornerstone

157. *Archimedes quote:* BrainyQuote. Accessed January 16, 2017. https://www.brainyquote.com/quotes/quotes/a/archimedes101761.html.

158. *let's look at the timeline of the richest people in world history:* Gladwell, Malcolm. *Outliers: the story of success.* New York: Back Bay Books, Little, Brown and Company, 2008, pgs. 58-61.

159. *Discussion of leverage and The 80/20 Principle:* Koch, Richard. *The 80/20 principle: the secret of achieving more with less.* New York: Currency, 1998, pgs. 4, 7-9.

160. *Kate Zabriskie quote:* Walter, Ekaterina. "40 Eye-Opening Customer Service Quotes." Forbes. March 4, 2014. Accessed January 16, 2017. http://www.forbes.com/sites/ekaterinawalter/2014/03/04/40-eye-opening-customer-service-quotes/#425696074dc8.

161. *Al Ries and Jack Troute quote:* Ries, Al, and Jack Trout. *The 22 immutable laws of marketing: violate them at your own risk.* New York, NY: HarperBusiness, 1993, p. 15.

162. *American Indian Proverb quote:* Kerpen, Dave. "13 Quotes to Inspire Your Inner Storyteller." Inc.com. January 17, 2014. Accessed January 16, 2017. http://www.inc.com/dave-kerpen/you-need-to-become-a-better-storyteller-heres-some-inspiration.html.

163. *Tom Peters quote:* Peters, Tom. "The Brand Called You." Fast Company. August 31, 1997. Accessed January 16, 2017. http://www.fastcompany.com/28905/brand-called-you.

164. *Studies have found that we are increasingly living in a world where people will have their own brands and sell their skills to those who need them:* The future of work: A journey to 2022. PDF. PricewaterhouseCoopers. http://www.pwc.com/gx/en/managing-tomorrows-people/future-of-work/assets/pdf/future-of-work-report-v23.pdf, p. 21.

165. *"If you're going to be a brand, you've got to become relentlessly focused on what you do that adds value, that you're proud of, and most important, that you can shamelessly take credit for," said Tom Peters:* Peters, Tom. "The Brand Called You." Fast Company. August 31, 1997. Accessed January 16, 2017. http://www.fastcompany.com/28905/brand-called-you.

166. *"Shaping a career narrative is like building your own brand, and you need to be able to sell it to potential employers," says college expert Jeffrey Selingo:* Selingo, Jeffrey. *There Is Life After College.* HarperCollins, 2016, p. 241.

167. *"Not only must you be an ideal candidate—you have to show them that you are":* Selingo, Jeffrey. *There Is Life After College.* HarperCollins, 2016, p. 241.

168. *Napoleon Hill quote:* BrainyQuote. Accessed January 24, 2017. https://www.brainyquote.com/quotes/quotes/n/napoleonhi152848.html.

169. *Seth Godin quote:* Godin, Seth. *The Dip: A Little Book That Teaches You When To Quit (And When To Stick).* New York: Portfolio, 2007, pp. 11-12.

170. *Reid Hoffman quote:* Hoffman, Reid, and Ben Casnocha. *The start-up of you.* New York: Crown Business, 2012, p. 29.

171. *Alain de Botton quote:* "Quotes About Work Life Balance." GoodReads. Accessed February 06, 2017. http://www.goodreads.com/quotes/tag/work-life-balance.

172. *This is a simple metaphor called the "Celery Test":* Sinek, Simon. *Start with why: how great leaders inspire everyone to take action.* New York: Portfolio, 2009.

173. *Jay Z quote:* Goodreads. Accessed January 16, 2017. http://www.goodreads.com/quotes/333793-i-m-not-a-businessman-i-m-a-business-man.

174. *There are more than 40 million students and recent college graduates on LinkedIn:* "About LinkedIn." LinkedIn Newsroom. Accessed January 16, 2017. https://press.linkedin.com/about-linkedin.

175. *Over 98 percent of recruiters use LinkedIn and over 94 percent of them have successfully hired:* Arruda, William. "Why College Freshmen Need To Major In LinkedIn." Forbes. August 26, 2014. Accessed January 16, 2017. http://www.forbes.com/sites/williamarruda/2014/08/26/why-college-freshmen-need-to-major-in-linkedin/2/#76e31ab12d5e.

176. *For the most ambitious students wanting to expand their personal brand:* Gillett, Rachel. "The Best (And Worst) Times To Post On Social Media (Infographic)." Fast Company. September 25, 2014. Accessed January 16, 2017. http://www.fastcompany.com/3036184/how-to-be-a-success-at-everything/the-best-and-worst-times-to-post-on-social-media-infograph.

177. *To get a 48 percent bump in retweets, use a picture:* Gillett, Rachel. "The Best (And Worst) Times To Post On Social Media (Infographic)." Fast Company. September 25, 2014. Accessed January 16, 2017. http://www.fastcompany.com/3036184/how-to-be-a-success-at-everything/the-best-and-worst-times-to-post-on-social-media-infograph.

178. *To maximize exposure, post Mondays – Thursdays at 1pm – 3pm:* Gillett, Rachel. "The Best (And Worst) Times To Post On Social Media (Infographic)." Fast Company. September 25, 2014. Accessed January 16, 2017. http://www.fastcompany.com/3036184/how-to-be-a-success-at-everything/the-best-and-worst-times-to-post-on-social-media-infograph.

179. *LegalZoom offers legal services for a fraction of the price and has serviced over 3.6 million customers:* "About Us." Legalzoom.com. May 27, 2016. Accessed January 16, 2017. https://www.legalzoom.com/about-us.

180. *as every thirty days projects are viewed nearly 65 million times:* "Take Creative Control." About Behance. Accessed January 16, 2017. https://www.behance.net/about.

College Selection HACK

181. *Peter Cappelli quote:* Cappelli, Peter. *Will college pay off?: a guide to the most important financial decision you will ever make.* New York: PublicAffairs, 2015.

182. *William Deresiewicz quote:* Deresiewicz, William. *Excellent sheep: the miseducation of the American elite and the way to a meaningful life.* New York, NY: Free Press, 2014, p. 7.

183. *Only about 1 percent of graduates come from Elite Colleges:* Thompson, Derek. "The Thing Employers Look For When Hiring Recent Graduates." The Atlantic. August 19, 2014. http://www.theatlantic.com/business/archive/2014/08/the-thing-employers-look-for-when-hiring-recent-graduates/378693/.

184. *Jase Robertson quote:* "Hunting Sayings and Quotes." Wise Old Sayings. http://www.wiseoldsayings.com/hunting-quotes/.

185. *Since 1972, the returns of attending an Elite College have been rising:* Hoxby, Caroline M. "The Return to Attending a More Selective College: 1960 to the Present." Department of Economics, Harvard University, 1998. http://www.nyu.edu/classes/jepsen/hoxby-selective.pdf.

186. *Elite College graduates earn several million dollars more than the General College graduate:* Selingo, Jeffrey J. *College (un)bound: the future of higher education and what it means for students.* Boston: Houghton Mifflin Harcourt, 2013.

187. *Jeff Hunter quote:* Wagner, Tony, and Ted Dintersmith. *Most likely to succeed: preparing our kids for the innovation era.* New York, NY: Scribner, 2015.

188. *Warren Buffett quote:* "Warren Buffett Quotes." BrainyQuote. Accessed January 28, 2017. https://www.brainyquote.com/quotes/quotes/w/warrenbuff398945.html.

189. *Mark Zuckerberg...scored a perfect SAT exam. Eduardo Saverin...made $300,000 in a summer making bets on heating oil:* The Social Network: The Social Network. Directed by David Fincher. Performed by Jesse Eisenberg, Andrew Garfield, Justin Timberlake. United States: Sony Pictures Home Entertainment, 2011. Film.

190. *90 percent of all students scored in their high school classes top ten percent:* Deresiewicz, William. *Excellent sheep: the miseducation of the American elite and the way to a meaningful life.* New York, NY: Free Press, 2014. Page 196.

191. *graduates from Elite Colleges carry less than 40 percent in student loans...and more than half of all Ivy League students graduate without any type of student loan:* Powell, Farran. "Map: 25 Universities Where Grads Have the Least Debt." U.S. News & World Report. January 12, 2017. Accessed January 28, 2017. http://www.usnews.com/education/best-colleges/paying-for-college/articles/2017-01-12/map-25-universities-where-grads-have-the-least-debt.

192. *graduates from Elite Colleges make millions of dollars more than graduates from General Colleges:* Selingo, Jeffrey J. *College (un)bound: the future of higher education and what it means for students.* Boston: Houghton Mifflin Harcourt, 2013.

193. *Abraham Lincoln quote:* "Abraham Lincoln Quotes." BrainyQuote. Accessed January 28, 2017. https://www.brainyquote.com/quotes/quotes/a/abrahamlin109275.html.

194. *General Colleges, where 99 percent of students go:* Thompson, Derek. "The Thing Employers Look For When Hiring Recent Graduates." The Atlantic. August 19, 2014. http://www.theatlantic.com/business/archive/2014/08/the-thing-employers-look-for-when-hiring-recent-graduates/378693/.

195. *employers have repeatedly said that college reputation is one of the least important considerations in making the hiring decision:* The Chronicle of Higher Education. The Role of Higher Education in Career Development: Employer Perceptions. Washington, DC: 2012. http://www.chronicle.com/items/biz/pdf/Employers%20Survey.pdf.

196. *Studies show that there are 1.5 million professors in the U.S.:* "Fast Facts." National Center for Education Statistics. Accessed February 07, 2017. https://nces.ed.gov/fastfacts/display.asp?id=61.

197. *"Accredited Colleges" are colleges overseen by a third-party organization charged with assessing the colleges' quality:* Selingo, Jeffrey J. *College (un)bound: the future of higher education and what it means for students.* Boston: Houghton Mifflin Harcourt, 2013, p. 132.

198. *One-third of all employers will consider a school they've never heard of as a negative factor in the hiring decision:* The Chronicle of Higher Education. The Role of Higher Education in Career Development: Employer Perceptions. Washington, DC: 2012. http://www.chronicle.com/items/biz/pdf/Employers%20Survey.pdf.

199. *Employers have even said that online degrees are "undesirable":* The Chronicle of Higher Education. The Role of Higher Education in Career Development: Employer Perceptions. Washington, DC: 2012. http://www.chronicle.com/items/biz/pdf/Employers%20Survey.pdf.

200. *when comparing against all other college types (e.g. private, public, regional), employers rated online colleges as the least desirable:* The Chronicle of Higher Education. The Role of Higher Education in Career Development: Employer Perceptions. Washington, DC: 2012. http://www.chronicle.com/items/biz/pdf/Employers%20Survey.pdf.

201. *Zig Ziglar quote:* "Do Things That Count." Ziglar Inc. July 14, 2016. Accessed January 28, 2017. https://www.ziglar.com/quotes/positive-kids/.

202. *a whopping one in four colleges offers a negative return on investment:* Lavelle, Louis. "College ROI: What We Found." Bloomberg. Bloomberg, 9 Apr. 2012. Web; see also Cappelli, Peter. *Will college pay off?: a guide to the most important financial decision you will ever make.* New York: PublicAffairs, 2015, p. 102.

203. *Oliver Goldsmith quote:* "Quotes About Questions." *Goodreads.* Goodreads, 2016. Web.

204. *For the Class of 2016, the average graduate had $37,172 in student loans:* "A Look at the Shocking Student Loan Debt Statistics for 2016." *Student Loan Hero. Student Loan Hero,* 2016. Web.

205. *Today, nearly $417 billion in student loans—roughly 39 percent of all student loans ($68 billion)—are in deferment:* Miller, Ben. "A Closer Look at Student Loan Deferment and Forbearance." *New America.* New America, 26 Feb. 2015.

Web.

206. *At more than 1,000 colleges, at least half of students defaulted or failed to pay down debt within seven years of gradating:* Fuller, Andrea. "Student Debt Payback Far Worse Than Believed." *The Wall Street Journal*. January 18, 2017. Accessed January 28, 2017. http://www.wsj.com/articles/student-debt-payback-far-worse-than-believed-1484777880.

207. *studies have found that the most successful college graduates have below $10,000 in student loans: What parents and students should know about navigating school to prepare for the jobs of tomorrow.* New York, NY: William Morrow, an imprint of HarperCollins Publishers, 2016. Print.

208. *Nearly 20 percent of all college graduates with student loans eventually give up on their preferred line of work:* Bowyer, Chris. "Overqualified and Underemployed: The Job Market Waiting for Graduates." *Forbes*. Forbes, 15 Aug. 2014. Web.

209. *Studies show that graduates are not earning more over the course of a career, by having graduated from a more expensive college:* Dale, Stacy Berg, and Alan B. Krueger. "Estimating the Payoff to Attending a More Selective College: An Application of Selection on Observables and Unobservable." *The Quarterly Journal of Economics* (Nov 2002): 1524. The Atlantic. Web.

210. *employers love major public colleges the most:* The Chronicle of Higher Education. The Role of Higher Education in Career Development: Employer Perceptions. Washington, DC: 2012. http://www.chronicle.com/items/biz/pdf/Employers%20Survey.pdf.

211. *graduates "are often the most prepared and well-rounded academically, and companies have found they fit well into their corporate cultures":* Evans, Teri. "Penn State Tops Recruiter Rankings." *The Wall Street Journal*. The Wall Street Journal, 13 Sept. 2010. Web.

212. *Among the top five employer-preferred colleges are:* Evans, Teri. "Penn State Tops Recruiter Rankings." *The Wall Street Journal*. The Wall Street Journal, 13 Sept. 2010. Web.

213. *employers actually have a bias against students from liberal arts schools:* Selingo, Jeffrey J. *There is life after college: what parents and students should know about navigating school to prepare for the jobs of tomorrow.* New York, NY: William Morrow, an imprint of HarperCollins Publishers, 2016. Print. Page 36.

214. *employers actually prefer liberal arts college least when compared to major public colleges, private colleges, and regional colleges:* The Chronicle of Higher Education. The Role of Higher Education in Career Development: Employer Perceptions. Washington, DC: 2012. http://www.chronicle.com/items/biz/pdf/Employers%20Survey.pdf.

215. *Davidson, a top 10 liberal arts schools in the country:* "How Does Davidson College Rank Among America's Best Colleges?" Davidson College - Profile, Rankings and Data | Davidson College | US News Best Colleges. Accessed January 28, 2017. http://colleges.usnews.rankingsandreviews.com/best-colleges/davidson-college-2918.

216. *Ron Popeil quote:* "Ron Popeil." Biography.com. August 05, 2016. Accessed January 28, 2017. http://www.biography.com/people/ron-popeil-177863.

217. *Mark Cuban quote:* Cuban, Mark. "Advice to High Schoolers and College Grads." South by Southwest. Austin, TX. 12 July 2014.

218. *Virginia residents, simply by going to a Virginia community college, are virtually guaranteed admission into the University of Virginia:* "University of Virginia." *U.S. News & World Report*. U.S. News & World Report, 2016. Web. 30 Dec. 2016.

219. *Wizard of Oz quote: Wizard of Oz.* Dir. Victor Fleming. Perf. Judy Garland, Frank Morgan, Ray Bolger. United States: MGM/UA, 1939. Film.

220. *employers love local schools:* "Frequently Asked Questions: 2017 Best Colleges Rankings." U.S. News & World Report. September 12, 2016. Accessed December 30, 2016. http://www.usnews.com/education/best-colleges/articles/rankings-faq.

221. *regional schools have an almost identical affect on the hiring process:* The Chronicle of Higher Education. The Role of Higher Education in Career Development: Employer Perceptions. Washington, DC: 2012. http://www.chronicle.com/items/biz/pdf/Employers%20Survey.pdf.

222. *the 20,000 to 40,000 interns who flock to D.C. each summer:* "Generation i." The Economist. September 06, 2014. Accessed January 28, 2017. http://www.economist.com/news/international/21615612-temporary-unregulated-and-often-unpaid-internship-has-become-route.

223. *Maya Angelou quote:* "Maya Angelou Quotes." BrainyQuote. Accessed February 07, 2017. https://www.brainyquote.com/quotes/quotes/m/mayaangelo101310.html?src=t_change.

224. *Studies show that more than one-third of students transfer colleges, and of those who do, 45 percent decide to transfer more than once:* Leavitt, Elly. "Study: More than 33% of undergrads transfer college at least once." USA Today. July 15, 2015. Accessed January 28, 2017. http://college.usatoday.com/2015/07/15/one-third-of-undergrads-transfer-colleges/.

225. *Shane Hunt quote:* "What's Really Important About The College You Attend: Part I." Score at the Top. March 30, 2016. http://www.scoreatthetop.com/blog-1/what-s-really-important-about-the-college-you-attend-part-i.

226. *a better predictor of lifetime success is not the name of your alma mater but rather the best school that rejected your college application:* Redburn, Tom. "Economic View; Ivy League or Also-Ran? Does it Matter?" *The New York Times*, April 21, 2002. http://www.nytimes.com/2002/04/21/business/economic-view-ivy-league-or-also-ran-does-it-matter.html.

Megatrends HACK

227. *Erica Schmidt quote:* Schmidt, Eric, Jonathan Rosenberg, and Alan Eagle. *How Google works.* London: John Murray, 2014, p. 134.

228. *Ray Kurzweil, a futurist and chief engineer at Google:* PricewaterhouseCoopers. *The future of work: A journey to 2022.* New York City, NY, 2014. http://www.pwc.com/gx/en/managing-tomorrows-people/future-of-work/assets/pdf/future-of-work-report-v23.pdf.

229. *Shia LaBeouf quote:* "Productivity Quotes." BrainyQuote. Accessed December 31, 2016. http://www.brainyquote.

com/quotes/keywords/productivity.html.

230. *Throughout the 1990s Mark Cuban:* Feloni, Richard. "Mark Cuban shares the most important lesson he learned in his 20s." *Business Insider,* March 25, 2015. http://www.businessinsider.com/mark-cubans-most-important-lesson-from-his-20s-2015-3.

231. *Cuban sold Broadcast.com to Yahoo! for $5.7 billion:* "Yahoo! buying BCST.com." CNN Money, April 1, 1999. http://money.cnn.com/1999/04/01/deals/yahoo/.

232. *50 percent of college students today are underemployed:* Parcells, Nathan. "What 50,000 Students Have to Say About College Recruiting." Looksharp. July 1, 2015. https://www.looksharp.com/blog/what-50000-students-have-to-say-about-college-recruiting.

233. *Napoleon quote:* "Quotes About Luck." Goodreads. 2016. http://www.goodreads.com/quotes/tag/luck.

234. *Jeff Bezos quote:* "2012 re:Invent Day 2: Fireside Chat with Jeff Bezos & Werner Vogels." *Amazon Web Services* (video blog), November 29, 2012. https://www.youtube.com/watch?v=O4MtQGRIIuA.

235. *Anthony Carnevale quote:* Selingo, Jeffrey J. *College (un)bound: the future of higher education and what it means for students.* Boston: Houghton Mifflin Harcourt, 2013, p. 8.

236. *Eric Schmidt quote:* Schmidt, Eric, Jonathan Rosenberg, and Alan Eagle. *How Google works.* London: John Murray, 2014, p. 134.

237. *Peter Diamandis quote:* Diamandis, Peter H., and Steven Kotler. *Bold: how to go big, achieve success, and impact the world.* New York: Simon & Schuster Paperbacks, 2016.

238. *Morano is the oldest person in the world:* Walker, Peter. "The oldest person in the world says 'being single' is the reason she's still alive." The Independent. November 29, 2016. Accessed March 04, 2017. http://www.independent.co.uk/news/people/oldest-person-alive-italian-emma-morano-celebrate-117th-birthday-a7444951.html.

239. *there is a one in three chance of people in developed countries living to 100:* Gilbert, Dan. "The behavior behind living longer." I Might Live How Long? May 3, 2013. http://www.bringyourchallenges.com/i-might-live-how-long.

240. *the number of people over the age of 60 will more than double between 2010 and 2030:* Ernst & Young Global Limited. *Megatrends 2015.* 2015. http://www.ey.com/Publication/vwLUAssets/ey-megatrends-report-2015/$FILE/ey-megatrends-report-2015.pdf.

241. *By 2030, the world's population of people over age 65 will be one billion:* Future State 2030: The global megatrends shaping governments. PDF. KPMG International, February 2014. https://assets.kpmg.com/content/dam/kpmg/pdf/2014/02/future-state-2030-v3.pdf.

242. *Within the next minute, the global population will increase by 145 people:* Anticipating problems, finding solutions Global Annual Review 2014. PDF. PricewaterhouseCoopers, 2014. https://www.pwc.com/gx/en/global-annual-review/assets/pwc-global-annual-review-2014.pdf.

243. *By 2030, more than 1.2 billion additional people will have been born:* Ernst & Young Global Limited. *Megatrends 2015.* 2015. http://www.ey.com/Publication/vwLUAssets/ey-megatrends-report-2015/$FILE/ey-megatrends-report-2015.pdf.

244. *"We are going to be short 100,000 doctors...":* Ferriss, Tim. "Tony Robbins and Peter Diamandis (XPRIZE) on the Magic of Thinking BIG." *The Tim Ferriss Show* (video blog), October 7, 2014. http://fourhourworkweek.com/2014/10/07/global-learning-xprize/.

245. *the World Health Organization estimates a global shortage of 4.3 million healthcare workers:* World Health Organization. *Health Workers.* 2006. http://www.who.int/whr/2006/06_chap1_en.pdf.

246. *Synthetic Genomics, a leading medical research company:* Fikes, Bradley J. "Modified pigs to grow humanized lungs." *The San Diego Union-Tribune,* May 6, 2014. http://www.sandiegouniontribune.com/business/biotech/sdut-synthetic-genomics-pigs-lung-therapeutics-2014may06-story.html.

247. *the market for synthetic biology is projected to be $38.7 billion:* Singh, Ranjan . "Synthetic Biology Market by Products (DNA Synthesis, Oligonucleotide Synthesis, Synthetic DNA, Synthetic Genes, Synthetic Cells, XNA) and Technology (Genome Engineering, Microfluidics Technologies, DNA synthesis & sequencing technologies) - Global Opportunity Analysis and Industry Forecast, 2013 - 2020." *Allied Market Research Report,* May 2014. Accessed December 30, 2016. https://www.alliedmarketresearch.com/synthetic-biology-market.

248. *Human Longevity is a company paving the way:* Regalado, Antonio. "J. Craig Venter to Offer DNA Data to Consumers." *MIT Technology Review,* September 22, 2015. https://www.technologyreview.com/s/541516/j-craig-venter-to-sell-dna-data-to-consumers/.

249. *In 2015, President Obama announced a $215 million investment:* Burton, Thomas M., Jonathan D. Rockoff, and Ron Winslow. "Obama Announces $215 Million Precision-Medicine Genetic Plan." *The Wall Street Journal,* January 30, 2015. http://www.wsj.com/articles/obama-to-lay-out-215-million-precision-medicine-plan-1422615602.

250. *a "decade-long, billion-dollar initiative" to develop "precision medicines,":* Ross, Alec. *The industries of the future.* New York, NY: Simon & Schuster, 2016, p. 52.

251. *Americans over the age of 50 will control approximately $7.1 trillion in wealth:* Oxford Economics. *The Longevity Economy.* Oxford, UK: 2013. http://www.aarp.org/content/dam/aarp/home-and-family/personal-technology/2013-10/Longevity-Economy-Generating-New-Growth-AARP.pdf.

252. *According to Cisco:* Nedeltchev, Plamen. "The Internet of Everything is the New Economy." Cisco. September 29, 2015. http://www.cisco.com/c/en/us/solutions/collateral/enterprise/cisco-on-cisco/Cisco_IT_Trends_IoE_Is_the_New_Economy.html.

253. *took the telephone 76 years to reach half the U.S. population. The smartphone did it in less than a decade:* "Global megatrends: Technological breakthroughs by Bob Moritz." YouTube. October 06, 2014. Accessed January 30, 2017. https://www.

youtube.com/watch?v=XioGwX_iNfg.

254. *experts believe that such forces will add $2.2 trillion in opportunities by 2025 alone:* Manyika, James, Sree Ramaswamy, Somesh Khanna, Hugo Sarrazin, Gary Pinkus, Guru Sethupathy, and Andrew Yaffe. "Digital America: A tale of the haves and have-mores." McKinsey Global Institute. December 2015. http://www.mckinsey.com/industries/hightech/our-insights/digital-america-a-tale-of-the-haves-and-have-mores.

255. *Smartphones and tablets are everywhere:* Kotler, Steven, and Peter H. Diamandis. *Bold: how to go big, achieve success, and impact the world.* New York: Simon & Schuster, 2015, p. 42.

256. *To demonstrate just how widespread sensors have become:* Kotler, Steven, and Peter H. Diamandis. *Bold: how to go big, achieve success, and impact the world.* New York: Simon & Schuster, 2015, pgs. 42-43.

257. *ShotSpotter's urban gunfire detection system: ShotSpotter.* ShotSpotter Flex. Newark, CA, 2014. Accessed December 30, 2016. http://www.shotspotter.com/system/content-uploads/ShotSpotter-Flex-Datasheet.pdf.

258. *By 2023, Stanford predicts, the sensor industry will represent a multi-trillion dollar industry: T Sensors Summit for Trillion Sensor Roadmap.* Proceedings of T Sensors Summit, Stanford University. October 25, 2013. http://tsensorssummit.org/Resources/Why%20TSensors%20Roadmap.pdf. Pages 5 & 6.

259. *By 2020, the number of Internet-connected devices is expected to explode to 50 billion:* Clark, Don. "'Internet of Things' in Reach." *The Wall Street Journal,* January 5, 2014. http://www.wsj.com/articles/SB100014240527023036406045792965808929732264.

260. *the size of the entire U.S. economy is $1.5 trillion:* "The Internet of Everything is the New Economy." Cisco. September 29, 2015. http://www.cisco.com/c/en/us/solutions/collateral/enterprise/cisco-on-cisco/Cisco_IT_Trends_IoE_Is_the_New_Economy.html.

261. *John Chambers forecast:* Ross, Alec. *The Industries of the Future.* New York, NY: Simon & Schuster, 2016.

262. *Amazon set the drone world ablaze when it announced its entry into the drone market:* Gross, Doug. "Amazon's drone delivery: How would it work?" CNN, December 2, 2013. http://www.cnn.com/2013/12/02/tech/innovation/amazon-drones-questions/.

263. *in 2015, Walmart applied for permission to begin testing drones:* O'Brien, Mike. "Walmart Enters Drone Airspace with Amazon, Google." *Multichannel Merchant,* October 27, 2015. http://multichannelmerchant.com/news/walmart-enters-drone-airspace-amazon-google-27102015/.

264. *Google X hopes to launch its drone service by 2017:* King, Hope. "Google X hopes to launch drone deliveries by 2017." *CNN Tech,* November 2, 2015. http://money.cnn.com/2015/11/02/technology/google-drone-delivery/.

265. *such as writing poetry:* Schwartz, Oscar. "Can a computer write poetry?" TED, May 2015. http://www.ted.com/talks/oscar_schwartz_can_a_computer_write_poetry.

266. *creating trendy furniture:* Blazehlts. "Robot With A Chainsaw Carving Stools." *YouTube,* January 23, 2013. https://www.youtube.com/watch?v=vgvlP87Ju5Y&feature=youtu.be.

267. *serving as a human receptionist:* NBC News. "The Frighteningly Human Robot." *YouTube,* April 21, 2015. https://youtu.be/JhUSRs_HgWI.

268. *"Robotics is the fastest growing industry in the world":* "Robotics, Artificial Intelligence (AI) and Automation." Littler. 2017. https://www.littler.com/robotics-artificial-intelligence-ai-and-automation.

269. *accessed financial information of more than 40 million customers:* Riley, Charles, and Jose Pagliery. "Target will pay hack victims $10 million." *CNN,* March 19, 2015. http://money.cnn.com/2015/03/19/technology/security/target-data-hack-settlement/.

270. *The damage to Target was enormous, losing billions of dollars:* Ross, Alec. *The Industries of the Future.* New York, NY: Simon & Schuster, 2016.

271. *James Clapper, director of national intelligence, warned Congress:* Ross, Alec. *The Industries of the Future.* New York, NY: Simon & Schuster, 2016.

272. *by 2020, the cyber security market will reach nearly $170 billion:* Morgan, Steve. "Cybersecurity Market Reaches $75 Billion In 2015; Expected To Reach $170 Billion By 2020." *Forbes,* December 20, 2015. http://www.forbes.com/sites/stevemorgan/2015/12/20/cybersecurity%E2%80%8B-%E2%80%8Bmarket-reaches-75-billion-in-2015%E2%80%8B%E2%80%8B-%E2%80%8Bexpected-to-reach-170-billion-by-2020/.

273. *Alex Ross quote recommending cybersecurity to college student:* Ross, Alec. *The Industries of the Future.* New York, NY: Simon & Schuster, 2016.

274. *every two days we create as much information as we did from the dawn of civilization up until 2003:* Siegler, MG. "Eric Schmidt: Every 2 Days We Create As Much Information As We Did Up To 2003." *TechCrunch,* August 4, 2010. http://techcrunch.com/2010/08/04/schmidt-data/.

275. *An Oxford study found:* Oxford Economics. *Digital Megatrends 2015.* Oxford, 2015. https://www.oxfordeconomics.com/Media/Default/Thought%20Leadership/advisory-panels/Digital_Megatrends.pdf.

276. *"Big Data," sophisticated predictive analytics, is solving the problem:* "The Internet of Everything is the New Economy." Cisco. September 29, 2015. http://www.cisco.com/c/en/us/solutions/collateral/enterprise/cisco-on-cisco/Cisco_IT_Trends_IoE_Is_the_New_Economy.html.

277. *basketball teams use Big Data:* Maheswaran, Rajiv. "The math behind basketball's wildest moves." TED, March 2015. http://www.ted.com/talks/rajiv_maheswaran_the_math_behind_basketball_s_wildest_moves#t-226800.

278. *Michael Dell, founder of Dell computers, said:* Bort, Julie. "Tech billionaire Michael Dell says 'big data' is the next trillion-dollar tech industry." *Business Insider,* December 10, 2015. http://www.businessinsider.com/dell-big-data-is-next-trillion-dollars-2015-12.

279. *over 75 percent of the global population has access to a mobile phone:* KPMG. *Future State 2030.* February 2014. https://

home.kpmg.com/xx/en/home/insights/2015/03/future-state-2030.html.

280. *In some countries, more people have access to a mobile phone:* KPMG. *Future State 2030.* February 2014. https://home. kpmg.com/xx/en/home/insights/2015/03/future-state-2030.html.

281. *showcased poor Chinese farmers using their limited money to buy cell phones:* McArdle, Megan. "What's Better: Cell Phones or Indoor Toilets?" *The Daily Beast,* January 3, 2013. http://www.thedailybeast.com/articles/2013/01/03/what-s-better-cell-phones-or-indoor-toilets.html.

282. *consumer spending via mobile is projected to increase from $204 billion in 2014 to $626 billion in 2018:* Ernst & Young Global Limited. *Megatrends 2015.* 2015. http://www.ey.com/Publication/vwLUAssets/ey-megatrends-report-2015/$FILE/ey-megatrends-report-2015.pdf.

283. *according to an Oxford study, respondents believe that mobile technologies are more likely to help business than "any other technology":* Oxford Economics. *Digital Megatrends 2015.* Oxford, 2015. https://www.oxfordeconomics.com/Media/Default/Thought%20Leadership/advisory-panels/Digital_Megatrends.pdf.

284. *companies are increasingly turning toward "cloud computing":* Oxford Economics. *Digital Megatrends 2015.* Oxford, 2015. https://www.oxfordeconomics.com/Media/Default/Thought%20Leadership/advisory-panels/Digital_Megatrends.pdf.

285. *"I can be a small business that can suddenly serve 20 or 30 million customers":* Oxford Economics. *Digital Megatrends 2015.* Oxford, 2015. https://www.oxfordeconomics.com/Media/Default/Thought%20Leadership/advisory-panels/Digital_Megatrends.pdf.

286. *Experts predict that the public cloud services industry will balloon to a $141 billion:* Columbus, Louis. "Roundup Of Cloud Computing Forecasts And Market Estimates, 2016" *Forbes,* March 13, 2016. http://www.forbes.com/sites/louiscolumbus/2016/03/13/roundup-of-cloud-computing-forecasts-and-market-estimates-2016/#5ca1a6e974b0.

287. *Parts of the suits were 3-D printed:* Global News. "3D Printing: Make anything you want." *YouTube,* January 28, 2013. https://www.youtube.com/watch?v=G0EJmBoLq-g.

288. *a process where physical items are built layer-by-layer:* Serlenga, Pierluigi and François Montaville. "Five Questions to Shape a Winning 3-D Printing Strategy." *Bain & Company,* July 20, 2015. http://www.bain.com/publications/articles/five-questions-to-shape-a-winning-3d-printing-strategy.aspx.

289. *computers are now able to add layers of plastic, metal, glass, leather, and even chocolate:* Diamandis, Peter H. "3D Printing & Technology Convergence." *Diamandis.com*(web log). Accessed December 30, 2016. http://www.diamandis.com/blog/3d-printing-technology-convergence.

290. *3-D printers have begun printing [organs]:* Global News. "3D Printing: Make anything you want." *YouTube,* January 28, 2013. https://www.youtube.com/watch?v=G0EJmBoLq-g.

291. *3-D printing has been called a "Wal-mart in your home":* Global News. "3D Printing: Make anything you want." *YouTube,* January 28, 2013. https://www.youtube.com/watch?v=G0EJmBoLq-g.

292. *a global manufacturing market valued at over $10 trillion:* Serlenga, Pierluigi and François Montaville. "Five Questions to Shape a Winning 3-D Printing Strategy." *Bain & Company,* July 20, 2015. http://www.bain.com/publications/articles/five-questions-to-shape-a-winning-3d-printing-strategy.aspx.

293. *By 2018, 3-D printing is projected to pass $12 billion:* Serlenga, Pierluigi and François Montaville. "Five Questions to Shape a Winning 3-D Printing Strategy." *Bain & Company,* July 20, 2015. http://www.bain.com/publications/articles/five-questions-to-shape-a-winning-3d-printing-strategy.aspx.

294. *By 2022, more people will be middle class than poor:* KPMG. *Future State 2030.* February 2014. https://home.kpmg.com/xx/en/home/insights/2015/03/future-state-2030.html.

295. *an expansion in global wealth created 920,000 new millionaires:* "Global HNWI Population and Wealth Expanded, but at a Slower Pace." Capgemini. 2016. https://www.worldwealthreport.com/Global-HNWI-Population-and-Wealth-Expanded.

296. *over 200 countries have vowed to reduce net carbon emissions to zero by 2050:* Vaughan, Adam. "Zero carbon emissions target to be enshrined in UK law." *The Guardian,* March 14, 2016. https://www.theguardian.com/environment/2016/mar/14/zero-carbon-emissions-target-enshrined-uk-law.

297. *By 2030, the share of electricity generated by renewable energy could reach 50 percent:* Ernst & Young Global Limited. *Megatrends 2015.* 2015. http://www.ey.com/Publication/vwLUAssets/ey-megatrends-report-2015/$FILE/ey-megatrends-report-2015.pdf.

298. *experts say that annual spending on energy efficiencies needs to increase from $130 billion today to $550 billion by 2035:* Ernst & Young Global Limited. *Megatrends 2015.* 2015. http://www.ey.com/Publication/vwLUAssets/ey-megatrends-report-2015/$FILE/ey-megatrends-report-2015.pdf.

299. *Experts predict that there must be a 50 percent increase in food supply:* KPMG. *Future State 2030.* February 2014. https://home.kpmg.com/xx/en/home/insights/2015/03/future-state-2030.html.

300. *in the last century, water usage has been growing at more than twice the rate of population growth:* Ernst & Young Global Limited. *Megatrends 2015.* 2015. http://www.ey.com/Publication/vwLUAssets/ey-megatrends-report-2015/$FILE/ey-megatrends-report-2015.pdf.

301. *By 2030, nearly half the global population may face water scarcity:* Ernst & Young Global Limited. *Megatrends 2015.* 2015. http://www.ey.com/Publication/vwLUAssets/ey-megatrends-report-2015/$FILE/ey-megatrends-report-2015.pdf.

302. *"If nothing is done, we will run out of water faster than we will run out of oil":* KPMG. *Future State 2030.* February 2014. https://home.kpmg.com/xx/en/home/insights/2015/03/future-state-2030.html.

303. *the Earth's average surface temperature rose at a rate six times higher than from 1890 to 1950:* Ernst & Young Global

Limited. *Megatrends 2015.* 2015. http://www.ey.com/Publication/vwLUAssets/ey-megatrends-report-2015/$FILE/ey-megatrends-report-2015.pdf.

304. *The United Nations forecasts that the number of people in large cities:* Ernst & Young Global Limited. *Megatrends 2015.* 2015. http://www.ey.com/Publication/vwLUAssets/ey-megatrends-report-2015/$FILE/ey-megatrends-report-2015.pdf.

305. *countries are racing to rebuild their dated infrastructure:* Ernst & Young Global Limited. *Megatrends 2015.* 2015. http://www.ey.com/Publication/vwLUAssets/ey-megatrends-report-2015/$FILE/ey-megatrends-report-2015.pdf.

306. *The cost of adapting to climate change for developing countries:* Ernst & Young Global Limited. *Megatrends 2015.* 2015. http://www.ey.com/Publication/vwLUAssets/ey-megatrends-report-2015/$FILE/ey-megatrends-report-2015.pdf.

307. *By 2030, almost two-thirds of the world's population will reside in cities:* KPMG. *Future State 2030.* February 2014. https://home.kpmg.com/xx/en/home/insights/2015/03/future-state-2030.html.

308. *trillions of dollars of opportunities are now moving into some of the world's biggest urban areas:* KPMG. *Future State 2030.* February 2014. https://home.kpmg.com/xx/en/home/insights/2015/03/future-state-2030.html.

309. *the median (think average) house in San Francisco cost $1.2 million:* Vekshin, Alison. "San Francisco's Housing Mania May Finally Have Reached Its Limit." *Bloomberg,* June 17, 2016. http://www.bloomberg.com/news/articles/2016-06-17/san-francisco-s-housing-mania-may-finally-have-reached-its-limit.

310. *getting prices back down in San Francisco to rates found in 1995:* Abbey-Lambertz, Katie. "There's A Profoundly Simple Explanation For San Francisco's Housing Crisis." *Huffington Post,* June 2, 2016. http://www.huffingtonpost.com/entry/san-francisco-housing-crisis_us_5750a95ee4b0eb20fa0d682e.

311. *Cities all across the nation, including Minneapolis:* Schaust, Sam. "Twin Cities Housing Market Caught In A Supply Crunch As Demand Intensifies." *Twin Cities Business,* April 14, 2016. http://tcbmag.com/News/Recent-News/2016/April/Twin-Cities-Housing-Market-Caught-In-A-Supply-Crun.

312. *Washington D.C.:* Zippel, Claire. "DC's housing affordability crisis, in 7 charts." *Greater Greater Washington,* April 30, 2015. http://greatergreaterwashington.org/post/26526/dcs-housing-affordability-crisis-in-7-charts/.

313. *and New York:* Senison, Heather. "NYC real estate sales: Increased demand in 'affordable market'." *AMNewYork,* April 20, 2016. http://www.amny.com/real-estate/nyc-real-estate-sales-increased-demand-in-affordable-market-1.11713086.

314. *nearly four times the size of China's economy:* Riley, Charles and Ivory Sherman. "World's Largest Economies." *CNN,* January 18, 2017. http://money.cnn.com/news/economy/world_economies_gdp/

315. *must be invested by 2030:* KPMG. *Future State 2030.* February 2014. https://home.kpmg.com/xx/en/home/insights/2015/03/future-state-2030.html.

316. *one billion people—nearly one in seven people in the world—live inside city slums:* KPMG. *Future State 2030.* February 2014. https://home.kpmg.com/xx/en/home/insights/2015/03/future-state-2030.html.

317. *That number could spike to two billion by 2030 if not addressed quickly:* KPMG. Future State 2030. February 2014. https://home.kpmg.com/xx/en/home/insights/2015/03/future-state-2030.html.

318. *billions of people, including the 60 percent of people are currently offline:* "Offline and falling behind: Barriers to Internet adoption." McKinsey&Company. September 2014. http://www.mckinsey.com/industries/high-tech/our-insights/offline-and-falling-behind-barriers-to-internet-adoption.

319. *Google [providing Internet coverage]:* "Project Loon." Google. 2017. http://www.google.com/loon.

320. *Facebook [providing Internet coverage]:* Zuckerberg, Mark. *Facebook* (web log), March 27, 2014. https://www.facebook.com/zuck/posts/10101322049893211.

321. *Elon Musk [providing Internet coverage]:* Thompson, Cadie. "Elon Musk is one step closer to making his ambitious $10 billion satellite internet business a reality." *Business Insider,* June 10, 2015. http://www.businessinsider.com/space-x-is-trying-to-serve-up-internet-service-from-space-2015-6.

322. *Richard Branson [providing Internet coverage]:* "OneWeb." OneWeb. 2017. http://oneweb.world.

323. *Paul Jacobs [providing Internet coverage]:* "OneWeb." OneWeb. 2017. http://oneweb.world.

324. *By 2030, half of the world will have Internet connection:* KPMG. *Future State 2030.* February 2014. https://home.kpmg.com/xx/en/home/insights/2015/03/future-state-2030.html.

325. *Facebook has 1.59 billion users:* Constine, Josh. "Facebook Climbs To 1.59 Billion Users And Crushes Q4 Estimates With $5.8B Revenue." *TechCrunch,* January 27, 2016. https://techcrunch.com/2016/01/27/facebook-earnings-q4-2015.

326. *In 2012, roughly 12 people built Instagram in less than two years:* Cutler, Kim-Mai. "From 0 To $1 Billion In Two Years: Instagram's Rose-Tinted Ride To Glory." *TechCrunch,* April 9, 2012. https://techcrunch.com/2012/04/09/instagram-story-facebook-acquisition/.

327. *Groupon, seen as a relatively new company, has over 50 million subscribers:* Oxford Economics. *Digital Megatrends 2015.* Oxford, 2015. https://www.oxfordeconomics.com/Media/Default/Thought%20Leadership/advisory-panels/Digital_Megatrends.pdf.

328. *there are more likes per day on Facebook than Google searches:* Frier, Sarah. "Inside Facebook's Decision to Blow Up the Like Button." *Bloomberg,* January 27, 2016. http://www.bloomberg.com/features/2016-facebook-reactions-chris-cox.

329. *estimated that by 2020 more than 40 percent of the American workforce would be made up of "contingent workers":* Intuit. *Intuit 2020 Report.* October 2010. http://http-download.intuit.com/http.intuit/CMO/intuit/futureofsmallbusiness/intuit_2020_report.pdf.

330. *In 2025, crowdfunding will rise to $96 billion:* Ernst & Young Global Limited. *Megatrends 2015.* 2015. http://www.ey.com/Publication/vwLUAssets/ey-megatrends-report-2015/$FILE/ey-megatrends-report-2015.pdf.

331. *reports indicate that China must add $1 trillion to $2.2 trillion per year:* Riley, Charles and Ivory Sherman. "World's Largest Economies." *CNN*, January 18, 2017. http://money.cnn.com/news/economy/world_economies_gdp/.

332. *"Companies will need a new playbook to capture the coming wave of growth":* Kuo, Youchi, Jeff Walters, Hongbing Gao, Angela Wang, Veronique Yang, Jian Yang, Zhibin Lyu, and Hongjie Wan. "The New China Playbook." BCG Perspectives. December 21, 2015. https://www.bcgperspectives.com/content/articles/globalization-growth-new-china-playbook-young-affluent-e-savvy-consumers/?linkId=19756240#chapter1.

Major Selection HACK

333. *John Maynard Keyes quote:* "John Maynard Keynes Quotes." BrainyQuote. Accessed January 30, 2017. https://www.brainyquote.com/quotes/quotes/j/johnmaynar385471.html.

334. *Michigan State offers more than 150 majors:* "Learn it all." Office of Admissions | Michigan State University. Accessed January 30, 2017. https://admissions.msu.edu/academics/majors.asp.

335. *Central Florida offers over 200 majors:* "UCF Academics - College Undergraduate Degree & Graduate Degree - Florida Majors and Academic Programs." University of Central Florida. Accessed January 30, 2017. http://www.ucf.edu/academics/.

336. *Arizona State offers a whopping 350 majors:* "Academic programs." ASU Students Site. Accessed January 30, 2017. https://students.asu.edu/programs.

337. *80 percent of all students change their major at least once, and the average college student changes his or her major at least three times over a college career:* Ramos, Yuritzy. "College students tend to change majors when they find the one they really love." Borderzine. March 15, 2013. Accessed January 30, 2017. http://borderzine.com/2013/03/college-students-tend-to-change-majors-when-they-find-the-one-they-really-love/.

338. *nearly a third of all college graduates wish they had picked a different major:* "The Rising Cost of Not Going to College." Pew Research Center's Social & Demographic Trends Project. February 11, 2014. Accessed January 30, 2017. http://www.pewsocialtrends.org/2014/02/11/the-rising-cost-of-not-going-to-college/.

339. *Yogi Berra quote:* "Mistakes Quotes." BrainyQuote. Accessed December 30, 2016. https://www.brainyquote.com/quotes/keywords/mistakes_2.html.

340. *List of Ultra Specific Majors:* Cappelli, Peter. *Will college pay off?: a guide to the most important financial decision you will ever make.* New York: PublicAffairs, 2015.

341. *graduates with degrees no longer needed in the marketplace often face higher unemployment rates than graduates with a high school diploma only:* Georgetown University, McCourt School of Public Policy. *The Economic Value of College Majors.* Washington, DC, 2015. https://cew.georgetown.edu/wp-content/uploads/HardTimes2015-Report.pdf.

342. *For liberal arts majors, the idea is about breadth, not depth:* Bogart, Julie. "What Are Liberal Arts?" My College Guide. Accessed January 27, 2017. http://mycollegeguide.org/articles/liberal-arts-degrees/what-are-liberal-arts.

343. *graduates who majored in the arts and psychology have nearly twice the unemployment rate compared to those who majored in other more technical fields:* Carnevale, Anthony P., and Ban Cheah. *From Hard Times to Better Times: College Majors, Unemployment, and Earnings.* Georgetown University, Center on Education and the Workforce. Washington, DC, 2015. https://cew.georgetown.edu/wp-content/uploads/HardTimes2015-Report.pdf.

344. *the average liberal arts graduate entering the workforce makes a meager $29,000:* Georgetown University, McCourt School of Public Policy. *The Economic Value of College Majors.* Washington, DC, 2015. https://cew.georgetown.edu/wp-content/uploads/Economic-Value-of-College-Majors-Full-Report-v2.compressed.pdf.

345. *only $1,000 more than the average high school graduate:* Gao, George. "14 striking findings from 2014." *Pew Research Center,* December 22, 2014. http://www.pewresearch.org/fact-tank/2014/12/22/14-striking-findings-from-2014/.

346. *some liberal arts majors, such as fine arts, start off earning as little as $20,000:* "Median Initial Earnings Growth in Early Career, by Major." The Hamilton Project. November 20, 2014. http://www.hamiltonproject.org/charts/median_initial_earnings_growth_in_early_career_by_major.

347. *Meet Stewart Butterfield:* Anders, George. "That 'Useless' Liberal Arts Degree Has Become Tech's Hottest Ticket." *Forbes,* August 17, 2015. http://www.forbes.com/sites/georgeanders/2015/07/29/liberal-arts-degree-tech/#7a2272b-b5a75.

348. *Description of Slack Technologies:* "#44 Slack." *Forbes,* January 2015. http://www.forbes.com/companies/slack/.

349. *Stewart Butterfield quote:* Anders, George. "That 'Useless' Liberal Arts Degree Has Become Tech's Hottest Ticket." *Forbes,* August 17, 2015. http://www.forbes.com/sites/georgeanders/2015/07/29/liberal-arts-degree-tech/#7a2272b-b5a75.

350. *"You generally don't see people majoring in Philosophy, or other soft majors, except in top schools":* Rampell, Catherine. "Do Elite Colleges Produce the Best-Paid Graduates." *The New York Times,* July 20, 2009. http://economix.blogs.nytimes.com/2009/07/20/do-elite-colleges-produce-the-best-paid-graduates.

351. *A Washington Post report explains:* Ferdman, Roberto. "Where to go to college if you want the highest starting salary." *The Washington Post,* September 11, 2014. https://www.washingtonpost.com/news/wonk/wp/2014/09/11/where-to-go-to-college-if-you-want-the-highest-starting-salary/.

352. *a college graduate with at least three years of experience will out-earn students freshly out of graduate school:* Otani, Akane. "When a Graduate Degree Just Isn't Worth it." *Bloomberg,* February 20, 2015. http://www.bloomberg.com/news/articles/2015-02-20/when-a-graduate-degree-just-isn-t-worth-it.

353. *recently 59 percent of graduates with a masters degree remained underemployed:* Bowyer, Chris. "Overqualified and Underemployed: The Job Market Waiting for Graduates." *Forbes,* August 15, 2014. http://www.forbes.com/sites/thecollegebubble/2014/08/15/overqualified-and-underemployed-the-job-market-waiting-for-graduates/.

354. *Quote from fortune cookie:* Ferriss, Timothy. *The 4-hour work week: escape 9-5, live anywhere, and join the new rich.*

Chatham: Vermilion, 2011.

355. *Tim Kreider quote:* Kreider, Tim. *We learn nothing: essays and cartoons.* New York: Free Press, 2012.

356. *Jeff Selingo quote:* Selingo, Jeff. "Want to Graduate With Job-Ready Skills? Don't Major in Business." *LinkedIn,* February 19, 2015. https://www.linkedin.com/pulse/want-graduate-job-ready-skills-dont-major-business-jeff-selingo.

357. *Skills Ready majors are majors that either fix things or fix people:* Selingo, Jeffrey. *There Is Life After College.* HarperCollins, 2016.

358. *"Today…STEM competencies are needed in a broader reach of occupations, and their use is growing outside of STEM":* Carnevale, Anthony, Nicole Smith, and Michelle Melton. *STEM.* Executive Summary. Center on Education and the Workforce, Georgetown University. Washington, DC, 2014. https://cew.georgetown.edu/wp-content/uploads/2014/11/stem-execsum.pdf.

359. *STEM graduates are expected to receive the highest starting salaries among all college graduates:* "STEM Grads Projected to Earn Class Of 2016's Highest Average Starting Salaries." National Association of Colleges and Employers. January 27, 2016. http://www.naceweb.org/s01272016/stem-grads-earn-highest-starting-salaries.aspx.

360. *Engineering graduates will earn double that of Education graduates:* Close, Kerry. "STEM Majors Will Earn Highest Starting Salaries This Year." *Time,* January 21, 2016. http://time.com/money/4189471/stem-graduates-highest-starting-salaries/.

361. *the average salary for a STEM graduate has continued to climb for years:* "STEM Grads Projected to Earn Class Of 2016's Highest Average Starting Salaries." National Association of Colleges and Employers. January 27, 2016. http://www.naceweb.org/s01272016/stem-grads-earn-highest-starting-salaries.aspx.

362. *projected to have the largest wage growth over the course of a career:* Georgetown University, McCourt School of Public Policy. *The Economic Value of College Majors.* Washington, DC, 2015. https://cew.georgetown.edu/wp-content/uploads/Economic-Value-of-College-Majors-Full-Report-v2.compressed.pdf.

363. *STEM graduates continue to find themselves as one of the most in-demand majors among employers:* "Employers Are Looking to Hire Class of 2016 Business and Technical Grads." National Association of Colleges and Employers. December 9, 2015. http://www.naceweb.org/s12092015/employers-want-business-technical-graduates.aspx?terms=top%20degrees%20in%20demand.

364. *reports the Wall Street Journal concerning a study that analyzed thousands of graduates:* Eide, Eric R. and Michael J. Hilmer. "Do Elite Colleges Lead to Higher Salaries? Only for Some Professions." *The Wall Street Journal,* January 31, 2016. http://www.wsj.com/articles/do-elite-colleges-lead-to-higher-salaries-only-for-some-professions-1454295674.

365. *Studies show STEM majors study 50 percent more than business majors:* Arum, Richard, and Josipa Roksa. *Academically adrift: limited learning on college campuses.* Chicago: University of Chicago Press, 2011.

366. *Business majors are the most in-demand major out of any other major, even topping STEM majors:* "Employers Are Looking to Hire Class of 2016 Business and Technical Grads." National Association of Colleges and Employers. December 9, 2015. http://www.naceweb.org/s12092015/employers-want-business-technical-graduates.aspx?terms=top%20degrees%20in%20demand.

367. *Business majors are one of two non-STEM majors included inside the top-five highest paying majors:* Georgetown University, McCourt School of Public Policy. *The Economic Value of College Majors.* Washington, DC, 2015. https://cew.georgetown.edu/wp-content/uploads/Economic-Value-of-College-Majors-Full-Report-v2.compressed.pdf.

368. *Business majors are projected to have the second-highest wage growth over the course of a career:* Georgetown University, McCourt School of Public Policy. *The Economic Value of College Majors.* Washington, DC, 2015. https://cew.georgetown.edu/wp-content/uploads/Economic-Value-of-College-Majors-Full-Report-v2.compressed.pdf.

369. *Business majors are the most common major:* Georgetown University, McCourt School of Public Policy. *The Economic Value of College Majors.* Washington, DC, 2015. https://cew.georgetown.edu/wp-content/uploads/Economic-Value-of-College-Majors-Full-Report-v2.compressed.pdf.

370. *salaries for Business majors—more than any other major—maintain the most variability:* Georgetown University, McCourt School of Public Policy. *The Economic Value of College Majors.* Washington, DC, 2015. https://cew.georgetown.edu/wp-content/uploads/Economic-Value-of-College-Majors-Full-Report-v2.compressed.pdf.

371. *the average annual salary of many Business majors can be as low as $43,000 or as high as $100,000+:* Georgetown University, McCourt School of Public Policy. *The Economic Value of College Majors.* Washington, DC, 2015. https://cew.georgetown.edu/wp-content/uploads/Economic-Value-of-College-Majors-Full-Report-v2.compressed.pdf.

372. *Highly Marketable Business Majors:* Georgetown University, McCourt School of Public Policy. *The Economic Value of College Majors.* Washington, DC, 2015. https://cew.georgetown.edu/wp-content/uploads/Economic-Value-of-College-Majors-Full-Report-v2.compressed.pdf.

373. *Least Marketable Business Majors:* Georgetown University, McCourt School of Public Policy. *The Economic Value of College Majors.* Washington, DC, 2015. https://cew.georgetown.edu/wp-content/uploads/Economic-Value-of-College-Majors-Full-Report-v2.compressed.pdf.

374. *"Career-Related" majors: majors chosen with a specific, technical career in mind:* Georgetown University, McCourt School of Public Policy. *The Economic Value of College Majors.* Washington, DC, 2015. https://cew.georgetown.edu/wp-content/uploads/Economic-Value-of-College-Majors-Full-Report-v2.compressed.pdf.

375. *Career-Related majors include Education, Social Work, and Healthcare:* Georgetown University, McCourt School of Public Policy. *The Economic Value of College Majors.* Washington, DC, 2015. https://cew.georgetown.edu/wp-content/uploads/Economic-Value-of-College-Majors-Full-Report-v2.compressed.pdf.

376. *Healthcare majors have some of the lowest unemployment rates, including nearly 50 percent less than the average Liberal Arts graduate:* Carnevale, Anthony P., Ban Cheah, and Jeff Strohl. *Hard Times: College Majors, Unemployment, and*

Earnings. Georgetown University, Center on Education and the Workforce. Washington, DC, 2014. https://cew. georgetown.edu/wp-content/uploads/2014/11/Unemployment.Final_.update1.pdf.

377. *and even lower than students with graduate degrees in nearly every field:* Carnevale, Anthony P., Ban Cheah, and Jeff Strohl. *Hard Times: College Majors, Unemployment, and Earnings.* Georgetown University, Center on Education and the Workforce. Washington, DC, 2014. https://cew.georgetown.edu/wp-content/uploads/2014/11/Unemployment. Final_.update1.pdf.

378. *Education and Social Work majors sport low unemployment rates and leads to some of the most predictable, stable salaries:* arnevale, Anthony P., Ban Cheah, and Jeff Strohl. *Hard Times: College Majors, Unemployment, and Earnings.* Georgetown University, Center on Education and the Workforce. Washington, DC, 2014. https://cew.georgetown.edu/ wp-content/uploads/2014/11/Unemployment.Final_.update1.pdf.

379. *employers inside Career-Related majors often mention practical experience as one of the most important line items on a resume:* The Chronicle of Higher Education. *The Role of Higher Education in Career Development: Employer Perceptions.* Washington, DC: 2012. http://www.chronicle.com/items/biz/pdf/Employers%20Survey.pdf.

380. *Tom Peters quote:* "Tom Peters Quotes." BrainyQuote. Accessed January 27, 2016. https://www.brainyquote.com/ quotes/authors/t/tom_peters.html.

381. *Anthony Carnevale quote:* Georgetown University, McCourt School of Public Policy. *The Economic Value of College Majors.* Washington, DC, 2015. https://cew.georgetown.edu/wp-content/uploads/Economic-Value-of-College-Majors-Full-Report-v2.compressed.pdf.

382. *Studies show that the first job of 47 percent of college graduates is unrelated to their college major:* O'Shaughnessy, Lynn. "New study shows careers and college majors often don't match." CBS, November 15, 2013. http://www.cbsnews. com/news/new-study-shows-careers-and-college-majors-often-dont-match/.

383. *27 percent of college graduates have never worked in a field related to their major:* Stahl, Ashley. "Six Reasons Why Your College Major Doesn't Matter." *Forbes,* August 12, 2015. http://www.forbes.com/sites/ashleystahl/2015/08/12/six-reasons-why-your-college-major-doesnt-matter/#3cf67a167977.

384. *In 1937, the average lifespan of an S&P 500 company…was 75 years: Future State 2030: The global megatrends shaping governments.* PDF. KPMG International, February 2014. https://assets.kpmg.com/content/dam/kpmg/ pdf/2014/02/future-state-2030-v3.pdf.

385. *Studies show, however, thanks to increasing rate of change, ten years from now, more than 40 percent of today's top companies will no longer exist:* Diamandis, Peter H., and Steven Kotler. *Bold: how to go big, create wealth and impact the world.* New York: Simon & Schuster Paperbacks, 2016.

386. *on average, a person will have held over six jobs by the age of 26:* Miller, Adam. "3 things millennials want in a career (hint: it's not more money)." *Fortune,* March 26, 2015. http://fortune.com/2015/03/26/3-things-millennials-want-in-a-career-hint-its-not-more-money/.

387. *will have held 15 to 20 jobs before their career is over:* Economy, Peter. "10 Warning Signs You Should Not Take That Job Offer." *Inc,* December 17, 2015. http://www.inc.com/peter-economy/10-warning-signs-you-should-not-take-that-job-offer.html.

388. *Millennials change jobs every four years:* Meister, Jeanne. "The Future Of Work: Job Hopping Is the 'New Normal' for Millennials." *Forbes,* August 14, 2012. http://www.forbes.com/sites/jeannemeister/2012/08/14/job-hopping-is-the-new-normal-for-millennials-three-ways-to-prevent-a-human-resource-nightmare/#6f6d6cc5508.

389. *half of them are considering leaving their employer within the next two years:* "The Deloitte Millennial Survey 2016." Deloitte. 2016. https://www2.deloitte.com/global/en/pages/about-deloitte/articles/millennialsurvey.html.

390. *Echo360, a multi-million dollar education technology company revolutionizing classroom learning:* "Echo 360." Crunchbase. January 27, 2017. https://www.crunchbase.com/organization/echo360#/entity.

391. *Peter Cappelli quote:* Cappelli, Peter. *Will college pay off?: a guide to the most important financial decision you will ever make.* New York: PublicAffairs, 2015.

392. *In 1979, young workers received an average of 2.5 weeks of training per year:* Philips, Matthew. "It's Not a Skills Gap: U.S. Workers Are Overqualified, Undertrained." *Bloomberg,* August 19, 2014. http://www.bloomberg.com/news/ articles/2014-08-19/its-not-a-skills-gap-u-dot-s-dot-workers-are-overqualified-undertrained.

393. *only 21 percent of employees received any training in the previous five years:* "Accenture Study Finds U.S. Workers Under Pressure to Improve Skills, But Need More Support from Employers." Accenture. November 16, 2011. https:// newsroom.accenture.com/news/accenture-study-finds-us-workers-under-pressure-to-improve-skills-but-need-more-support-from-employers.htm.

394. *companies are creating entire recruiting programs designed to hire only the top talent, while passing over everyone else:* PricewaterhouseCoopers. *The future of work: A journey to 2022.* New York City, NY, 2014. http://www.pwc.com/ gx/en/managing-tomorrows-people/future-of-work/assets/pdf/future-of-work-report-v23.pdf (stating 31 percent of HR professionals are gearing their talent strategies for only the best candidates and offering them long-term job security and reward).

395. *Studies have shown that graduates with a Skills Ready majors…scored significantly higher on critical thinking and problem-solving abilities:* Arum, Richard, and Josipa Roksa. *Academically adrift: limited learning on college campuses.* Chicago: University of Chicago Press, 2011.

396. *It's these raw abilities—critical thinking and problem solving—that employers most want:* Korn, Melissa. "Your College Major Is a Minor Issue, Employers Say." *The Wall Street Journal,* April 10, 2013. http://blogs.wsj.com/ atwork/2013/04/10/your-college-major-is-a-minor-issue-employers-say/.

397. *Margin Call quote: Margin Call.* Directed by J.C. Chandor. Performed by Zachary Quinto, Stanley Tucci, and Kevin

Spacey. USA: Before the Door Pictures, 2011. Film.

398. *Studies have found that the difference between the highest-and lowest-paying college majors equals $3.4 million:* Georgetown University, McCourt School of Public Policy. *The Economic Value of College Majors.* Washington, DC, 2015. https://cew.georgetown.edu/wp-content/uploads/Economic-Value-of-College-Majors-Full-Report-v2.compressed.pdf.

399. *that's four times the amount a typical high school graduate earns in a lifetime:* Hershbein, Brad and Melissa S. Kearney. "Major Decisions: What Graduates Earn Over Their Lifetimes." *The Hamilton Project,* September 29, 2014. http://www.hamiltonproject.org/papers/major_decisions_what_graduates_earn_over_their_lifetimes/.

400. *one study found that nearly 25 percent—one in four students—is made worse off by college:* Cappelli, Peter. *Will college pay off?: a guide to the most important financial decision you will ever make.* New York: PublicAffairs, 2015.

401. *each of the top 25 highest paying majors are all Skills Ready majors:* Georgetown University, McCourt School of Public Policy. The Economic Value of College Majors. Washington, DC, 2015. https://cew.georgetown.edu/wp-content/uploads/Economic-Value-of-College-Majors-Full-Report-v2.compressed.pdf.

402. *The majors with the lowest salaries are those that emphasize creativity:* Hershbein, Brad and Melissa S. Kearney. "Major Decisions: What Graduates Earn Over Their Lifetimes." *The Hamilton Project,* September 29, 2014. http://www.hamiltonproject.org/papers/major_decisions_what_graduates_earn_over_their_lifetimes.

403. *as much as forty percent of students graduate with a double major:* Selingo, Jeff. "The Rise of the Double Major." *The Chronicle of Higher Education,* October 11, 2012. http://www.chronicle.com/blogs/next/2012/10/11/the-worrying-rise-of-double-majors/.

404. *math-loving people persons earn salaries that are much higher than just technical experts alone:* Torres, Nicole. "It's Never Been More Lucrative to Be a Math-Loving People Person." *Harvard Business Review,* September 2, 2014. https://hbr.org/2014/09/its-never-been-more-lucrative-to-be-a-math-loving-people-person.

405. *studies show that by adding a technical skill, Liberal Arts graduates can nearly double their job prospects: The Art of Employment: How Liberal Arts Graduates Can Improve Their Labor Market Prospects.* PDF. Burning Glass, August 2013. http://burning-glass.com/wp-content/uploads/BGTReportLiberalArts.pdf.

Grades HACK

406. *Francis Chan quote:* Goodreads. Accessed January 16, 2017. http://www.goodreads.com/quotes/249877-our-greatest-fear-should-not-be-of-failure-but-of.

407. *Tom Peters quote:* Sethi, Ramit. "Your College is Not a Technical School." I Will Teach You To Be Rich. November 17, 2005. Accessed February 03, 2017. http://www.iwillteachyoutoberich.com/blog/your-college-is-not-a-technical-school/.

408. *other employers consider grades to be one of the "most significant" influences in the hiring process:* "Job Outlook 2016: The Attributes Employers Want to See on New College Graduates' Resumes." National Association of Colleges and Employers. November 18, 2015. Accessed February 03, 2017. http://www.naceweb.org/s11182015/employers-look-for-in-new-hires.aspx.

409. *According to studies, the minimum GPA most employers expect to see is a 3.0 GPA:* "Job Outlook 2016: The Attributes Employers Want to See on New College Graduates' Resumes." National Association of Colleges and Employers. November 18, 2015. Accessed February 03, 2017. http://www.naceweb.org/s11182015/employers-look-for-in-new-hires.aspx.

410. *Sir Ken Robinson quote:* Robinson, Ken, and Lou Aronica. *Creative schools: the grassroots revolution that's transforming education.* New York: Viking, 2015.

411. *Ernst & Young recently announced that it scrapped its previous practice of requiring new employees to have at least a 3.0 GPA:* Lam, Bourree. "The Best Job Candidates Don't Always Have College Degrees." The Atlantic. September 24, 2015. Accessed February 03, 2017. https://www.theatlantic.com/business/archive/2015/09/ernest-young-degree-recruitment-hiring-credentialism/406576/.

412. *Ramit Sethi quote:* Sethi, Ramit. "Your College is Not a Technical School." I Will Teach You To Be Rich. November 17, 2005. Accessed February 03, 2017. http://www.iwillteachyoutoberich.com/blog/your-college-is-not-a-technical-school/.

413. *Laszlo Bock quote:* Bryant, Adam. "In Head-Hunting, Big Data May Not Be Such a Big Deal." The New York Times. June 19, 2013. Accessed February 03, 2017. http://www.nytimes.com/2013/06/20/business/in-head-hunting-big-data-may-not-be-such-a-big-deal.html?pagewanted=2&_r=2&.

414. *"You have to compete against everyone else who will be trying to get jobs using the same criteria: grades":* Sethi, Ramit. "Your College is Not a Technical School." I Will Teach You To Be Rich. November 17, 2005. Accessed February 03, 2017. http://www.iwillteachyoutoberich.com/blog/your-college-is-not-a-technical-school/.

415. *"Any customer can have a car painted any color that he wants so long as it is black":* "Henry Ford Quotes (Author of My Life And Work)." Henry Ford Quotes (Author of My Life And Work). Accessed February 03, 2017. https://www.goodreads.com/author/quotes/203714.Henry_Ford.

416. *the average GPA is close to a 3.5 and 45 percent of all grades administered are A's:* Deresiewicz, William. *Excellent sheep: the miseducation of the American elite and the way to a meaningful life.* New York, NY: Free Press, 2014.

417. *"I would always hire a B-student who can show me she understands technology and is passionate about what she does…":* Sethi, Ramit. "Your College is Not a Technical School." I Will Teach You To Be Rich. November 17, 2005. Accessed February 03, 2017. http://www.iwillteachyoutoberich.com/blog/your-college-is-not-a-technical-school/.

418. *William of Occam quote:* "William of Occam Quotes." BrainyQuote. Accessed February 03, 2017. https://www.brainyquote.com/quotes/quotes/w/williamofo142887.html.

419. *RateMyProfessor statistics:* "RateMyProfessors.com – Find and rate your professor or campus." Rate My Professors

- Review Teachers and Professors, School Reviews, College Campus Ratings. Accessed February 03, 2017. http://www.ratemyprofessors.com/About.jsp.

420. *To identify what not to read, ask yourself the following questions:* Nathan, Rebekah. *My freshman year: what a professor learned by becoming a student.* New York: Penguin, 2006, p. 138.

421. *Research shows that when people read, their eyes jump around, thereby slowing down the reading process:* Ferriss, Tim. "How to Triple Your Reading Speed in 20 Minutes." YouTube. June 04, 2015. Accessed February 03, 2017. https://www.youtube.com/watch?v=jeOHqI9SqOI.

422. *studies show that classes, on average, are a little less than 50 percent full:* Nathan, Rebekah. *My freshman year: what a professor learned by becoming a student.* New York: Penguin, 2006, p. 120.

423. *nearly 25 percent of students miss a year's worth of classes:* "The cost of skipping class, by the numbers." USA Today. February 26, 2016. Accessed February 18, 2017. http://college.usatoday.com/2016/02/26/the-cost-of-skipping-class-by-the-numbers-3/.

424. *John Reed quote:* Kaufman, Josh. *The personal MBA: master the art of business.* New York, NY: Portfolio/Penguin, 2012.

425. *This approach doesn't work for three reasons:* Wagner, Tony, and Ted Dintersmith. *Most likely to succeed: preparing our kids for the innovation era.* New York, NY: Scribner, 2015.

426. *experts have optimized the learning process by boiling it down to the following four-step process:* "The first 20 hours – how to learn anything." YouTube. March 14, 2013. Accessed February 03, 2017. https://www.youtube.com/watch?v=5Mg-BikgcWnY&feature=youtu.be.

427. *Studies show that the average person pulls out their phone 85 times a day:* Mazzeo. "Breaking Digital Addiction." Medium. January 12, 2017. Accessed February 03, 2017. https://medium.com/@mazzeo/breaking-digital-addiction-3deaa3072153#.79913gya6.

428. *Internet searches take up 60 percent of people's working hours:* Barker, Eric. "How To Manage Your Time: 5 Secrets Backed By Research." Barking Up The Wrong Tree. Accessed February 03, 2017. http://www.bakadesuyo.com/2015/11/how-to-manage-your-time/.

429. *Studies show that even the mere presence of a phone limits productivity:* Rosen, Larry, and Alexandra Samuel. "Conquering Digital Distraction." Harvard Business Review. June 2015. Accessed February 03, 2017. https://hbr.org/2015/06/conquering-digital-distraction.

430. *studies show that twenty hours of study time (that's it!) is all that is required to learn a subject:* "The first 20 hours – how to learn anything." YouTube. March 14, 2013. Accessed February 03, 2017. https://www.youtube.com/watch?v=5Mg-BikgcWnY&feature=youtu.be.

431. *Studies show that out of these batching periods, learning occurs best in 45 to 50 minute learning intervals:* Newport, Cal. *How to win at college: simple rules for success from star students.* New York: Broadway Books, 2005.

432. *To take learning to the next level:* Ferriss, Timothy. *The 4-hour chef: the simple path to cooking like a pro, learning anything, and living the good life.* Boston: New Harvest, 2012.

433. *Alfred Montapert quote:* "Problems Quotes." BrainyQuote. Accessed February 03, 2017. http://www.brainyquote.com/quotes/keywords/problems.html.

434. *Chris Sacca quote:* Ferriss, Tim. "Chris Sacca on Being Different and Making Billions." Podcast. May 30, 2015. Accessed February 3, 2017. http://tim.blog/2015/05/30/chris-sacca, min 1:16:00.

435. *Margaret Fuller quote:* "Quotes About Exceptions (25 quotes)." GoodReads. Accessed February 03, 2017. http://www.goodreads.com/quotes/tag/exceptions.

436. *to intern at JP Morgan you need a 3.2 GPA:* "Jobs & Internships." JPMorgan Chase. Accessed February 03, 2017. http://careers.jpmorgan.com/student/jpmorgan/careers/us/programs/summerug/intern.

437. *every year, about 3 million students enroll in a post-college program:* "Fast Facts." National Center for Education Statistics. Accessed February 03, 2017. http://nces.ed.gov/fastfacts/display.asp?id=372.

438. *Graduate admissions offices typically evaluate a candidate on three equal bases:* Crotty, James Marshall. "Undergraduate Grades Are Crucial To Your Future Academic Life: Get Them Right." Forbes. August 31, 2014. Accessed February 03, 2017. http://www.forbes.com/sites/jamesmarshallcrotty/2014/08/31/undergraduate-grades-are-the-most-important-factors-in-your-future-academic-life-get-them-right/#7878b10b7c13.

439. *For some natural sciences and top med schools, the value can be more like one-half grades and one-half relevant test:* Crotty, James Marshall. "Undergraduate Grades Are Crucial To Your Future Academic Life: Get Them Right." Forbes. August 31, 2014. Accessed February 03, 2017. http://www.forbes.com/sites/jamesmarshallcrotty/2014/08/31/undergraduate-grades-are-the-most-important-factors-in-your-future-academic-life-get-them-right/#7878b10b7c13.

440. *Some of the elite graduate schools, such as Harvard, like to see a 3.5 GPA or better:* Welsh, Matt. "Tips on Getting into Grad School." Scribd. Accessed February 03, 2017. https://www.scribd.com/document/104566089/Grad-School-Tips.

Internships HACK

441. *Jon Medina quote:* "Brain Rules Quotes by John Medina." GoodReads. Accessed January 17, 2017. https://www.goodreads.com/work/quotes/2257186-brain-rules-12-principles-for-surviving-and-thriving-at-work-home-and.

442. *Big Law is where 25-year old new law school graduates go to make $160,000:* "Salary Distribution Curves." National Association for Law. Accessed January 17, 2017. http://www.nalp.org/salarydistrib.

443. *a huge drop off in salary, where many law school graduates make as little as $40,000 per year:* "Salary Distribution Curves." National Association for Law. Accessed January 17, 2017. http://www.nalp.org/salarydistrib.

444. *Chico Mendes quote:* Facebook post. May 17, 2016. Accessed January 25, 2017. https://www.facebook.com/chicomendesbjj/photos/a.241056189258971.66195.197484886949435/1151734111524503/?type=3&theater.

445. *Studies show that no matter the industry:* The Role of Higher Education in Career Development: Employer Perceptions. PDF.

The Chronicle of Higher Education, December 2012. https://chronicle.com/items/biz/pdf/Employers%20Survey.pdf, p. 26.

446. *no matter the company size: The Role of Higher Education in Career Development: Employer Perceptions.* PDF. The Chronicle of Higher Education, December 2012. https://chronicle.com/items/biz/pdf/Employers%20Survey.pdf, p. 27.

447. *internships are the single most important credential during the hiring process: The Role of Higher Education in Career Development: Employer Perceptions.* PDF. The Chronicle of Higher Education, December 2012. https://chronicle.com/items/biz/pdf/Employers%20Survey.pdf, pgs. 11, 24.

448. *Matt Mullenweg quote:* "Matt Mullenweg on Polyphasic Sleep, Tequila, and Building Billion-Dollar Companies." *Tim Ferriss Blog* (audio blog), February 9, 2015. Accessed January 17, 2017. http://fourhourworkweek.com/2015/02/09/matt-mullenweg, min. 1:15:00.

449. *employers widely acknowledge that the primary focus of internships is to convert students into full-time, entry-level employees: 2015 Internship & Co-op Survey.* PDF. National Association of Colleges and Employers, 2015. http://www.naceweb.org/uploadedFiles/Content/static-assets/downloads/executive-summary/2015-internship-co-op-survey-executive-summary.pdf.

450. *in 2015, over half of all internships converted into full-time hires: 2015 Internship & Co-op Survey.* PDF. National Association of Colleges and Employers, 2015. http://www.naceweb.org/uploadedFiles/Content/static-assets/downloads/executive-summary/2015-internship-co-op-survey-executive-summary.pdf.

451. *Mikhail Gorbachev quote:* "Mikhail Gorbachev Quote." A-Z Quotes. Accessed January 17, 2017. http://www.azquotes.com/quote/786681.

452. *Over 75 percent of graduating students with internship experience reported they were either "very satisfied" or "extremely satisfied":* "Internship and Co-op Satisfaction and Conversion." National Association of Colleges and Employers. August 5, 2015. Accessed January 17, 2017. https://www.naceweb.org/s08052015/intern-co-op-satisfaction-conversion.aspx.

453. *in 2015, the average hourly wage for a bachelor's degree-level intern equaled $17.20: 2015 Internship & Co-op Survey.* PDF. National Association of Colleges and Employers, 2015. http://www.naceweb.org/uploadedFiles/Content/static-assets/downloads/executive-summary/2015-internship-co-op-survey-executive-summary.pdf.

454. *a six-year high:* "Average Hourly Wage Climbs for Interns, Dips Slightly for Co-ops." National Association of Colleges and Employers. May 13, 2015. Accessed January 17, 2017. http://www.naceweb.org/s05132015/2015-hourly-wages-interns-co-ops.aspx.

455. *Some of the highest-paying internships paid closer to $20.00 per hour:* "Average Hourly Wage Climbs for Interns, Dips Slightly for Co-ops." National Association of Colleges and Employers. May 13, 2015. Accessed January 17, 2017. http://www.naceweb.org/s05132015/2015-hourly-wages-interns-co-ops.aspx.

456. *Leonardo da Vinci quote:* Edberg, Henrik. "14 Inspirational Quotes on Simplifying Your Life." The Positivity Blog. Accessed January 17, 2017. http://www.positivityblog.com/index.php/2007/06/15/14-inspirational-quotes-on-simplifying-your-life/.

457. *Studies show that 93 percent of employers said that "relevant work experience" is the most important qualification to landing an internship:* Smith, Jacquelyn. "Experience Outweighs Educational Pedigree For Internship Candidates." Forbes. January 15, 2011. Accessed January 17, 2017. http://www.forbes.com/sites/jacquelynsmith/2011/01/15/experience-outweighs-educational-pedigree-for-internship-candidates-2.

458. *"relevant work experience" means simply demonstrating that you're passionate and interested in the field:* Smith, Jacquelyn. "Experience Outweighs Educational Pedigree For Internship Candidates." Forbes. January 15, 2011. Accessed January 17, 2017. http://www.forbes.com/sites/jacquelynsmith/2011/01/15/experience-outweighs-educational-pedigree-for-internship-candidates-2.

459. *Brandeis University dean quote:* Smith, Jacquelyn. "Experience Outweighs Educational Pedigree For Internship Candidates." Forbes. January 15, 2011. Accessed January 17, 2017. http://www.forbes.com/sites/jacquelynsmith/2011/01/15/experience-outweighs-educational-pedigree-for-internship-candidates-2.

460. *Four out of five students work part time during college:* Kingkade, Tyler. "Most College Students Work Part-Time Jobs, But Few Pay Their Way Through School: Poll." The Huffington Post. August 07, 2013. Accessed January 17, 2017. http://www.huffingtonpost.com/2013/08/07/college-students-jobs_n_3720688.html.

461. *Studies show that employers prefer to hire interns from on-campus recruiting activities: 2015 Internship & Co-op Survey.* PDF. National Association of Colleges and Employers, 2015. http://www.naceweb.org/uploadedFiles/Content/static-assets/downloads/executive-summary/2015-internship-co-op-survey-executive-summary.pdf.

462. *employers begin planning for internship recruitment seven months before the position is scheduled to start: 2015 Internship & Co-op Survey.* PDF. National Association of Colleges and Employers, 2015. http://www.naceweb.org/uploadedFiles/Content/static-assets/downloads/executive-summary/2015-internship-co-op-survey-executive-summary.pdf.

463. *research shows that students must intern by junior year:* Hansen, Katharine. "Networking Timetable For College Students." Quintessential. Accessed January 17, 2017. https://www.quintcareers.com/networking-timetable/.

464. *Confucius quote:* "Tools Quotes." BrainyQuote. Accessed January 17, 2017. http://www.brainyquote.com/quotes/keywords/tools.html.

465. *Cvent, a cutting edge technology company recently purchased by an investment firm for $1.65 billion:* Medici, Andy. "Cvent shareholders greenlight $1.65 billion sale to Vista Equity Partners." Washington Business Journal. July 13, 2016. Accessed January 17, 2017. http://www.bizjournals.com/washington/news/2016/07/13/cvent-shareholders-greenlight-1-65-billion-sale-to.html.

466. *Researchers have shown that time and time again that students who worked at high-status companies consistently land better jobs:* "The Hiring Advantage of High-status Firms." University of Pennsylvania. April 10, 2014. Accessed January 17,

2017. http://knowledge.wharton.upenn.edu/article/hiring-advantage-high-status-firms/.

467. *interviews are typically short—no more than 35 to 40 minutes:* McCoy, William. "How Long Do You Expect to Interview?" Our Everyday Life. Accessed January 17, 2017. http://everydaylife.globalpost.com/long-expect-interview-5354.html.

468. *Gary Vaynerchuk quote:* "Dear Interns." Gary Vaynerchuk Profile. June 3, 2016. Accessed January 17, 2017. https://www.facebook.com/gary/videos/10154185928643350/.

469. *One of the best pieces of advice I've received to establishing early wins at the office is to act like you're 35 years old:* Rodgers, Shane. "The career advice I wish I had at 25." LinkedIn. March 16, 2015. Accessed January 17, 2017. https://www.linkedin.com/pulse/career-advice-i-wish-had-25-shane-rodgers.

470. *Jobs was famous for saying, "But there's one more thing":* "Steve Jobs 'One more thing...' Complete Compliation (1999-2011)." January 01, 2014. Accessed January 17, 2017. https://www.youtube.com/watch?v=hyCzbXx9i-M.

471. *Leo Thom quote:* Thom, Leo. "No experience? No problem! 4 Ways to Land Your First Internship." Looksharp. January 5, 2015. Accessed January 17, 2017. https://www.looksharp.com/blog/experience-problem-4-ways-first-internship.

472. *nearly half of all internships are unpaid: The Class of 2014 Student Survey Report*. PDF. National Association of Colleges and Employers, 2014. http://career.sa.ucsb.edu/files/docs/handouts/2014-student-survey.pdf.

473. *expected to continue at that rate well into the future: The Class of 2014 Student Survey Report*. PDF. National Association of Colleges and Employers, 2014. http://career.sa.ucsb.edu/files/docs/handouts/2014-student-survey.pdf.

474. *nearly every college student—92 percent to be exact—having interned at least once prior to graduation: 2015 Internship & Co-op Survey*. PDF. National Association of Colleges and Employers, 2015. http://www.naceweb.org/uploadedFiles/Content/static-assets/downloads/executive-summary/2015-internship-co-op-survey-executive-summary.pdf

475. *"modern day exploitation":* Milligan, Susan. "Modern Day Exploitation." U.S. News & World Report. April 10, 2014. Accessed January 17, 2017. http://www.usnews.com/opinion/blogs/susan-milligan/2014/04/10/unpaid-internships-ncaa-athletes-and-modern-day-exploitation.

476. *"deeply unfair":* Venator, Joanna, and Richard V. Reeves. "Unpaid internships: Support beams for the glass floor." Brookings. July 7, 2015. Accessed January 17, 2017. http://www.brookings.edu/blogs/social-mobility-memos/posts/2015/07/07-unpaid-internships-reeves.

477. *nearly 80 percent of all employers agree that even an unpaid internship has a positive impact in the hiring process: The Role of Higher Education in Career Development: Employer Perceptions*. PDF. The Chronicle of Higher Education, December 2012. https://chronicle.com/items/biz/pdf/Employers%20Survey.pdf, p. 84.

Networking HACK

478. *Margaret Wheatley quote:* Ferrazzi, Keith, and Tahl Raz. *Never eat alone: and other secrets to success, one relationship at a time.* New York: Crown Business, 2014, p. 3.

479. *research shows that referred individuals are ten times more likely to be hired than other applicants:* Arruda, William. "Why College Freshmen Need To Major In LinkedIn." Forbes. August 26, 2014. Accessed January 17, 2017. http://www.forbes.com/sites/williamarruda/2014/08/26/why-college-freshmen-need-to-major-in-linkedin/#6d1f4a996a3b.

480. *Nicholas Sparks quote:* "A quote from The Lucky One." Goodreads. Accessed January 26, 2017. http://www.goodreads.com/quotes/489551-sometimes-the-most-ordinary-things-could-be-made-extraordinary-simply.

481. *African Proverb quote:* "A quote from Coming Attractions." Goodreads. Accessed January 17, 2017. http://www.goodreads.com/quotes/189589-in-africa-we-having-a-saying-if-you-want-to.

482. *Mathews 7:7 quote: Holy Bible: New International Version.* Grand Rapids, MI: Zondervan, 2011.

483. *Stanford conducted a study which found that people dramatically underestimate how likely others are to help:* Rigolglioso, Marguerite. "Francis Flynn: If You Want Something, Ask For It." Stanford Graduate School of Business. July 1, 2008. Accessed January 17, 2017. http://www.gsb.stanford.edu/insights/francis-flynn-if-you-want-something-ask-it.

484. *Reid Hoffman quote:* Hoffman, Reid, and Ben Casnocha. *The Start-Up Of You.* New York: Crown Business, 2012, p. 85.

485. *Over 2.6 billion people use email: Email Statistics Report, 2015-2019.* PDF. The Radicati Group, Inc., March 2015. http://www.radicati.com/wp/wp-content/uploads/2015/02/Email-Statistics-Report-2015-2019-Executive-Summary.pdf.

486. *On average, people send or receive 122 business emails per day: Email Statistics Report, 2015-2019.* PDF. The Radicati Group, Inc., March 2015. http://www.radicati.com/wp/wp-content/uploads/2015/02/Email-Statistics-Report-2015-2019-Executive-Summary.pdf.

487. *Studies show that the best email subject lines are overly straightforward...have up to a 900 percent open rate:* "Subject Line Comparison." MailChimp. Accessed January 17, 2017. http://mailchimp.com/resources/research/email-marketing-subject-line-comparison/.

488. *Ramit Sethi quote:* "How to Grow Your Network, with Ramit Sethi." YouTube. September 28, 2011. Accessed January 17, 2017. https://www.youtube.com/watch?v=Yb03mTqI2Io&feature=youtu.be, min. 2:00.

489. *do what billionaire and founder of Virgin Records, Richard Branson, recommends:* Branson, Richard. "Say yes." Virgin. Accessed February 16, 2017. https://www.virgin.com/richard-branson/say-yes.

490. *one expert networker developed the "five-minute" favor:* Grant, Adam. *Give and take: why helping others drives our success.* New York, NY: Penguin Books, 2014.

491. *For added effect, in class, sit within the "reverse T":* Nathan, Rebekah. *My freshman year: what a professor learned by becoming a student.* New York: Penguin, 2006.

492. *Lion King quote:* "It's a Small World (song)." Disney Wiki. Accessed January 17, 2017. http://disney.wikia.com/wiki/

It's_a_Small_World_(song).

493. *The theory states that anyone can reach anyone else in the world through a short chain of acquaintances:* Koch, Richard, and Greg Lockwood. *Superconnect: harnessing the power of networks and the strength of weak links.* New York: W.W. Norton & Co., 2010, p. 14.

494. *Keith Ferrazzi quote:* Raz, Tahl. "The 10 Secrets of a Master Networker." Inc.com. January 01, 2003. Accessed January 17, 2017. http://www.inc.com/magazine/20030101/25049.html.

495. *Robin Sharma quote:* Sharma, Robin. "Starting strong is good. Finishing strong is epic." Twitter. November 14, 2013. Accessed January 17, 2017. https://twitter.com/robinsharma/status/400981431976873986.

Non-Negotiable Skills HACK

496. *Michael LeBoeuf quote:* "Michael LeBoeuf Quotes." BrainyQuote. Accessed January 17, 2017. http://www.brainyquote.com/quotes/quotes/m/michaelleb158247.html.

497. *These complaints refer to the "skills gap":* Glinton, Sonari. "Is The 'Skills Gap' Really A Thing?" NPR. October 29, 2014. Accessed January 17, 2017. http://www.npr.org/2014/10/29/359892883/is-the-skills-gap-really-a-thing.

498. *studies show that over 80 percent of hiring managers said it was "difficult" to hire a candidate with the right skills:* Munk, Jonathan. "Universities can't solve our skills gap problem, because they caused it." TechCrunch. May 8, 2016. Accessed January 17, 2017. https://techcrunch.com/2016/05/08/universities-cant-solve-our-skills-gap-problem-because-they-caused-it/.

499. *over 63 percent of CEOs admit they are "extremely concerned" about the availability of skills they need right now:* "Are you ready for tomorrow's workforce?" PricewaterhouseCoopers. Accessed January 17, 2017. http://www.pwc.com/gx/en/services/advisory/consulting/risk/resilience/publications/ceo-survey-talent-demographics.html.

500. *only 11 percent of business leaders think colleges are preparing graduates to be successful in the workplace:* Weathers, Lucia Anderson. "Today's business leaders say,." Lumina Foundation. February 25, 2014. Accessed January 17, 2017. https://www.luminafoundation.org/news-and-views/today-s-business-leaders-say-it-s-what-you-know-not-where-you-go-when-making-hiring-decisions-new-study-shows.

501. *Derek Bok, former Harvard president quote:* Arum, Richard, and Josipa Roksa. *Academically adrift: limited learning on college campuses.* Chicago: University of Chicago Press, 2011, p. 1.

502. *Tony Wagner quote:* Wagner, Tony. *The Global Achievement Gap.* New York: Basic Books, 2008, p. 14.

503. *a national survey found that over 93 percent of business leaders indicated that they are more important than a candidate's undergraduate major:* "Employers More Interested in Critical Thinking and Problem Solving Than College Major." Association of American Colleges & Universities. April 10, 2013. Accessed January 17, 2017. https://www.aacu.org/press/press-releases/employers-more-interested-critical-thinking-and-problem-solving-college-major.

504. *The Non-Negotiable Skills can be easily remembered as the "3 C's":* Wagner, Tony, and Ted Dintersmith. *Most Likely To Succeed: Preparing Our Kids For The Innovation Era.* New York, NY: Scribner, 2015, pp. 223-24.

505. *Maya Angelou quote:* "A quote by Maya Angelou." Goodreads. Accessed January 17, 2017. https://www.goodreads.com/quotes/5934-i-ve-learned-that-people-will-forget-what-you-said-people.

506. *Rodney Brooks...presented a TED Talk showcasing a robotic initiative:* "Rodney Brooks: Why we will rely on robots." YouTube. June 28, 2013. Accessed January 17, 2017. https://www.youtube.com/watch?v=nA-J0510Pxs.

507. *Oxford University to release a study that found 47 percent of all U.S. jobs are in danger of being replaced by computers:* Frey, Carl Benedikt, and Michael A. Osborne. *The Future Of Employment: How Susceptible Are Jobs To Computerisation?* PDF. University of Oxford, September 17, 2013. http://www.oxfordmartin.ox.ac.uk/downloads/academic/The_Future_of_Employment.pdf.

508. *Examples of lawyers, financiers, and corporate executives using automation:* Chui, Michael, James Manyika, and Mehdi Miremadi. "Four fundamentals of workplace automation." McKinsey & Company. November 2015. Accessed January 17, 2017. http://www.mckinsey.com/insights/business_technology/four_fundamentals_of_workplace_automation.

509. *"The reason is that computers are still very poor at simulating human interaction":* Deming, David. *The Growing Importance of Social Skills in the Labor Market.* PDF. Harvard University, August 2015. http://scholar.harvard.edu/files/ddeming/files/deming_socialskills_august2015.pdf, p. 36.

510. *value of communication skills is at an all-time high:* Rapacon, Stacy. "The skills employers really want." CNBC. December 02, 2015. Accessed January 17, 2017. http://www.cnbc.com/2015/12/01/the-skills-employers-are-looking-for.html.

511. *employers have said that communication is the most important out of the 3 C's:* Rapacon, Stacy. "The skills employers really want." CNBC. December 02, 2015. Accessed January 17, 2017. http://www.cnbc.com/2015/12/01/the-skills-employers-are-looking-for.html.

512. *Mark Twain quote:* Quotes for Public Speakers (No. 1) – Mark Twain." Manner of Speaking. March 25, 2016. Accessed January 17, 2017. https://mannerofspeaking.org/2009/12/07/quotes-for-public-speakers-no-1/.

513. *employers complain that communication is one of the 3 C's that graduates lack most: The Role of Higher Education in Career Development: Employer Perceptions.* PDF. The Chronicle of Higher Education, December 2012. https://chronicle.com/items/biz/pdf/Employers%20Survey.pdf, p. 29.

514. *Toastmasters facts and figures:* "Who We Are." Toastmasters International -Who We Are. Accessed January 26, 2017. https://www.toastmasters.org/About/Who-We-Are.

515. *Daniel Bernstein quote:* "Daniel J. Bernstein Quotes." BrainyQuote. Accessed January 17, 2017. http://www.brainyquote.com/quotes/quotes/d/danieljbe442326.html.

516. *nearly 40 percent of students enter college requiring courses in remedial writing:* Selingo, Jeffrey J. *College (un)bound: the*

HACKiversity

future of higher education and what it means for students. Boston: Houghton Mifflin Harcourt, 2013, p. 93.

517. *Nearly 36 percent of graduates failed to show any improvement in their writing skills since freshman year:* Selingo, Jeffrey J. *College (un)bound: the future of higher education and what it means for students.* Boston: Houghton Mifflin Harcourt, 2013, p. 25.

518. *powers over 24 percent of the web:* McKinnon, Jenni. "WordPress.org vs WordPress.com: A Definitive Guide For 2015." WPMU DEV Blog. January 12, 2016. Accessed January 26, 2017. https://premium.wpmudev.org/blog/wordpress-org-vs-wordpress-com-2015/.

519. *John D. Rockefeller quote:* Carnegie, Dale. *How to win friends and influence people.* New York: Simon and Schuster, 1981.

520. *Karen Bruett quote:* Wagner, Tony. *The Global Achievement Gap.* New York: Basic Books, 2008, p. 15.

521. *more than 80 percent of employers look for leaders of organizations:* "Job Outlook 2016: The Attributes Employers Want to See on New College Graduates' Resumes." National Association of Colleges and Employers. November 18, 2015. Accessed January 17, 2017. http://www.naceweb.org/s11182015/employers-look-for-in-new-hires.aspx.

522. *Bill Gates quote:* Hickle, Tim. "20 Quotes From History's 20 Top Entrepreneurs." Verge. February 5, 2014. Accessed January 17, 2017. http://vergehq.com/2014/02/05/top-entrepreneur-quotes/.

523. *Wikipedia…printing it out in its entirety would require more than four football fields of shelving:* O'Donnell, Jim. "This Is What Happens When You Try to Print Out the Entirety of Wikipedia." Slate Magazine. March 10, 2016. Accessed January 17, 2017. http://www.slate.com/blogs/future_tense/2016/03/10/michael_mandiberg_s_art_installation_prints_out_the_entirety_of_wikipedia.html.

524. *Peter Diamandis is fond of saying that Google affords today's student access to more information than Bill Clinton had during his presidency:* Diamandis, Peter. "Mobile is Eating the World." Blog. Accessed January 17, 2017. http://www.diamandis.com/blog/mobile-is-eating-the-world.

525. *One study even found that, thanks to the increasing speed of technology and change, four-year degrees are becoming outdated by a student's junior year:* Nedeltchev, Plamen. "The Internet of Everything is the New Economy." Cisco. September 29, 2015. Accessed January 17, 2017. http://www.cisco.com/c/en/us/solutions/collateral/enterprise/cisco-on-cisco/Cisco_IT_Trends_IoE_Is_the_New_Economy.html.

526. *That skill is called "creative problem solving":* Maggitti, Patrick. "Be the Problem-Solver." U.S. News & World Report. June 2, 2015. Accessed January 17, 2017. http://www.usnews.com/opinion/knowledge-bank/2015/06/02/3-critical-thinking-skills-business-graduates-need-to-succeed.

527. *"Smart Creatives," a term coined by Google:* Schmidt, Eric, Jonathan Rosenberg, and Alan Eagle. *How Google Works.* London: John Murray, 2014, p. 17.

528. *A Smart Creative is someone with technical depth, business savvy and creative flair:* Schmidt, Eric, Jonathan Rosenberg, and Alan Eagle. *How Google Works.* London: John Murray, 2014, p. 18.

529. *Eric Schmidt, Google's former CEO, said this means that a Smart Creative is a computer scientist, or at least understands the structure of the systems:* Schmidt, Eric, Jonathan Rosenberg, and Alan Eagle. *How Google Works.* London: John Murray, 2014, p. 18.

530. *Paul Graham quote:* Sethi, Ramit. "Your College is Not a Technical School." I Will Teach You To Be Rich. November 17, 2005. Accessed January 17, 2017. http://www.iwillteachyoutoberich.com/blog/your-college-is-not-a-technical-school/.

531. *Robert Heinlein quote:* Lombardi, Esther. "Robert Heinlein Quotes." About.com Education. Accessed January 17, 2017. http://classiclit.about.com/od/heinleinrobert/a/aa_rheinleinqu.htm.

532. *In his book There Is Life After College, author Jeffrey Selingo refers to students with specialized knowledge as "I-shaped" people:* Selingo, Jeffrey J. *There Is Life After College.* New York, NY: William Morrow, an imprint of HarperCollins Publishers, 2016, p. 30.

533. *"T-shaped," as Selingo calls them:* Selingo, Jeffrey J. *There Is Life After College.* New York, NY: William Morrow, an imprint of HarperCollins Publishers, 2016, p. 30-31.

534. *Chris Messina, developer at Uber, describes a Generalist:* Messina, Chris. "The full-stack employee." Medium. April 7, 2015. Accessed January 17, 2017. https://medium.com/chris-messina/the-full-stack-employee-ed0db089f0a1#.l739tku1d.

535. *It's called the "Halo Effect":* Rosenzweig, Philip M. *The Halo Effect.* London: Pocket, 2008, p. 50.

Bringing It to a Close

536. *Aristotle quote:* Tiscione, Kristen Robbins. *Aristotle's Tried and True Recipe for Argument Casserole.* PDF. Perspectives: Teaching Legal Research and Writing, Fall 2006. https://info.legalsolutions.thomsonreuters.com/pdf/perspec/2006-fall/2006-fall-9.pdf.

537. *Mother of H. Jackson Brown quote:* Lovell, Cindy. "That's What He Said: Quoting Mark Twain." The Huffington Post. November 18, 2013. Accessed February 07, 2017. http://www.huffingtonpost.com/cindy-lovell/thats-what-he-said-quotin_b_4282800.html.

538. *Ralph Waldo Emerson quote:* Emerson, Ralph Waldo. "Success." The Ralph Waldo Emerson Society. Accessed February 07, 2017. http://emerson-legacy.tamu.edu/Ephemera/Success.html.

539. *Albert Einstein quote:* "A quote by Albert Einstein." Goodreads. Accessed February 07, 2017. http://www.goodreads.com/quotes/272021-the-significant-problems-we-have-cannot-be-solved-at-the.

540. *Wayne Gretzky quote:* "Wayne Gretzky Quotes." BrainyQuote. Accessed February 07, 2017. https://www.brainyquote.com/quotes/quotes/w/waynegretz131510.html.

541. *Despite some speculation that every college is poised to undergo major disruptions:* "Interview with Peter Thiel, Billionaire

Investor and Company Creator." *Tim Ferriss* (audio blog), September 9, 2014. Accessed February 11, 2017. http://tim.blog/2014/09/09/peter-thiel/.

542. *Isaac Newton quote:* "Isaac Newton Quotes." BrainyQuote. Accessed March 08, 2017. https://www.brainyquote.com/quotes/quotes/i/isaacnewto135885.html.

CPSIA information can be obtained
at www.ICGtesting.com
Printed in the USA
LVOW13s0136231217
560596LV00016B/1351/P

9 780692 924488